SHADOW
ON
THE TETONS

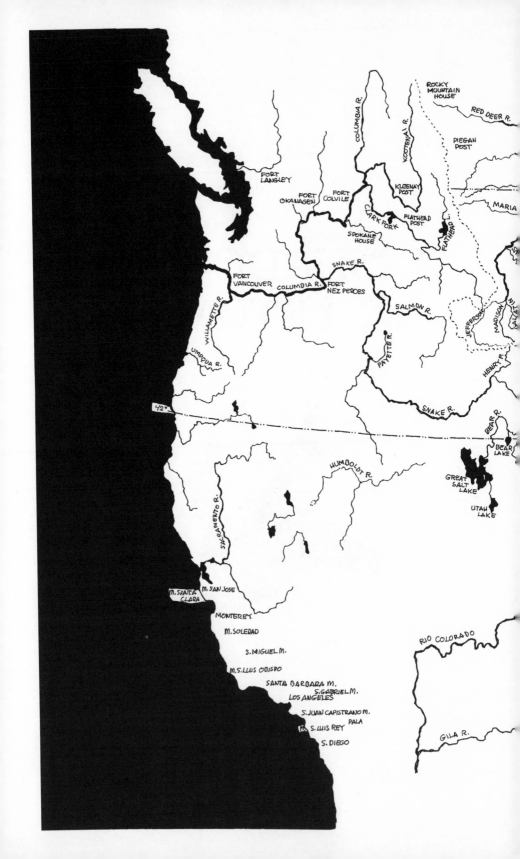

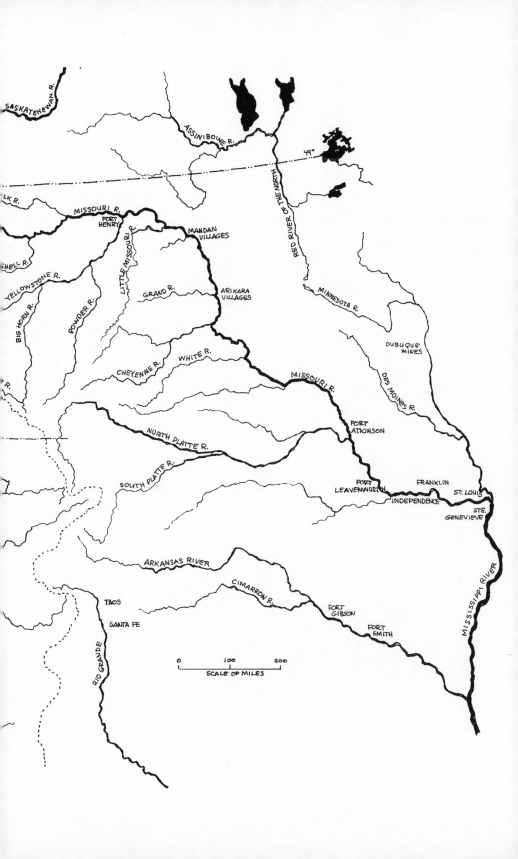

SHADOW
ON THE TETONS

DAVID E. JACKSON and the
Claiming of the American West

by John C. Jackson

Mountain Press Publishing Company
Missoula, 1993

Cover art by Dick Gravender

Library of Congress Cataloging-in-Publication Data

Jackson, John C., 1931-
  Shadow on the Tetons :   David E. Jackson and the claiming of the
American West   /   by John C. Jackson.
  Includes bibliographical references and index.
  ISBN 0-87842-295-1
  1. Jackson, David Edward, 1788-1837. 2. Fur traders—Rocky
Mountains—Biography.   3. Fur trade—Rocky Mountains—History—
19th century.   4. Frontier and pioneer life—Rocky Mountains.   5.
Rocky Mountains—History.   I. Title.
F721.J13   1993
978' .02'092-dc20   93-11610
[B]   CIP

Printed in the U.S.A.

Mountain Press Publishing Company

This is dedicated to Lucille and Marian.

Contents

David E. Jackson in the uniform of the 19th Infantry, black and white copy of a color miniature in the possession of the Jackson family descendents in West Virginia. —Hays Collection

Preface

My inspiration for recovering the life and discovering the overlooked accomplishments of the American fur trader David E. Jackson came from his great-grandson, Carl D. W. Hays. Hays devoted his life to collecting every scrap of information on his forbearer and pressed his research into areas where less committed scholars had not ventured. Carl's death in 1979 left the project unfinished, and I have undertaken to complete it.

In the impressive number of historical studies that redefine and interpret the American West, David Jackson appears closely associated with the development of the Rocky Mountain fur trade. Jackson's name is still attached to the beautiful valley near the center of fur-trade operations, but historians have written little about his role in that business.

When David E. Jackson and his associates went up the Missouri River in spring 1822, the mountain hunt represented the last bonanza trapping for the 200-year-old North American fur trade. When he returned to Missouri eight years later the fur business was already declining and the emphasis of those trying to wring money from the West had shifted to territorial possession.

By the time Jedediah Smith, David E. Jackson, and William L. Sublette formed their partnership, the mountain beaver hunt had hit its peak. Smith conducted one of the trapping brigades and explored new trapping areas. Sublette operated the transportation system that supplied the mountain hunters and carried their returns back to market. During the eight years that Jackson remained in the mountains he supervised field operations and planned trapping strategies. Through his maturity and attention to the business Jackson provided stability and thereby profits to keep the dangerously undercapitalized partnership solvent and the mountain men at their work.

The trading firm of Smith, Jackson & Sublette provided the only representation of United States interests during a time when the British

Empire, represented by the Hudson's Bay Company, contested for economic dominance of the disputed Oregon Country. The three partners were set against an older, larger, and better capitalized institution of the Hudson's Bay Company with the formation of a continental nation at stake.

As a saddle businessman, David Jackson kept his paperwork to a minimum and left few written records. We see him only as the eyes of his competitors reflect him, especially in newly recovered evidence from the archives of the Hudson's Bay Company. That evidence contributes significantly to this revised history of the mountain fur trade featuring Jackson.

This book reconsiders the mountain fur trade between 1822 and 1830, viewing it as a business rather than as aimless trapper adventures. Synthesizing previous publications and new documentation, it reassesses the contributions of the main figures and reappraises the effect of British and American competition. It considers the Indian point of view as a significant and consistent factor of mountain politics. The focus on David E. Jackson demonstrates the continuity of one western experience that was firmly rooted in the founding of the new union and significantly contributed to the realization of a continental nation.

Among those who helped in this study, Alvin M. Josephy, Jr., has been a consistent friend. Shirlee Anne Smith, the former head archivist of the Hudson's Bay Archives, guided my search for the British reaction to Jackson. Gene W. Setzer of Jackson Hole Preserve gave me the support that allowed me to complete my research without his blinking at postcard reports from a roaming jackalope. My deepest gratitude is due the staff of the Hudson's Bay Company Archives, the Missouri Historical Society in St. Louis, the Jackson County (Missouri) Historical Society, the Archives of British Columbia, the Mexican Archives of New Mexico, the California Mission Archives at Santa Barbara, and the Bancroft Library. Individuals who contributed in special ways include Lucille Basler, Don Berry, Edwin R. Bingham, Beverly Bishop, Patricia J. Bryan, Victor C. Dahl, Dorothy Upton Davis, Nancy Ehrlick, Janice Fox, James Goodrich, David Lavender, Bill McGaw, Fred Rosenstock, C. L. Sonnichsen, Father Vergilio, and Thane White. My horseback and packing education is due to Ed Widman, Scotty Rohwer, and Deaver Noland.

Prologue

"Leve! Leve! Leve!"

POCKETS OF GLACIAL ICE on the jagged peaks above the trapper camp turned golden as the sun climbed over the Continental Divide and injected shafts of light into the long valley on the east side of the Trois Tétons. On the old command of "Leve! Leve! Leve!," borrowed from the French voyageurs, bearded men rolled from their dirty buffalo robes and began to poke up the ashes of the campfires of the night before. While they were still warming their rheumatic joints in the gathering light, the nighthawks gathered the pony herd that had been grazing in a lush meadow. The last brigade of the mountain partnership of Jedediah Smith, David E. Jackson, and William Sublette was getting underway. Carrying the beaver pelts of the 1830 spring hunt, they were on their way to meet Bill Sublette at the junction of the Wind and Big Horn rivers.

This day, like most, began in a chorus of curses, grunts, and snorts as the men and the animals came to their daily contest. Working in pairs, each duo of packers cinched a wooden packframe on a quivering horse or mule and hung a buffalo-skin-covered bundle on each side. They dropped a third pack into the hollow on top of the load, which then weighed between about 150 and 200 pounds. The hitches binding everything to the animal were thrown with strips of crudely braided buffalo hide, called *shaganappi*, made by Shoshoni Indian women and purchased for a few beads.

We can only imagine the noisy camp because, as the resting place of a phantom outfit that left no records, it has no recorded history. Standing in the middle of the confusion, pensively chewing on a cold buffalo rib, was David E. Jackson. His men called him "Ol' Jackson" or "Old Davy" but he thought of himself as a Virginia farm boy who had spent the last eight years growing old in the mountains while pulling the tail of John Bull.

The bourgeois wore a thick layer of Snake country dust and Kootenai mud, mixed with some horse manure. Washing exposed the tender Jackson hide. Jackson wore a decent shirt, a blanket capote taken out of stores, and greasy buckskin pants. Some joked that Jackson's pants could stand up by themselves, and the fat of many a mess of hump ribs kept them waterproof.

David Jackson made his living supplying beaver fiber for fine headwear, but the broad-brimmed plains hat he wore was made from raccoon hair, which lasted nearly as long and cost a lot less. Because sweat had softened his hat, Jackson used a band of Indian beadwork to tighten its crown and keep its fit reasonable. He wore a bandana to keep from burring his perpetual sunburn. David had little taste for ostentation, and from a distance he was difficult to distinguish from any other trapper, a mountain métis, or an Indian.

Living in a world of hard saddles and cold blankets, David Jackson had been horse bit, kicked, stomped, trampled, gouged, goaded, confused, exasperated, and abused. His accumulated scars bespoke his experience. Most of his packers, though, were still boys, some who came out the previous year with the supply caravan and were getting their education under the master teacher.

Real mountaineers preferred to trap on their own, selling their pelts at the rendezvous sites designated by Jackson. The trader-trapper relationship had been strained since Smith, Jackson & Sublette raised prices three years earlier. The partners failed to convince the hunters that the price of goods reflected the cost of doing business, chilling the former sense of comradeship. And new competitors were calculating shortcuts to fortune. They could have "the skin game" all to themselves—Jackson was going home.

Home. Even in the shadow of these magnificent mountains he held onto his memories of the green Virginia hills and brother George's snug little farm on the edge of the Ozarks. Sister-in-law Catharine wrote last year that her husband was drinking too much, and she needed David to come home to do something about it. In contrast, Jackson's wife, Juliet, never suggested that she needed him at home. Forty-five years old by now, she had managed on her own while he was away in the mountains.

Even though his wife gave him no encouragement to return, Jackson was anxious to see how his sons had turned out. While he was conducting the mountain "survival school" for the sons of other fathers, he had neglected his own children. If David had been a backward-looking man, he might have allowed himself some regret.

David took pride in knowing that the men who followed him stayed alive. During the past winter he watched Jedediah Smith struggle with a burdened conscience as he answered to his stern God for the men who had been killed following him in "Californy."

Although he lived by the skin game, Jackson had never trapped a skin. Sometimes he let his black servant and companion, Jim, try wading in icy waters, but Jackson found that work too hard on a man for what little he got out of it. The Hudson's Bay Company (HBC) tricked its half-breed and Indian employees into servitude by loading them with debts they could never quite clear, and the independent mountaineers tried to forget their misery by blowing everything they earned in a brief drunk.

Jim brought up Jackson's saddled horse and hustled off to load the rest of their camping gear. Swinging up into the new-fangled Grimsby saddle that Sublette brought out last year, Jackson settled himself for another long day.

The defter hands were already shouting "ketch up! ketch up!" in the hope of stampeding laggards into an embarrassing mistake. David rode through the confusion, and a string of laden horses and chattering packers fell in behind him. They followed the old Indian track that led toward Togwotee Pass, a trail scoured wide and bare by lodge poles dragged behind ponies.

Reining off the trail to a hump where he could look back toward the valley, Jackson took a last look at the place that carried his name. His mentor, Andrew Henry, had been the first to describe it to him. Jackson and Sublette came down this trail for the first time five years earlier, high on expectations. Jackson's Hole contained many dreams.

The early morning shadows pointed toward the valley where David could see the braided channels of the Snake River sparkling between the aspens. The lake caught the first sun, and the glittering silver water began to reflect the inverted mountains.

The sun warming his back reminded the packtrain boss that they would have to ride high today before breaking across the pass into the Wind River valley. They would be sweating before noon. As the Tetons brightened, David rode toward the last high place he would have to cross.

1

"If ever he had a chosen people"

THE PIONEER SETTLEMENTS cowering on the upper Monongahela River had lived for fourteen years in terror of Indian attack, but the autumn of 1788 was an eddy of relative peace in the maelstrom of border warfare. During the Revolution painted Indian warriors came as British irregulars trying to draw troops away from the formal war. In the worst year, 1782, the community had to abandon the local stockade and retreat to consolidated forts at Clarksburg and Tygart Valley. Missing many pioneer names, the census of 1784 revealed the cost. The Hagle, Fink, White, Painter, Tanner, and Schoolcraft families fell in the four years of frontier war. Indians had killed twenty white settlers and carried sixteen away as captives.

After the end of the Revolutionary War the Indians returned to discourage pioneer expansion and defend the boundary of the Ohio River. In 1788 frontier folk took small comfort from the few horse raids of the previous year because they knew the Indians would keep coming. The farmers were disgusted when their veteran scouts were called away to guard the New England colony at Marietta, located on the Indian side of the Ohio River and sure to bring reprisals. The war-weary frontiersmen protested that their crops would stand unharvested and their families lie undefended, while the Army protected the interests of distant speculators.

Autumn frosts had already singed the hardwood trees as the family of John and Elizabeth Jackson gathered to celebrate the wedding of Mary Sarah, the last of their daughters living at home. A rider came whooping down the trail to receive the whiskey bottle customarily called "Black Betty." He carried the first drink back to the groom's party escorting Philip Reger to his bride. The guests from across the holler arrived already primed on good Monongahela rye.

A backwoods feast of beef, pork, fowl, venison, and roasted bear followed the preacher's brief words. Elizabeth's kitchen garden provided potatoes, cabbage, and roasting ears. Her oven turned out heaps of corn pone and wild-fruit pies. The hosts later set aside the luncheon tables so the guests could dance squares and couples until the fiddler collapsed or the sun broke over Big Indian Knob. Black Betty whirled and curtsied with the dancers.

The father of the bride was a small, slight man, but Elizabeth Jackson stood a full six feet tall. Too many years in the wilderness had grayed her once blond hair without altering her commanding presence. Her genes obviously prevailed in five capering sons and three whirling daughters, all tall, big-boned, and blue of eye.[1]

The second-oldest son, Edward Jackson, seated his pregnant wife, Mary, where she could watch the dancing and tend their firstborn, George, bedded among his cousins as though they were a nest of puppies. Edward welcomed a chance to drink and compare thoughts with his older brother George, who now lived across the hills on the West Fork of the Monongahela. During the Revolution the brothers served together as woods rangers and militia officers, but George followed the new Harrison County government to Clarksburg.

George Jackson went to Richmond a few months earlier as a delegate to the Virginia Convention to consider the ratification of a new federal constitution. After casting one of the fourteen favorable votes in that crucial test of the new document, George returned home confident that the new nation had finally devised a replacement for the tired Articles of Confederation.

Seaboard Americans might have disputed the idea that these isolated hill-country hamlets, threatened border stations, and muddy river landings inspired the citizens of the new nation. But the frontiersmen carving out new counties from the wilderness were strengthening a grass roots belief in democracy.

The Jackson clan played its part in this grass roots democracy. Monongalia County gave birth to Harrison County, which in turn produced Randolph County. Each division created new offices, and naturally the Jacksons, leaders in community defense, claimed the rewards.

Edward Jackson, the former militia leader, became justice of the peace, sheriff's bondsman, and, by getting seven of eleven possible votes, county surveyor. Even the distant governor of Virginia recommended him as "a man of probity and good character." The same session of the county court appointed him captain of the militia and named his younger brother, John Jr., lieutenant.[2]

George Jackson operated an ordinary—a tavern and inn—at Clarksburg, a progressive new community that already had a courthouse, real roads, and even an academy. He saw to it that the Harrison County Court gave his brother Edward permission to build a mill on the West Fork. George insisted that Edward get started with that project because a man had to keep up with his opportunities. But the Jacksons, like hill bears, needed space for their ranges, and Edward wasn't content to become a mere miller in a political arena dominated by his brother.

At Westfall's Fort in Tygart Valley, Edward met the daughter of David Haddon and later returned to court and marry her. The couple lived in a two-story log house, as strong as a fort, on Edward's land claim on Fink's Run. After three years their taxable property had increased to ten cows and two horses.

The pioneers who broke across the Appalachian Mountains saw endless blue ridges and rolling forests spreading before them. Like hungry children gorging on sweet fruit, they feasted on sprawling claims and became addicted to possessing land. They would have agreed with Thomas Jefferson that "those who labor in the earth are the chosen people of God, if ever he had a chosen people." They felt they earned their place through the stiff price of blood spilled to conquer it. The forested, rolling hills were a land bank, and community growth was a means of increasing their investment.

Immigrant parents, remembering the rack rents imposed by Old World landlords that had driven them from the homeland, resented absentee speculators who tried to exploit old deeds or war claims. Anything that smelled of aristocratic privilege the new settlers found repugnant.

Soon after the wedding, when the first snow muffled the leaves and made tracking easy, the Jacksons went on the fall hunt. Edward was away in the woods when Mary delivered their second son one day before Halloween 1788, but his mother, who had borne her children in lonely cabins and rickety forts, came over to help. They named the big baby boy David Edward Jackson.

Recognizing that the clan would have problems sorting out cousins, Edward Jackson proposed that each family code their children with the father's initial. Unfortunately the logic was lost on most of the brothers. George and John Jackson tried to follow the system, but it collapsed when the youngest brother, Henry Jackson, could not conceive twenty-two names beginning with "H."

Edward Jackson's absence during the birth of his son was in keeping with the nature of his work. Surveying, military service, and private business often took him away for long periods of time—common for a man of affairs in an age of slow travel and great distances.

Largely self-educated, Edward puzzled out land definition from texts including *Gibson's Surveying* and passed that skill on to his youngest brother, Henry, and their nephew John George Jackson. In the almost cashless frontier society, mapping earned fees and subsidized the location of desirable tracts in unclaimed territory. By selling his knowledge to several eastern land speculators who invested in Revolutionary War script, Edward formed associations with influential and wealthy men of the eastern establishment, including financier Henry Banks. Edward, listed among Virginia's fifty-two delegates to its House of Representatives who received public land grants of ten thousand acres, eventually shared title with Banks to over fifty thousand acres.[3]

In July 1788 Methodist circuit rider Bishop Francis Asbury pondered the influence of such frontier landlords as he rode to Clarksburg for the quarterly session of his floating church. While staying in George Jackson's ordinary, Asbury concluded that "the great landholders who are industrious will soon show the effects of the aristocracy of wealth, by lording it over their poorer neighbors, and by securing to themselves, all the offices of profit and honor. On the one hand savage warfare teaches them to be cruel: and on the other, the preaching of [rival churches] poisons them with error of doctrine: good moralists they are not, and good Christians they cannot be, unless they are better taught." Mary Jackson sat in the tiny congregation to hear Asbury's pessimistic sermon.[4]

In 1789 another preacher, Jedediah Morse, gave a more optimistic vision of the frontier future. He foresaw the new country soon comprehending millions of souls and determined that "the Mississippi was never designed as the western boundary of the American Empire." In his geographical compendium Morse picked fur-trader Jonathan Carver's name for that western goal, Oregon. Morse's words bespoke the Buckhannon yearling's destiny—David E. Jackson would head west.[5]

Indians raided the Monongahela-area settlements in September 1789, shattering the illusion of peace. Eyeing land as a way to pay off the war debt, the new nation appropriated eastern Ohio from the tribes who aided the British during the Revolution. Upset by dispossession, and goaded by bitter Loyalist refugees into becoming pawns in a cynical imperial policy, the tribesmen fought back.

In April 1791 raiders attacked a family on the West Fork near Edward's mill site, proving to the Jacksons that it was too dangerous for the family to move into an exposed area. Four years later, when tomahawks cut down the Bozarth family, hard men in stained buckskins came to Col. Edward Jackson's house. The Jackson children listened in wonder as the men reported killing the Indians and displayed fresh scalps.

9

The Battle of Fallen Timbers discouraged further Indian resistance, and on 9 September 1795 the chastened Shawnee returned three captive Bozarth children, the last sufferers of the border warfare. But peace and treaties failed to mitigate the bitter hatred of Indians smoldering in the frontiersmen.[6]

Mary Haddon Jackson died in spring 1796, and Edward sent his children to live with relatives. Six-month-old Rebecca, two-year-old Polly, four-year-old Rachael, and six-year-old Jonathan went to understanding aunts and uncles. But eight-year-old David and ten-year-old George, as old as their father and uncle had been when they accompanied Grandfather across the mountains, continued to live with Edward, or with their grandparents when he was away.

Grandmother Elizabeth kept the family legends and gave her grandchildren a strong sense of the continuity of their tribe. When the family gathered around the fireplace to peel apples and smoke in the flickering darkness, she told how Grandfather John left northern Ireland as a boy and moved to the great city of London, where he began an apprenticeship in the carpenters' guild. In 1748 he crossed the Atlantic Ocean with a house built then disassembled in England for reassembly on the Maryland shore.

Grandmother had been an orphan living with a maiden aunt, until the aunt's death provided her a small inheritance. Carefully unwrapping an old kerchief, Grandmother Elizabeth showed the children what remained of the gold coins that had financed her voyage to America. She planned to join relatives who had emigrated before her but, to her dismay, found they had all died. She was alone in a strange new world. Grandfather married her in Cecil County, Maryland.[7]

George and David Jackson were more interested in Grandfather's story of crossing the Allegheny Mountains in 1768 with Uncle George and their father padding behind. Anticipating the treaty of Fort Stanwix by a year, they crossed the old Iroquois war trail and slashed out a corn patch along Turkey Run. Planting was important to Grandmother's morality tale because roots made them different from the long hunters who crossed the mountains for extended deer hunts. Those worthless men returned home with hides to trade for more powder and shot and wasted their lives in a wild, roaming existence. She insisted substantial people made something of themselves.

George and David visited the hollow tree up the run where the long-hunting Pringle brothers lived like wilderness Robinson Crusoes. The folded mountains and dark valleys of the upper Buckhannon River were poor places for hard-scrabble farms but a rich playground for youngsters. They used the runs and brooks as trails and worked along the ridges until they could see out across the sea of trees to the smoky horizon. They learned to recognize walnut, beech, poplar, oak, maple, chestnut, ash, gum, and hemlock trees, all of which had specific uses in the pioneer economy. In spring they fished with hooks, nets, gigs, trotlines, and even brush seines. They picked berries in the summer and gathered nuts in the fall. In the winter they ran trap lines for snow birds, rabbits, and muskrats. They rarely caught beavers. Raucous coon hunts echoed in the nights as their elders guided the boys to become skilled woodsmen—marksmen, hunters, trackers, and horsemen.[8]

The fall hunt was the high point of the year when, like the Indians before them, the Jackson tribe went to live in distant camps and kill animals for winter meat. During Uncle George's legendary hunt on Skin Creek, he and three companions killed forty deer in a single day. Memories of warm blood gushing from a slashed throat and steam rising from an early morning gutting gave David Jackson a hunter's sense of primordial fulfillment.

During evenings around the campfire, the boys listened to their elders discuss the shaping of the new nation. Uncle George had been to Congress three times, where he served as a member of the House Committee on Indian Affairs. Always the champion of the frontier, when George retired in 1803 he wrote a circular letter to his constituents warning them of the dangers of Federalism, deficit spending, and an established state religion.

The boys' mentors now considered Spain's hold on the Mississippi River outlet at New Orleans the great western problem. Their elders indoctrinated the young Jacksons with the ideal of a greater continental nation while the boys poked the ashes of the campfire.[9]

Edward Jackson remarried in 1799. The boys' new stepmother was Elizabeth Brake, a German girl from the south branch of the Potomac. Her uncle, Jacob Brake, was a redeemed Indian captive who never managed to live down the stigma of that savage association.[10] During the Revolution Jacob marched in the militia with George Jackson or ran as a scout for Edward Jackson. Later Edward's two older daughters also found mates in the Brake family.[11]

Moving from Fink's Run, Edward and Elizabeth settled into a two-story log cabin by a bend of the West Fork River at Freeman's Creek. During the twenty years of their marriage she bore nine children. The first son, born in 1801, they named Cummins in honor of the Jackson clan matriarch.

Randolph Academy was chartered at Clarksburg in 1788, and as a founder and trustee Uncle George convinced Edward Jackson to spend $5 or $6 a term to educate his sons in grammar and arithmetic. During this time the boys stayed with their grandparents, just a short walk across the Elk Creek bridge to the academy situated behind the courthouse.

Rev. George Tower, the English schoolmaster, came to America in July 1794 and reached Clarksburg by November. Even in the rough frontier Tower maintained his intention of imparting a traditional English education laced with Presbyterianism. He encouraged his students to use his "large and select library" in the evenings. The Reverend and Mrs. Tower both smoked pipes and encouraged the practice among the scholars in the belief that it eased the difficult process of comprehension.[12]

Grandmother enthusiastically supported her countryman's teaching, and David Jackson applied himself. He learned to write in a simple, unadorned style, forming his letters well and spacing them properly with a careful but not fussy angle. By frontier standards he had adequate spelling and a sufficient vocabulary.

David grew familiar with Clarksburg, where many places bore the mark of the Jacksons—the toll bridge, the old mill, and the new saltworks operated by his father and cousin. John George Jackson inherited his father's office in the House of Representatives and became the notable public figure of the clan. He married Mary Payne, the sister-in-law of James Madison, at Montpelier in October 1800, and the future president accepted him into the Virginia dynasty. Meanwhile, Col. Edward Jackson pinned his expectations on David's younger brother, Jonathan, who rode with the congressman as squire and law student. As laudable as the settlers found frontier egalitarianism, they also realized good connections helped aspiring young men.

Serving as a delegate to the Virginia Assembly in 1803 and 1804 took the colonel away from the West Fork and put the home responsibilities on seventeen-year-old George and fifteen-year-old David. They rode through the corn bottoms to oversee the cycle of planting, weeding, and harvesting by slaves and hired neighbors, and learned the difficult art of supervising workers. At the sawmill the Jacksons monitored the dangerous machinery and learned to bargain with their neighbors. David saw the farm as a duty, but others envied the estate, which was as extensive as that of a feudal lord.[13]

When he rode between Freeman's Creek and Clarksburg David sometimes stopped to refresh himself at the home of Jedediah Waldo, a Yankee who came to the West Fork to raise a family of twelve tough border children. David also visited another interesting neighbor on Freeman's Creek, Capt. John Norris, a war veteran who told first-hand stories of General Washington's crossing of the Delaware and of the British surrender at Yorktown. The patriotic gore made for fine yarns, but the captain's daughter succeeded better in capturing David's attention.[14]

John Davis, an itinerant Baptist preacher, held church services at George Woofer's home in Clarksburg during the twenty years it took the community to establish a real church. By then some West Fork neighbors thought it was too late to redeem the Jacksons, who drank, swore, and raced horses. When he retired from Congress in 1802, David's Uncle George expressed faith in Christ and tolerance for the beliefs of others, but warned that "... when sects, creeds and denominations are raised up, and that by the protection of law, that then, your political liberty will cease." David learned to keep his religion as he might a poker hand, close to his vest.[15]

The West Fork country entered into a period of consolidation and development as the frontier passed westward. Col. Edward Jackson, proud of the fruits of his initiative and self-reliance, planned to stake his sons to substantial farms when they were ready to fly on their own. He wanted them to have a comfortable future, where diligence and attention to duty would spare them the uncertainties that had burdened his life. But his oldest sons rejected the gift. New land-clearing fires already burning in the West drew their attention.

President Jefferson's purchase of Louisiana in 1803 refocused national attention on the West. The return of Meriwether Lewis and William Clark in 1806 increased the nation's interest. Soon the governor of Upper Louisiana, Gen. James Wilkinson, was rattling his double-edged sword at the Spanish in the South and the British in the North. His associate, former Vice President Aaron Burr, was pandering to dissatisfied frontiersmen.

Wilkinson and Burr were opportunists willing to trade the emerging vision of a continental nation for personal ambition. The two men, both lesser heroes of the Revolution, felt dissatisfied with their share of the political spoils and hoped to gain power by playing up the idea that the East and the West were ungovernable as one country.

Frontiersmen distrusted the eastern establishment that controlled the new United States government. Reluctant to disperse funds for western defense, the eastern mercantile interests also acted with indifference to the stranglehold that Spain held over the world outlet for western products. The government also made one of its first targets for taxation—an early display of federal power—the frontier product, whiskey. The easterners who appeared when Indian conflicts threatened were often stuffy Army officers more concerned with personal careers than with frontier defense. But plenty of Yankees always showed up to claim lucrative federal offices. These complaints gained Wilkinson and Burr support from frontiersmen.

Burr, canvassing the West in the summer of 1805, met Wilkinson at Fort Massac to scheme a way to steal Texas by starting a war with Spain. Burr found an angel in the expatriate Harmon Blennerhasset, who was recreating his forfeited Irish estate on an island in the Ohio River. After some secret arrangements with Blennerhasset, Burr approached Congressman John George Jackson, who was away when Burr arrived at Clarksburg. Burr repeated the overtures in Washington, but Jackson, a loyal Republican and firm supporter of the Virginia political dynasty, remained hostile to the opportunist.[16]

When he returned from Congress in July 1806 John George discussed the situation with Colonel Edward, who was already aware of President Jefferson's public warning against the plotters. Near the end of the year the western Virginia and Ohio militia moved in to break up the arrangements on Blennerhasset's island. But some of the schemers slipped away in boats, leaving enough unanswered questions to excite cracker-barrel discussions during the winter.

Late in the afternoon of 18 April 1807 a messenger brought an urgent note to Jackson's mill from Congressman John George Jackson. Sympathetic western courts had failed to convict Burr of treason, and the United States was going to try him in Richmond. Chief Justice John Marshall, ever hostile to President Jefferson, had set the trial date for 22 May, which left the federal prosecutor insufficient time to prepare a case. On 6 April James Madison asked his brother-in-law to collect evidence of the conspiracy on the island and to send on the message bearer, Virginia Deputy Marshal Drew, to collect more witnesses in the West. The congressman made enough trips to Washington to know that journey should have taken Drew less than two weeks. The marshal was moving too slowly—the trial would be over before he ran down his witnesses. Congressman Jackson called on his cousin George, David's brother, "an active, enterprising, trustworthy young man," to ride with Drew and force a faster pace.

David was also ready to defend the Republic, but Congressman Jackson called on only one of the brothers. David had to endure three months of boring farm chores before he learned how the Jacksons answered the Aaron Burr conspiracy.

When the trail-worn George Jackson stepped down from his thin horse in mid-summer, the West Fork idealists were disillusioned. After sending his cousin racing west to collect witnesses, Congressman John George Jackson compiled evidence of the conspiracy in Wood County, Virginia, and at Marietta, Ohio. Unfortunately, in his haste he took ex parte depositions from witnesses, which gave Burr's panel of attorneys cause to object that the evidence had been collected without the presence of a defense representative. Burr's attorneys accused Congressman Jackson of directing the testimony, and Chief Justice John Marshall disallowed everything from the island. Other witnesses were unable to stand up under the hammering of the defense team, making the prosecution unable to prove a conspiracy on the island. The now-worthless downstream evidence meant George E. Jackson's hard ride across the Ohio Valley to Fort Massac was in vain. By September the court had acquitted Burr.[17]

Even though Burr was acquitted, the Richmond trial exposed the plot and the plotters' motives, impeaching the idea of western separatism. The Lewis and Clark expedition and the parallel explorations of Zebulon Pike opened new vistas about the West. George E. Jackson and his dutiful brother David felt the excitement. At Vincennes, Indiana, George spoke with their uncle, John Haddon, who encouraged them to take advantage of the new opportunities. Why would young men want to rust in the narrow, constraining valleys of Virginia?

Jackson's mill region of western Virginia.

2

"How my business stands"

GEORGE E. JACKSON'S severe case of western fever paralleled the similar enthusiasm of another upper Monongahela visionary. In 1807 Pittsburgh entrepreneur Henry M. Shreve floated a 35-ton barge of cargo down the Ohio and returned with a profitable load of furs. By early summer 1808 some upper Monongahela River iron smelters also decided to try the downstream market. They needed a trustworthy supercargo for their broad-horn flatboat load of pig iron, and Congressman Jackson gladly recommended his young cousin George as someone already acquainted with the West.[18]

David rode down to the landing to see George off. As his brother floated away, David stood on the shore thinking the eldest brother should have stayed to mind their father's business. He took small consolation in being considered the steadier hand in developing the West Fork properties.

The Jacksons had solid ties to the tidewater Virginia elite: David's uncle and cousin worked in the halls of government with Washington, Jefferson, Madison, and Monroe—the best political minds of the Virginia dynasty. His father was connected to the tobacco planters and capitalists who dabbled in western land speculation. If asked his patriotic orientation, Colonel Edward might have answered Virginian first and American second. As the western Virginians outdistanced the tidewater aristocracy, David was perched between two worlds—the autocratic tradition his father had created and the western opportunity that seduced his brother.

Operating the mill had its problems. The West Fork ran between steep hills but had little actual drop in elevation to generate water power. In 1806 the Jacksons extended the mill dam across the river to trap enough water for their shallow tub mill. (A conventional upright waterwheel could be no taller than the head of water behind the mill dam, but inventive mechanics got around that limitation by putting the wheel on its side, like a tub.) The millstones were set up to crack corn into coarse meal and were not adjustable for other grains. Because it was a long, difficult journey downstream to New Orleans, local farmers cooked much of their local corn and rye in neighboring whiskey stills.

Unlike his grandfather, who was fascinated by machinery, David found the ponderous rhythm of the grindstones dulling and preferred the dangerous energy of the sawmill. He favored cutting the planks and beams for the frame houses that were replacing pioneer log cabins. Characteristically, the colonel, who had a ready supply of lumber at his doorstep, saw no reason to improve the original two-level log house.[19]

The men cut poplar logs for lumber on the banks of upper Freeman's Creek and floated them down to the mill. Logging operations took David back to Millstone Creek, where Captain Norris and his daughter Juliet (who earlier had, more than her father's war stories, captured David's interest) lived. In a community with few eligible brides, Juliet being five years older than David did not impede their romance.

The couple's relationship deepened during their walks along the creek bank, and they agreed on a future together. Allowing for the intentions, or lack of restraint, of young lovers on the frontier, custom required contractual engagements. David and Juliet recorded their marriage bond on 31 October 1809, the day after David's twenty-first birthday, with both fathers standing as sureties.[20]

Two days later the exuberant groom's party rode to the Norris home where frontier minister John Davis performed the marriage ceremony. The bride wore a handmade dress of white cotton trimmed with Swiss embroidery, while the sheepish groom was decked out in old-style knee breeches and white cotton stockings. An all-night dance and serious drinking followed the wedding feast. The celebrants repeated the process the next day at a reciprocal "infair" held at the groom's home. After two days of celebrating the merrymakers finally allowed the couple to retreat to their new home, where they could still expect revelers to surprise them, preferably in bed, with a shivaree.[21]

In recognition of his son's coming of age, and in appreciation of his dedication, Edward Jackson gave David the pioneer land claim of David Sleeth, which lay just across the river from the mill.[22]

Juliet became pregnant almost immediately. They named their first son, born on 31 July 1810, Edward John Jackson to honor both grandfathers. Grandfather Norris proudly noted in the family bible a second son, named William Pitt Jackson, born at ten minutes after eleven on the night of 5 January 1812.

The unusual name indicated his father's political sensitivity when the United States was deeply concerned about the presence of the British Empire on its northern border. William Pitt Jackson's parents were expressing admiration for the "Great Commoner" who had engineered the British conquest of New France and later criticized attempts to recover the cost from the colonies. In upholding human rights in Parliament, Pitt roared, "the poorest man in his cottage may bid defiance to all the force of the Crown. It may be frail; its roof may shake; the wind may blow through it; the storm may enter; the rain may enter—but the King of England cannot enter: all his forces dare not cross the threshold of the ruined tenement."[23]

The younger William Pitt concerned himself with the Nootka controversy, northern Irish religious freedom, and South American independence from Spain. He died six years before David named his son.

David's most immediate appreciation of international politics came from his cousin, Congressman John George Jackson, who advocated that Americans resist the overbearing English. He shared his feelings, and the Washington newspapers, with his kinsmen. After the Revolution, and against the terms of the Treaty of Paris, the British continued meddling in American affairs. Finding the southwest Indian trade too lucrative to give up, the empire encouraged the Ohio Valley tribes to resist U.S. expansion.

Western Virginians would neither forget nor forgive the twelve years of border warfare preceding the Battle of Fallen Timbers in 1795, which finally disproved British pretensions. But Jay's Treaty allowed the British southwest traders to continue operating in U.S. territory, and, by 1810, the British were again inciting the tribes. The pugnacious new nation had no inclination to overlook the intrusion, and "War Hawks" in Congress wanted to call in the military.

The West Fork family's interest in the growing tension came from brother George E. Jackson's business venture in the dangerous Old Northwest. He had drifted to the Mississippi River frontier settlement of Ste. Genevieve, Missouri, just below St. Louis, and got into lead mining. During the winter of 1810-11 George went up the Mississippi River to trade with the Indian lead miners operating in the Dubuque area, where his main competitor was Nathaniel Pryor, a member of the Lewis and Clark expedition. He returned to Ste. Genevieve in the spring with part of the 29,900 pounds of lead transshipped through the Indian Trade Factory at Fort Madison, then wrote home that he planned to go upriver again as a lead miner and smelter. That plan was smashed when Indian fugitives from the inconclusive Tippicanoe battle descended on Pryor and another trader, killed two of their employees, and drove the survivors away. Like other indignant frontiersmen, George blamed the British southwest traders working out of old Prairie du Chien.[24]

By March 1812 the secretary of war, scrambling to get the inadequate regular Army on a war footing, raised the initial call for 1,500 Ohio troops by an additional 500. To help make up the Virginia quota of 1,200 men, the brigadier general of the Virginia Militia, John George Jackson, responded by dispatching 50 men from Harrison County.

Congressman Jackson, wounded in a duel growing out of his support of the Non-Intercourse Act of 1806, was already a crippled veteran of the British problem. Everyone knew that young men got started in public careers through United States Army commissions, but John George Jackson appalled his friends by looking for a Regular Army commission. He managed to obtain a commission for his younger brother, George Washington Jackson, in the newly forming 19th Infantry Regiment.

As the war came to a boil Harrison County organized a troop of mounted riflemen, offering their services to the county court on 12 June. The officers—Capt. James McCally, 1st Lt. Jonathan Jackson, 2d Lt. John Wilkerson, and Coronet David E. Jackson—stated their readiness to ride immediately to any place the Republic was threatened, a bit presumptuously because the government formally declared the War of 1812 three days later. The Army never accepted the troop into service.[25]

At the end of the first session of the 12th Congress, John George Jackson returned to Clarksburg, and on 26 June he informed his brother-in-law, now President James Madison, that he was at the disposal of the government. His band of friends organized as mounted riflemen and prepared themselves to ride behind his standard. Madison tried to steer Jackson into a civil commission to oversee the resurvey of the Virginia military tract in Ohio, but the hawkish congressman refused to be put off that easily.

American illusions evaporated in the ignominious surrender of Detroit, the capture of Mackinac, and the nightmare of the Fort Dearborn massacre. As a serious Indian threat developed near the end of August, Congressman Jackson wrote to the president that he expected that his volunteer officers "would be called upon to command companies, battalions, etc."[26] Unable to discover a way to project themselves into federal service, Jackson and his followers rode off without orders to join the army that General William Henry Harrison was assembling in central Ohio.

During the second week of October David Jackson rode up the old Indian war trails along the Muskingum River to the assembly point and training area at Franklinton (now Columbus, Ohio). The volunteers arrived on 21 October, prepared to serve even without pay.[27]

21

General Harrison's cynical treaties and pre-emptive attack on the Shawnee Indian confederacy precipitated the war, but the Battle of Tippicanoe made him wiser. Harrison realized that it was too late in the season to move an untrained army against the British forces holding Detroit and the lakes frontier. He would be better off spending the winter training an effective force.

Several previous Indian campaigns had disproved popular myths about the Revolutionary War minutemen, and to depend upon the notoriously unreliable militia called up for only three months was madness. Their obligations would expire before they reached any action. Some Harrison County militia marched as far as Sandusky, where they helped bury the dead of a previous American blunder, but General Harrison sent the Virginia mounted riflemen home.

Before leaving Franklinton David Jackson spoke with his cousin, Lt. George Washington Jackson, who encouraged him to seek a commission in the 19th Infantry.[28] Finally, commissioned as an ensign in the 19th Infantry, David got into the war on 29 July 1813. Within a week he was marching toward the sound of guns with a group of neighbor boys, including Juliet's brother, William Norris. David's note to Juliet on 7 August said something about his father's attitude toward runaway patriotism:

Dear Wife

I start this morning 7th of August 1813 on my march. John G. Jackson informs me that he expects an appointment for me to serve in the company that Washington Jackson is in and if you can send the Henry Bush mare to Clarksburg against Sunday evening, Captain Moore will send him on to Morgantown. I have been much disappointed in my father not coming to town according to agreement.

From your affectionate husband,
D. E. Jackson

Mrs. Juliet Jackson[29]

Marching north through Morgantown the recruits proceeded to the regimental rendezvous on the upper Muskingum River in Jefferson County, Ohio. Col. John Miller and Lt. Col. John Campbell were already in the field, and a Regular Army officer had charge of organizing and training the new companies. When Ensign Jackson reported to Maj. Sidney Jessup with an awkward, self-conscious salute, he disappointedly found himself assigned to inglorious recruiting duty.

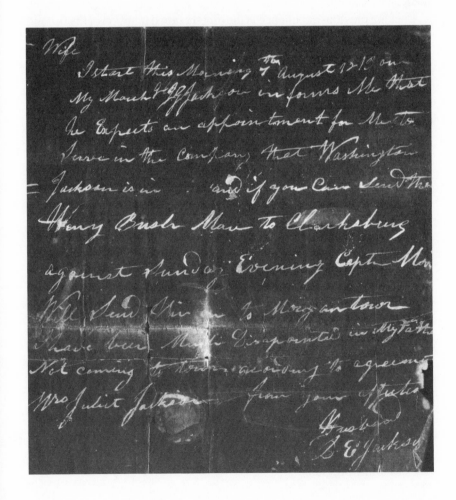

The federal government was poorly prepared for the war. Congress was so tardy in passing war measures that its forces lacked adequate artillery, and the hysterical call-up of militia resulted in a complete waste. Although authorized a military strength of 58,354 men, the United States had only 19,036 in federal service in February 1813.

The military district commander had responsibility for recruiting. He set up conscript depots and rendezvous points, and dispatched teams of officers and men to scour the countryside for likely prospects. Before sending him trudging off to duty, Ensign Jackson's superiors cautioned him to refuse any person "who has sore legs, scurvy, scald-head, rupture or other infirmities," but to accept a man of small size so long as the man was strong, active, well made, and healthy.

Lacking previous experience in the time-honored tradition of the fife and drum, Jackson developed his own recruiting technique. Though unpolished as a speaker, he learned patriotic oratory and resorted to whiskey treats and blatant good-fellowship. Regulations required administering the oath of office to new recruits within six days, but smart recruiters read it before their victims sobered up. David became fluent in the arguments that justified the war, including British intrusions and their incitement of Indians, to which David could attest from his brother's experience. But his best argument was that land grants would certainly reward real patriots.

David neglected to date the letter he sent to Juliet from Chillicothe, but he wrote it in the fall, when a homesick farmer thinks of planting.

Dear Wife

I now stop to inform you that I am well at presant if you get this in 10 days write to Urbanna and inform me how business is carried on in our part and if you can get Joseph White or some person to sead that field on the river or by the hous, get it done. Remember my best respects to your father and family [torn edge] Rachel, remember Sampson of Char[?]y.

from yours affectionately
D E Jackson

Mrs Juliet Jackson.

Sometime during his wandering David had a color miniature painted by one of those portrait artists who found a bonanza in lonesome sons and separated lovers. Innocent in interpretation and primitive in style, the little picture shows only David's profile. He wore his uniform coat with a high, stiff collar and stock, and the tall, varnished hat common in that period. His features are pronounced, with a rather beaky nose and a firm, jutting chin. The flattering Napoleonic treatment is the only known likeness of David.[30]

To offset boredom and assist his recruiting around Chillicothe, Jackson joined the Grand Lodge of Freemasons and wrote home asking for the words to a lodge song he had forgotten:

Dear wife

I have Nothing of importance to write only that William Norris had the Measels and has got nearly over them but has not had them bad and, as I told some of your friends that william would not think it advisable for their moving to the ohio, he is Satisfyed to stay where he is I have got one Recruit and took one deserter from amoung the bellepont torys and he Escaped the next Morning pleas shew this to your friends and at any time that you or any others will Write to me and give me a full statement how business is carried on it will be a pleasure and I wish you or Polly or some friend to write a Mason song and send Enclosed in a letter. The song that Polly knows (and they are cept in the Dark Untill we open their eyes) the Reason [is that] I am joining the grand lodge (and get wood and what you want Done for Mary, or any thing so that you Dont suffer)

Mrs Juliet Jackson

from your husband and friend
D E Jackson
30th January 1814.

Fraternities gave travelers an important advantage when they needed introductions to trustworthy strangers. The Masonic philosophy promised intellectual stimulation to young men in a pragmatic frontier world. The association accompanied David to the farthest reaches of the continent, even to his grave.

In October 1813 the Army had shattered the Indian confederacy and killed Tecumseh in the Battle of the Thames. The war shifted to eastern battlefields, and the understrengthed 19th Infantry merged with another regiment. As spring arrived David became ill, and because Jackson's Mill was only seventy miles away he went home to recuperate. Colonel Miller, who had lost track of the perambulating recruiter, reported on 14 April 1814 that Ensign Jackson was eligible for separation. Jackson had similar thoughts and penned a letter to the secretary of war.

> *West fork mills Harrison County*
> *Virginia May 7th 1814*

Sir

In leaving my family to enter into the service it was with a view of going into active service without delay and the encouragement met with in recruiting scarcely favored that expectation—but the recent transfer of our Regiment to the 26th whereby I am continued in the recruiting service seems to dispel the hopes I had entertained with so much confidence as of being called to the lines to complete my services.

A soldier enlisted by me who I considered a voluntary, and in the soundest principles of fairness & justice, was recently discharged on a habias corpiss—such consideration I think make it necessary that I shall resign when an order for me to serve in the lines cannot be procured—I ask the favor of you to accept of my resignation and am very respectfully your most obediant and very humble servant

> *D. E. Jackson*
> *Engsign 19th Regt U S. Infy*
> *Clarksburg May 21 Free*

The Honble John Armstrong
Secy of War
Washington City[31]

The Adjutant and Inspector General's Office had already acted on Colonel Miller's letter, striking Ensign Jackson from the rolls on 10 May 1814.

Lucky are the men who learn the poverty of war without the attendant lessons of blood. What failed to yield glory for the country hero gave rich insights about human nature, leadership, persuasion, dissimulation, politics, bureaucracy, and the inherent failure of using force to settle problems. The 26-year-old veteran put his tall, varnished hat away on the top shelf and became a farmer again. Traveling across the rich flatlands of the Ohio countryside showed David the inadequacy of his own mountain-pinched bottom lands, although he enjoyed taking his sons out into the fields with him. And last October, while he tramped around in Ohio, Juliet gave birth to the twin girls they named Mary Jones and Nancy Norris.

Some Jacksons pursued several new ventures. David's brother George had sent several letters, reporting that after the hostile Indians and British fur traders took over Prairie du Chien he had little hope of resuming operations at the Dubuque lead mines. Instead, George went into partnership with John McClanahan. They intended to construct and operate a sawmill near Ste. Genevieve, Missouri Territory, where George saw attractive possibilities for milling, lead mining, and farming.

David's younger brother Jonathan was pursuing a law career, and in January 1814 he was appointed collector of internal revenue. Their usually indulgent cousin, Congressman Jackson, who saw in Jonathan a weakness for gambling, refused to stand as his security in the appointment.[32]

Their father, the colonel, was busy forming another county in cooperation with a neighbor, Col. John McWhorter. As a first step toward forming Lewis County, Edward Jackson campaigned for election to the Virginia Assembly. During the three voting days at Clarksburg the candidates threw away the bung and treated the homespun electorate. The colonel won, the assembly passed the formation act in December, and by the following spring Edward was surveying the new county seat at Weston, conveniently near his home. Building a new town would keep the Jackson sawmill humming.[33]

Just when new business began claiming his attention, David received a call from his brother George in Missouri. McClanahan turned out to be an unlucky partner whose debt to the lawyer John Scott forced him to relinquish his half of the mill. In June 1815 Scott accepted George's note for $500, which allowed him to reclaim full ownership. But George, faced with running the entire operation, wrote home asking to hire two of Colonel Edward's experienced mill hands. Sometime in late 1815 David Jackson

headed west, escorting two slaves: Jack and nineteen-year-old Alex. He concluded a rental agreement with George at Ste. Genevieve dated 25 January 1816.[34]

The trip to Missouri gave the brothers an opportunity to discuss George's frustrated expectations for the upper Mississippi, which he blamed on the meddling British. Still, George's affairs were looking up: he had a pre-emption on 160 attractive acres of bottom land near his mill; and he had found a promising bride in Catharine McGreggor.[35] George needed only enough land for subsistence. He intended to support his new family with the sawmill or by lead mining, if the opportunity arose.

David also saw potential in this old French community on the west bank of the Mississippi. Halfway between the mouth of the Ohio and the mouth of the Mississippi, David expected Ste. Genevieve to develop into an important river metropolis. As soon as the government surveyors located the tracts dedicated to military warrants, David would be eligible for a claim. He agreed to return and help George get the sawmill going properly, but he first had to go home and convince Juliet about the opportunity.

With the guarantee of his brother's help, George E. Jackson made another attempt at upper-river lead mining. On 26 May 1816, when the land office at Kaskaskia—just across the river in Illinois—advertised leases for the Fever River mines, George submitted one of the first applications.[36]

David returned home to find his father deeply disappointed in Jonathan. The collector of internal revenue had failed to settle his accounts for 1815 and was short $3,500.76. A scandal could interfere with the campaign to get the new county approved in Richmond, but the stern colonel refused to bail him out. David was more understanding and loaned Jonathan $100.

Colonel Jackson was unhappy to learn that his main dependence was considering a move to Missouri. If David left, he would have to rely on fourteen-year-old Cummins E. Jackson.

The notion of moving to Missouri also got a chilly response across the river. Juliet was appalled by her husband's expectation that she would leave her family, friends, and familiar places to move to a raw frontier inhabited by foreigners, ruffians, and savages.

3

"Mr. Henery leaves here by land"

LANDOGOSHEN, HOW THOSE SETTLERS CROSSED the Mississippi for the federal land sales! The government had three million acres up for grabs. And before settlers had realized the full potential of their last forest clearing, they were already moving on to build new lives and make fortunes.

River ferries carried an average of fifty wagons a day from the muddy landings of American river bottoms to the golden coast of Missouri. Most of the newcomers trailed through St. Louis and St. Charles to Booneslick country; others rolled into the three southern counties—Ste. Genevieve, St. François, and Washington. The building boom needed the lumber from George Jackson's sawmill, and what locals didn't use could be shipped down the Mississippi to the expanding cotton plantations. The Jackson brothers, working together again, cut timber in the highlands and floated it down to the sawmill.

While logging on the spooky upper Fourche du Clos River, David Jackson drew down on a wolf and got into the skin game. Settlers made fences a low priority, exposing their roaming cattle and hogs to predators, which the county tried to control through a bounty system. In late 1817 the public-spirited David Jackson took the wolf's ears to a county officer who wrote out a note against the public treasury.

When the government advertised Fever River lead-mining leases in 1816, George Jackson was one of the first applicants; other speculators included Pierre Menard, William Morrison, and Andrew Henry—all of whom previously associated in fur-trapping adventures on the upper Missouri—and John Hay, who had traded on the Assiniboine River in British territory. The registrar and receiver issued Jackson a pre-emption certificate for lots 2, 27, 29, and 30, and forwarded his application to Washington, D.C., on 23 July. Washington disappointed Jackson and the others in September when it suspended the leasing process until the system could be better thought out.

On 26 October 1817, when his wife gave birth to a daughter, George felt the responsibility of caring for his family and decided to restrict his adventuring and stick close to his sawmill. This made David, by now committed to his western location, a supernumerary. A man with time on his hands in that place and time had little choice but to dig lead.

David had landed in one of the most cosmopolitan communities in mid-America. With its oddly designed old houses and French-speaking residents, Ste. Genevieve was tied to an old tradition. The French explorers—Jolliet, Father Marquette, and LaSalle—had brief but brilliant importance.

The city's economy had always rested on the coureur de bois. Those woods-running Indian traders caused New France great concern when they began looking to the English up the Ohio River for better prices. The French branded them as renegades for their disrespect of the state fur-trade monopoly. Many coureurs had settled around Kaskaskia, on the Illinois side of the river, and had intermarried among the local tribes. When the French garrison at Fort Chartres finally surrendered after the British conquest, many of the east-bank inhabitants, fearing English Protestantism, moved across the river into Spanish territory.

Several years before the American Revolution an English surveyor estimated that Americans on the east shore supported 1,273 "sencible men," while about 208 undiagnosed Frenchmen lived in Ste. Genevieve. Many inhabitants of Ste. Genevieve formed a genealogical tree with its roots in old Montreal and whose fruit had ripened into the métis of the middle river. The Valle family, already into their third inheritance of civic leadership, shared power with the Boyer, Beauvais, Pratte, Janis, Dufour, and Menard families.[37]

Even before the Louisiana Purchase, Ste. Genevieve had experienced several waves of American immigration from those eager for an opportunity to acquire Spanish land grants. More came soon after Israel Dodge raised the American flag on 10 March 1804. As David Jackson strolled around town he overheard conversations in middle-American French, Mississippi Valley Spanish, several bastardized Indian tongues, and a brand of frontier English that would have appalled his former teacher.

This frontier also feared Indians, and some older houses were still surrounded by pickets. *Poteaux en terre* and *poteaux sur solle* architectural styles reflected Old France, but the thatched roofs were giving way to shakes. While David's hometown in Virginia grew from and strung out along Main Street, Ste. Genevieve surrounded a public square bounded by the edifices of religion, government, and education. When the newcomers tried to plant a courthouse as the symbol of a new order in the center of the square, the old inhabitants protested until the authorities shifted it to the north side of the block.

The American population released the expansionist energy pent up by the War of 1812 in an optimistic rush toward the apparently limitless chance to get a start in western agriculture. But when the government began to dispense public lands in Missouri Territory, Spanish land grants and a maze of pre-emption claims clouded many titles. Before the government could sell any land, surveyors had to identify prior claims and assure those who settled before 1814 that they had first chance to purchase the land at minimum price. Because one hundred townships in Missouri had to be surveyed by the understaffed Illinois field office, the government found it would not have basic plats available until 1818.[38]

David Jackson felt frustrated in every expectation. Instead of operating a successful lumber mill while George tapped the Fever River lead mines, he had to share in the sawing. Instead of falling into a hot new property in Missouri, the government blocked David from getting land until it caught up with its duty to its citizens. Instead of reaping the golden promise, he stood neck deep in a goddamn lead pit, selling his ore piecework. He could not ask Juliet to join him in this uncertain situation, and he could not admit to a mistake by going home.

Digging lead near the new center of industry at Potosi put David in contact with an undesirable body of men.[39] The head ruffian, a killer named John Smith T. (for Tennessee), swaggered and intimidated everyone into excusing his excesses under the dueling code. His successful dueling tactic was to fire before the end of the count. George cautioned David that Smith T. had played a part in an earlier filibuster attempt on the Dubuque mines that greatly contributed to Indian unrest in that region.[40]

Most newcomers found the riverman Mike Fink and his depraved cronies—Ohio River riffraff left over from the war, Indian fighting, light piracy, and other excesses—equally repugnant. These men's Sunday entertainment usually consisted of drunken tests of marksmanship in which an inebriate held the target board between his knees. Fink particularly liked to terrorize his rotten girlfriend, Pittsburgh Blue, by forcing her to hold the mark.[41]

Jackson cut his teeth on Ohio Tories, and the rough crowd left him alone when he went into town on Saturday night for supplies and a drink. He preferred the conversation of more interesting men of enterprise, including Andrew Henry, the justice of the peace. Henry had known George Jackson for some time, and over a friendly cup of the local poison with David he related some remarkable adventures on the upper Missouri River.[42]

Henry came from York County, Pennsylvania, near the old trans-Allegheny Indian-trade supply towns. A disappointment in love and honor brought him to Ste. Genevieve in 1801. Six years later that same star-crossed romanticism led to a brief marriage and precipitous divorce from a daughter of the French community. In the summer of 1808 he had little to lose in joining Manuel Lisa's fur-trapping adventure up the Missouri River.[43]

The promising returns of the Spanish adventurer's 1807-1808 enterprise attracted other substantial Missourians. Pierre and Auguste Chouteau, Jr., Sylvestre Pratte, Benjamin Wilkerson, and Reuben Lewis (the brother of Upper Louisiana Governor Meriwether Lewis) joined Lisa's original backers, William Morrison and Pierre Menard. William Clark, rewarded with superintendency of the western Indians, compromised his position by entering into private business with his charges. The new organization required active participation by its members in field operations; the others excused Morrison of this requirement on his agreement to furnish a stand-in: Andrew Henry.[44]

Henry lacked the capital for his share of the adventure, but he had a good reputation among the Ste. Genevieve miners and boatmen. Soon he and his new friends were poling, rowing, and towing the heavy keelboats against the strong Missouri River current. That heavy work eroded their enthusiasm, and of the 350 men who started from St. Louis only 153 stayed on past Fort Osage, barely the beginning of the long journey. Partner Pierre Menard wrote that Henry kept the mutinous men in line by his "frank manner and honesty [which] admitted everything without beating around the bush."

Just beyond the Mandan villages they built a fort and wintered. Early in 1810 Menard took fifty men to work the boats up the Yellowstone while Henry and forty mounted hunters rode overland to the mouth of the Big Horn River. From there Henry and Menard took a trapping party to the head of the upper Gallatin River and down to the fabulous beaver reserves at the Three Forks of the upper Missouri River.[45]

They saw an ominous sign: the bones of western Indians killed in a battle with the Gros Ventres in spring 1808. John Colter had been with the intruders and had fired on the attackers. Later in the fall he and his trapping partner, John Potts, returned to the area and were surprised by Indians who riddled Potts with arrows until he looked like a porcupine and gave Colter a slim chance to race, naked, for his life. Colter's companions found his story sobering.

When the Henry-Menard party reached the place where the Three Forks of the upper Missouri River came together, they built a fort on a peninsula between the rivers. As inheritors of the long-hunter traditions of the trans-Appalachian frontier and of the Dan'l Boone-Kentucky legendry, they intended to trap in the hunting preserves bloodily conquered and savagely defended by the southern Blackfeet.

Henry and Menard learned the hard way that the Piegans fully understood the value of the beaver within their territory. They customarily traded pelts for guns, ammunition, and blankets at any British post, or, more conveniently, at Lisa's house on the middle Yellowstone. Direct trapping by whites violated the traditional relationship between the Indian hunters and visiting traders.[46]

Blackfoot retribution for the invasion of their hunting grounds came swiftly and emphatically with the killing of trappers Ayres and James Cheek. Three more men were missing and presumed slain: Freehearty "and his man, and a young man named Hull." The raiders took the men's traps, arms, and horses, and a sally from the fort to recover some of the property failed to dispel the dark cloud that settled over the Missouri Fur Company (MFC) enterprise.

Colter saw the light and after April 21 departed for St. Louis carrying Menard's letters. Later, former Lewis and Clark expedition hunter George Drouillard made another attempt to trap with some of his Shawnee kinsmen. The Bloods left his intestines draped around on bushes.[47]

Although several years had passed by the time David Jackson heard these stories in Ste. Genevieve, he saw that Andrew Henry took no pride in this thrilling yarn. Losing good men was nothing to brag about; still, Henry continued the saga.

Menard and Reuben Lewis pulled out for safer climes, but Henry convinced fifteen determined hunters to make another attempt beyond striking range of the watchful Indians. Peter Wiser, another Lewis and Clark alumnus, said they had a five- or six-day ride up the Madison branch of the Three Forks to safer trapping.[48] Henry's party crossed over the Continental Divide into the drainage of the upper Snake River and built several log huts. To the west stretched the forbidding barren sagebrush of the eastern Snake plains, punctuated by three volcanic buttes. East and south behind rolling foothills loomed the long wall of the Teton Range, a snow-crested rampart pointing southward like an endless promise.

The more understanding Indians they met on these buffalo-hunting plains told Henry that their trails led to good beaver hunting and to a spring trade fair in the Salmon River country. Some of the Snake Indians had their winter camps in the willow-sheltered river bottoms to the south. Beyond, in the Bear

River valley, tribes met to trade and fight at another intermountain rendezvous. The man who reached those annual Indian conclaves with trading goods could collect a fortune in beaver pelts without ever wetting his moccasins.

Henry's men scattered to hunt, and he took the opportunity to travel as far south as the headwaters of the Green River.[49] By spring they had exhausted their supplies, and Henry's hunters needed powder and lead to survive. Henry had to abandon the bonanza and return to Lisa's Big Horn fort, keeping well south of the dangerous Blackfeet. They built bullboat skin canoes and drifted their returns down the Yellowstone and Missouri to St. Louis. Henry recalled in newspaper reports that he "subsisted principally on roots, and having lost his clothes, dressed himself from head to foot in skins."[50]

Coming down the Missouri they met another Lisa party going up with the former Ste. Genevieve lawyer Henry Marie Brackenridge, who was interested in the route selected by Lewis and Clark.[51] They also met a contingent of the Pacific Fur Company heading upstream under the leadership of Wilson Price Hunt and Ramsay Crooks. Crooks, an experienced middle-Missouri River trader, and Hunt enjoyed the confidence of John Jacob Astor. Four of Henry's trappers returned to the mountains with them.

David recognized the names Crooks and Hunt as the same men his brother George saw descending the Mississippi when he was at the Dubuque mines.

Henry felt only slightly disappointed when the War of 1812 prevented him from returning to the killing ground. During the next few years he concentrated on mining, farming, and militia duty and let the memory of the shining mountains recede. Some said that he let slip "the most flattering prospect of future success" to stay on his Blackwater River farm with his new wife, Mary Fleming, a simple country girl unlikely to cause him any heartache.

David's drinking friends remembered that Robert Stuart brought the first Astorians back, reaching St. Louis in the spring of 1813. They had hard times crossing the plains but proudly reported that the Pacific Fur Company had beat the British to the mouth of the Columbia River; they then sent traders inland to such strange-sounding places as Okanagon and Spokane. But Astor lost the bright promise of American domination on the Columbia when his Canadian partners sold out to their brothers-under-the-skin of the British North West Company. The Americans turned the Pacific slope over to the British Empire for salvage.

On 29 April 1816 Congress passed a bill barring foreigners from the Indian trade within the borders of the United States. In 1818 the northern border was set along the 49th parallel of latitude as far as the crest of the Rocky Mountains. Unable to come to an acceptable division for conflicting territorial claims west of the mountains, the negotiators compromised on the joint occupancy of the Oregon Country.

A pessimistic military observer stalled at Council Bluffs in 1819 decided that the fur trade had "little importance from a pecuniary point of view" and should probably continue to be controlled by the government. The observer's comments were sour grapes—the United States Army had failed to push an expedition up the Missouri to the mouth of the Yellowstone. Military presence was supposed to inhibit British intrusion, but the fancy new-fangled steamboats were unable to breast the strong current, and the whole expedition stalled at Council Bluffs. The United States was unable to proceed to the mouth of the Yellowstone and "secure to us the fur trade and break up the intercourse between the British traders and the Indians."[52]

Andrew Henry, the pioneer of the Rocky Mountain trade, was just another countryman come into town for a drink and a hand of cards when David met him in Ste. Genevieve. He told a damn fine yarn but was only interested in local lead mining and modest community service. Jackson listened with interest to business proposals but felt content developing a land claim and a western home. Then the bubble burst.

To facilitate the distribution of public lands the government sold parcels on easy credit with a minimal down payment. Westerners considered the pre-emptive right to buy government land as good as the actual title, and they bought and sold that right before making anything except the initial down payment. To get in on the bonanza, settlers who arrived with little money took credit. And merchants, to meet the demands of their customers, ordered more goods on similar expectations. To handle such complex deals in a cashless country, banks printed their own banknotes without reserves adequate to back the paper. The frontier economy was overheating.

Realizing that its policies had created a dangerous situation, the government abruptly curtailed credit. The Second Bank of the United States called in its outstanding loans, and the land offices demanded cash. The East managed to suffer through the credit squeeze in 1818, but panic rapidly overtook the West through 1819 and 1820. As the tide of immigration slowed and new money disappeared, plans formulated on anticipated growth collapsed. When land prices tumbled, the speculator's market evaporated. Farmers were left holding crops they could not sell, and merchants stared at unsalable stock on their shelves. The Panic of 1819 shook the West as violently as the New Madrid earthquake had eight years earlier.[53]

The impartial disaster caused good men to suffer with fools. Mining entrepreneur Moses Austin lost everything in the collapse of the Bank of St. Louis, causing him to look south to Texas. Thomas James, one of Henry's Three Forks trappers, went legitimate as a river merchant and watched his dream sink. He then crawled up the Arkansas River to try to get started in the Santa Fe trade.

The Jackson clan suffered its losses, too. David's uncle John Jackson, Jr., a conservative western Virginia miller, tried to redeem his losses by floating a flatboat load of flour to New Orleans. He died in the lower Mississippi River miasmas, as much a victim of the economy as of the river fever.[54] In a territory that allowed imprisonment for debt, George Jackson faced humiliation because he sold lumber on credit to men unable to pay him.

When a note to lawyer John Scott came due on 1 July 1819, George faced the repossession of his Missouri enterprise. Four years later he was still trying to collect his mill debts.[55]

David Jackson luckily had made only conservative western investments. He had been waiting until the surveyors completed their work so he could file on a land claim. Now, with most of the land nearly worthless and with little to show for his efforts, he again faced the possible embarrassment of going home with his tail between his legs.

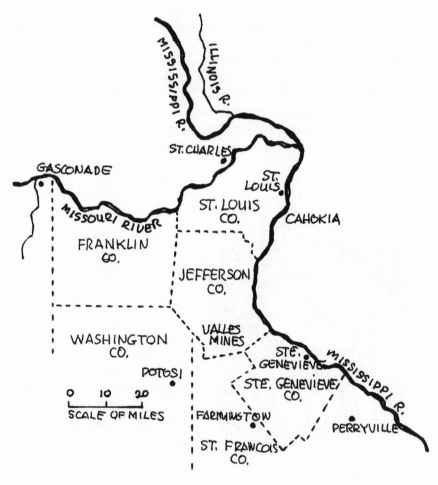

St. Louis/Ste. Genevieve region.

4

"All the high points of the mountains were in view"

FOR THE PRICE OF A DRINK IN BRUGER'S TAVERN some former western hunter could unravel the mysteries of western geography. Men around Ste. Genevieve could yarn about the upper Mississippi and the Red River as far north as Selkirk's colony; about trading on the Assiniboin and Saskatchewan rivers in the British northwest; about the lower, middle, and upper Missouri; about the Columbia and Snake rivers across the Continental Divide; or about the shallow Platte and tepid Arkansas of the central plains.

These men knew the interior of the continent from having been there, and their memories were generally trustworthy—pride kept them from being caught in lies or being corrected by lesser men. David sensed that more than the liquor was speaking when they mentioned the thrill of topping rises they had never crossed before, or of looking out across expanses as pure as when the first Frenchmen saw them.

In early 1822 David Jackson listened closely. He needed to know what he was getting into. The death of Manuel Lisa, the godfather of the Missouri trade, two years earlier had passed the supervision of the Missouri Fur Company to a former Kentucky hatter's apprentice. Joshua Pilcher came to St. Louis after the war to get closer to the fiber supply, and when the company designated him "Acting Partner on the Missouri," he inherited the whole show.[56]

The story that came back to the settlements was that in 1821 Pilcher pushed a small trading post up to the mouth of the White River, where boating problems forced him to pack his outfit overland. He had a crew of 180 men to keep gainfully employed and decided to risk sending a strong party up the White River and across to the middle Yellowstone where Lisa had traded with the Crows and even some Blackfeet. The adventure proved so successful that other Missouri entrepreneurs again became interested in the skin game.

David's acquaintance Andrew Henry had a good farm, a loving wife, and manageable debts, but Henry's oldest friend, William H. Ashley, was an unattached man of business with pressing debts and considerable ambition. Ashley, the son of a tidewater Virginian, came to Spanish Louisiana about the same time as Henry and joined him in lead mining around Ste. Genevieve. During the War of 1812 Ashley made enough from the manufacture of gunpowder to speculate in St. Louis real estate with another Washington County man, Lionel Brown. Brown unwisely took exception to a remark of the duelist John Smith T., which gained him a bullet hole in the center of his forehead. Ashley continued riding high as the agent for an English investor with a $26,000 line of credit. When they elected him lieutenant governor of the new state of Missouri, the voters, and even his close friends, did not realize that Ashley was dancing on the edge of financial disaster.[57]

In the excited reports of the MFC successes on the upper Missouri, Ashley began to see the fur trade as his financial salvation. As a man of business rather than action, he needed a partner to organize and lead the field operations. Sometime late in 1821 Ashley convinced his old friend Andrew Henry to undertake a joint venture the following spring. Ashley would serve as the downstream capitalist and Henry the upstream wintering partner. Henry began looking for a trustworthy field staff among the lead miners while Ashley advertised for enterprising young men in St. Louis.

With a population of only four thousand in 1822, St. Louis had many merchants and commercial men with special interests, and everyone knew something about everyone else's business. Just a day after Ashley and Henry ordered $6,000 worth of goods to outfit their operation, on 8 September 1821, Thomas Hempstead wrote to warn his partner, Joshua Pilcher. The supplies came from the same outfitter who supplied the MFC: Oliver Bostwick, the agent for David Stone & Company of Boston. The Ashley-Henry operation probably got terms similar to the latter's: credit due twelve months after delivery at the cost of 6 percent, doubled for late payment.[58]

In January the partners visited the United States Army commandant at St. Louis to apply for a trapping license. Ashley and Henry found Brig. Gen. Henry Atkinson testy because he had recently broken his leg for the second time. They intended to trap and trade with the Indians of the Yellowstone, and the general felt obliged to point out that the Army and other trappers had yet to resolve past differences with the Blackfeet. Hunting on their lands might create yet another incident that could interfere with the government's plans for negotiation. Atkinson denied the license.[59]

Ashley and Henry then applied for a license directly to the secretary of war in a petition presented by the entire Missouri congressional delegation: Senators David Barton and Thomas Hart Benton and Representative John Scott. Within a week the secretary of war responded: "I have agreeably to your recommendation and request of 1 March 1822 issued licenses to Gen'l

W. H. Ashley & Maj Henry as soon as they have executed their bonds, as required by law."[60] Clerical delays held up the licenses until 11 April, but Henry left St. Louis earlier expecting his authorization to follow him up the Missouri River.[61]

The Indians took only enough beaver skins to satisfy their immediate needs, and the dangerously undercapitalized partners intended to boost fur production by direct trapping. Just a few lone-wolf trappers worked up the river, so the Ashley-Henry party needed to import trappers. In an arrangement similar to Lisa's in 1809, Ashley-Henry offered contracts that provided transportation to the beaver country and a supply of powder, lead, and traps on credit. In return the hunters would help the enterprise ascend the river, build a central depot, and defend it if necessary. In addition, they owed Ashley-Henry half of their first year's catch and could dispose of the remaining pelts as they saw fit, presumably by selling to the conveniently near and financially fair Ashley-Henry buyers.

The partners expected to make a profit on the goods they sold to the hunters, but, more important, they saved paying salaries and still managed to shift a good part of the capital to the trappers.

Andrew Henry identified the enterprise's biggest disadvantage as its lack of enforceable control over the hunters; however, he remained confident in his own ability to lead and knew from previous experience that Indian trouble would teach the men to stick together. For an honest and dependable second-in-command Henry turned to a Danish mining friend, John H. Weber, who had a quarterdeck sense of authority and enough education to handle the necessary book work.[62] To raise cash, Henry and Weber sold some jointly held land in Washington County and looked for others with spare funds to invest.[63]

Henry's brother-in-law, Nicholas Fleming, joined the group as its surgeon. The 1822 tax assessments for the three counties listed the names Chapman, Cunningham, Evans, Fitzpatrick, Gale, Galbraith, Ham, Kirker, and Tullock. Those families apparently entrusted their kinsmen to Henry and Weber, who recruited as many as fifty men from the mining region.

Because George E. Jackson was a former Indian trader who knew how to handle himself in difficult situations, Henry might have approached him with a clerk's job. But George had some large debts and a family that needed him, which Henry understood because he was reluctantly leaving his own wife and baby daughter. George's brother, David, however, had experience as a former army officer and was accustomed to supervising men. Mature enough at thirty-three to command respect, David Jackson was one of the few men in the country who had the sound judgment to handle his affairs without falling into debt.[64]

Like other disappointed republicans with the pioneer fixation on land, David Jackson blamed the government for the panic and economic upset. Since real estate turned into a slow road to fortune, he stood ready for any reasonable alternative. When Henry and Weber offered him a role in their enterprise, he welcomed the crossroad in his career but still took two months to make up his mind.

During the previous year David had boarded at the home of Joseph Hertich, who ran a school on a portion of his father-in-law's land.[65] David had assembled some livestock to begin a ranch. Entering the fur trade and running off with the long hunters would mean abandoning corn-patch thinking. It would mean turning his back on steady achievement for a risky flyer in an unfamiliar field. It would extend by two or three years the separation from his wife, Juliet, and his children. Walking along the Mississippi shore to order his thoughts David noticed how the Missouri waters discolored the river. He imagined that the silt came from the heart of the continent. At the last moment David E. Jackson committed to an irresistible adventure. He would turn his cattle and slave herdsman over to George.

The brothers made a carefully specific contract covering "the term of three years or until his Return from the Expedidition that he is about to take up the Missouri." The men valued the cattle and horses at $410, but instead of receiving cash David allocated the stock to George as payment for their care and as credit against the debt he owed their father for rental of the slave. If disputes over increases arose, two good men could arbitrate them.[66]

Hempstead described Henry's departure from St. Louis to Pilcher: "General Ashley's company starts this day with one boat and one hundred and fifty men by land and water." A member of the party later recalled only one hundred men, which suggests that fifty came by horseback from the mining region. Hempstead portrayed the crew pessimistically: "The men are all generally speaking untried and of every description and nation, when you see them you will judge for yourself."[67]

Benjamin O'Fallon, the agent for the Upper Missouri Indian Agency at Fort Atkinson, saw the group similarly and fired an apprehensive letter off to Secretary of War Calhoun:

> The [Sioux] Indians high up the Missouri Continue to insult our traders: but I hear of no late depredations I understand that License has been granted to Messrs Ashley & Henry to trade, trap and hunt, on the

upper Missouri—I have not seen it, but am in hopes that limits have been prescribed to their hunting and trapping on Indian Lands, as nothing is better Calculated to alarm and disturb the harmony so happily existing between us and the Indians in the vicinity of Council Bluffs.

As I can see no probability of the military expeditions progressing up the Missouri this year; I think there is no impropriety in allowing hunting and trapping above the Mandans, on the lands of Indians who are unfriendly to us, and under foreign influence; but as soon as we have an opportunity of counteracting that influence and producing a good understanding between us and the Indians, then, hunting and trapping should be prohibited and our traders confined alone to a fair and equitable trade with them.[68]

Prospective trappers, whose forbearers had driven the Delawares and Iroquois from the Susquehanna and Shenandoah valleys and then crossed the Appalachian Mountains to appropriate the Ohio country, gave slight consideration to the territorial rights of Indians. Now the United States puzzled over what to do with the last tribesmen clinging to eastern reservations. The government's attempt to ensure fair trading through properly supervised Indian trade factories came under fire from such opportunists as John Jacob Astor, who claimed the system inhibited free enterprise. The only factory on the Missouri was Fort Osage, about twenty miles below the mouth of the Kansas River.

Jackson and the mining-region recruits rode overland to intercept the first Ashley-Henry keelboat, which left St. Louis on 3 April 1822. Bypassing St. Louis, they apparently missed meeting Ashley, who could not readily distinguish between the Jackson brothers.

David Jackson probably wore miner's clothes: red shirt, tough pants tucked into his boots, and a broad-brimmed hat. He carried an all-purpose butcher knife used for gutting, skinning, hoof-trimming, eating, and self-defense. Flint and steel, some gun tools, and a pistol rounded out his equipment. His rifle carried an eastern gunsmith's mark; Jacob Hawken was just beginning to earn his reputation as the St. Louis armorer to the plainsmen. David and his body servant, Jim, sat worn Virginia saddles on their horses.[69]

Facing a 1,700-mile upriver pull, Andrew Henry meant to travel light. The majority of the outfit would follow later in a second boat sent by Ashley. The sixty- to eighty-foot-long keelboat could use a square sail when the wind cooperated, but most of the time its passengers had to row, tow, or pole it. Setting their long poles in the river's muddy bottom, the boatmen put the other end against their shoulder and trudged the length of a catwalk stretching alongside the boat. Each trip from the bow to the stern moved the heavy keelboat another forty or fifty feet. Mike Fink and his brutish boatmen were going to walk up the river backwards. When the current got too strong they had to go ashore and drag the damn thing with long towlines. Smaller pirogues (log canoes) and skiffs accompanied the keelboat as tenders or auxiliary transport. The shore party rode apart from that grueling labor and kept a bright eye for fresh game.

On 26 April the expedition paused to catch a second wind at Franklin, Missouri. Ezekiel Williams, the former MFC trapper, came out to see the spectacle. He crossed the river from his Cooper County home to greet old acquaintances, including Major Henry, and to cackle at the innocents by telling them the Blackfeet would rob them and "git yer hair."[70]

An eleven-year-old boy, whose father displayed the Masonic emblem on his tavern sign and exchanged secret handshakes with Henry and Jackson, saw the expedition more romantically. Young Caleb Bingham soaked up images with the hungry eye of a kid who knew he must draw.[71]

Unwilling to waste cargo space on food, Andrew Henry fed his party a diet of deer, elk, black bear, wild turkey, and raccoon; soon these became as monotonous as Mama's corn mush and scarce, too, because other river parties also hunted their way inland, depleting the game near the river. When empty bellies rubbed against backbones some weaklings wanted to turn back, and the expedition almost lost its historian, Daniel Potts. He and eight disgruntled men left the boat near the White River only to discover that going back was as bad as going on.[72]

David's duties as clerk required his occasional presence on board the keelboat, which allowed him to sit in the shade of the deckhouse and listen to Henry explain the skin game. The major intended to leapfrog the river trading posts of the established middle Missouri River traders—Berthold & Chouteau, Pratte & Vasquez, and the old MFC—by going up the Missouri next spring. He had heard of new competition by two St. Louis backers, William P. Tildon and S. S. Dudley, fronting for some British former traders. Tildon and Dudley were in the Lac Traverse Sioux trade but planned to come overland to the Mandan villages. By then Ashley-Henry expected to be far up the Missouri.[73]

As the party climbed the ladder of Indian tribes—Omaha, Ponca, Sioux, Arikara, and Mandan—it met the "durtey, Kind, pore & extravigent" people that William Clark encountered eighteen years earlier. Since Clark's visit the river people had learned to increase the passage tolls they charged travelers.

The boatmen sweating at the cordelle (towline) despised the Indians, but what the travelers resented as simple bribery the Indians viewed as a polite response to their hospitality. The single-minded parties were incapable of bridging a hundred years of cultural misunderstanding, and Henry was prepared to avoid Indian trouble with a few gifts.

Below the MFC's Cedar Fort the travelers entered the territory of Yankton and Teton Sioux. Major Henry came ashore at the Arikara villages near the mouth of Grand River to exchange forty or fifty of their tired horses for fresh animals. The new mounts allowed the shore party to take an overland shortcut to the Mandan villages at Heart River, where they saw tribesmen dressed in splendid painted hides, feathers, horns, and decorated trade cloth. Those sophisticated folk who had known traders for over eighty years understood how to be indulgent hosts.[74]

Because Henry used the horses to lighten the boat, the pack string and flotilla arrived in tandem at the mouth of the Little Missouri on 15 August 1822 when they found three hundred of the plains-ranging Assiniboin Indians waiting to meet them. Henry invited the leaders aboard his keelboat for a parley and treats. Meanwhile, some young warriors stampeded the horse herd and ran off twenty-two horses, some with packs still on them. The partnership not only lost $1,840 in goods and horseflesh, it suffered the indignity of being outwitted.[75]

Around the first of September the expedition reached the mouth of the Yellowstone River, where Henry stopped to build a strong central depot. This location gave him the option of trapping the Yellowstone or the Missouri. The men constructed the post on the south bank of the Missouri about a quarter-mile above the entry of the Yellowstone. The site was pleasant, even beautiful to the aesthetically minded among the party. The men soon surrounded four cottonwood-log houses with a palisade enclosure that had only one gate.[76]

As a result of Henry's trading en route, both to keep up friendly relations with the river tribesmen and to draw off furs from the opposition, he already had a few packs of beaver before the men began trapping in earnest. The lists of employees and other organizational details did not survive Ashley's management, however, making it impossible for us to determine exactly how many hunters had turned back.[77]

After helping build the fort the hunters began to learn their new profession under nearly ideal conditions. The water still ran warm, and the riverside trees glowed with autumn color. The beavers' coats were beginning to thicken for winter, but it was still too early for the best-quality pelts. The men lazing around the depot were surprised when William H. Ashley rode in on the first of October. He brought bad news.

Henry's eagerness to get on the river left the task of recruiting a crew of eighty for the second keelboat to Ashley. The general had no intention of going upriver himself and assigned the supervision of the boat to Daniel D. S. Moore, a clerk of the St. Louis Circuit Court. Ashley hired Hiram Scott, a young bankrupt, as the clerk and entrusted the steering to the boat captain, or patron, Joseph Marchand. About twenty miles below Fort Osage the boat's mast snagged an overhanging tree. The keelboat swamped and sank with a $10,000 cargo aboard. The crew waited on the river bank to see what Ashley wanted to do.

In the face of disaster the appalled partner acted credibly. In three frantic weeks Ashley sold three choice town lots to raise $2,600 and buy another outfit. Previous expeditions must have nearly cleaned out the St. Louis suppliers' stock, and the inexperienced Ashley put together a poor outfit. He decided he could not risk the partnership's last hope to anyone else, so he traveled west with the outfit.[78]

At Fort Atkinson, near Council Bluffs, Ashley learned that Robert Jones and Michael J. Immell brought down thirty packs of good Crow beaver as returns from the 1821-22 Big Horn post outfit and planned to return to that lucrative area with sixty trappers.[79] Immell accompanied Henry in 1810-11, so Ashley knew the MFC would make an attempt on the Three Forks. By forcing the pace Ashley got ahead of Jones and Immell, bought horses from the Arikaras, and rode overland to inform Henry that they were now in a race for the best beaver grounds.

Ashley's arrival at Fort Henry on the first of October preceded the second keelboat's by two weeks. With the general were the reformed Daniel Potts and a tall, lanky new recruit named Jedediah Smith. If Smith met David Jackson at this time, he omitted it from the memoir he wrote eight years later.

The partners agreed that Ashley would return to St. Louis with the furs so far accumulated, use them to mend financial fences, and finagle another outfit for next spring. Ashley pulled away in a large pirogue, leaving Henry with about ninety-seven men including those hired to guard the depot. The arrival of the second boat allowed the hunters to outfit and get ready to trap. The earlier brush with the Assiniboin reinforced that they stick together.[80]

The first trapping brigade went up the Yellowstone with Capt. John Weber as the bourgeois and David E. Jackson as the petite bourgeois, or clerk. Weber planned to take canoes as far as the mouth of Powder River, buy horses from the River Crow, and make a late hunt. He decided to avoid the

Big Horn because the MFC trapped there last year and would surely return. Some men, including Smith and Chapman, hunted for meat on the lower Yellowstone and took "what Beaver we could conveniently."[81]

The Missouri Fur field superintendent, Joshua Pilcher, stopped at the Mandan villages and sent his 43-man Yellowstone brigade on under Jones and Immell. They headed for the Big Horn post and caught up with Weber and Jackson just below the mouth of the Powder River.

The Ashley-Henry men worked their pirogues upstream in the low channels shadowed by brilliant autumn willows and cottonwoods. Cut banks and crumbling bluffs limited their views from the water, but climbing the banks revealed a new world of long horizons where the Yellowstone country glowed like gold beneath a pale blue, endless sky. Beyond the rolling expanse of ocher grass and olive earth rose distant mountains already crowned with snow. David's knowledge of the pinched, shadowed valleys of western Virginia began giving way to a new sense of space and time measured by distance.

The Yellowstone rapids discouraged the idea of taking the pirogues higher. Packing their outfit on their few horses, Weber and his men hunted up the Powder River as it flowed through barren, soluble country that clouded it with fine sand. British traders had examined the murky stream that led toward the Big Horn Mountains as early as 1805, and the Americans came to it as exploiters rather than discoverers.

As Weber and his men worked their way up the Powder, Major Henry took twenty-one men up the Missouri to set up an outpost at the mouth of the Milk River. They made such good time paddling that instead of stopping at the Milk, Henry decided to go on to the mouth of the Musselshell. They arrived at the end of November and, after building cabins and securing the outfit, Henry returned to the central depot with eight men. Going down he met hunters Smith and Chapman leading the land party, whose hope for a late hunt was spoiled when the river "frose to the emmence thickness of four feet."[82]

The bored men sharing close quarters at Fort Henry soon got on each other's nerves. The others found Mike Fink, Bill Carpenter, and Levi Talbot intolerable, and everyone was relieved when the three retreated to a den they dug into the river bank. The remaining men killed time playing cards, drinking, or dancing to the fiddling of the amiable major.

Somewhere on the upper Powder, perhaps as far as the sheltering Big Horn Mountains, Captain Weber wintered his little band of trappers.

Because they lacked the proper equipment and experience to live in the open, they probably enjoyed the hospitality of the Crow Indians.[83]

Blinking from smoke that refused to exit the hole in the top of the buffalo-hide tepee, David Jackson must have felt centuries away from everything he knew. He lay wrapped in a vermin-infested buffalo robe next to Indians that his background taught him to detest. But he was beginning to float, as these strange folk did, in a world without fully known dimensions.

Across the Big Horn Mountains, in the Wind River valley, the Mountain Crow were hosting another band of wanderers, a mixed bag of fourteen Iroquois hunters and some homesick Astorians who were looking for a way to escape from debt bondage to the HBC. The men just coming into the mountains and those who had been there too long were about to collide.

5

"This territory being trapped by both parties"

DURING THE WINTER OF 1822-23 American and British traders were already moving toward competitive collision. The movement of the Ashley-Henry and Missouri Fur Company keelboats on the Missouri paralleled a brigade of Hudson's Bay Company York boats stemming the South Saskatchewan (Bow) River. As Andrew Henry passed the Mandan villages, Chief Factor Donald McKenzie was approaching the Gros Ventre camps. While the Americans hunched against the winter at Fort Henry, their British counterparts shivered in leather lodges at the mouth of the Red Deer River about 280 miles to the northwest.[84]

The Mandan villages had witnessed international competition before, when Spanish officers tried to forbid British intrusion in 1795. The Lewis and Clark party noticed foreigners at that place when they went up the Missouri, and a North West Company expedition actually crossed behind them to test the potential of the Yellowstone River. In 1805 the first United States governor of Upper Louisiana limited unauthorized intrusion, but the lack of a force to police the edict failed to discourage British traders from exploiting American resources. Indians using British fuzees slew the first American hunters on the upper Missouri, and after Andrew Henry retreated from the Blackfeet in 1810 the Indians traded some of his slain hunters' property at Edmonton House on the North Saskatchewan. Across the mountains Astor's Pacific Fur Company met the North West Company head to head at the mouth of the Columbia River in 1811, and lost.

The boundary compromise of 1818 drew a line across the northern plains but left the Oregon Country west of the Rocky Mountains under a frustrating compromise of joint occupancy. Building on the Astorian experience, the North West Company began trapping the Snake River in 1818. Instead of waiting for unreliable Indians to bring in furs Donald McKenzie sent out engaged or obligated trappers to take them in the field. The Bannock and Shoshoni Indians dared not oppose these strong brigades, but McKenzie's men met determined resistance when they tried to work the headwaters of the upper Missouri. Accustomed to older trading conventions, the southern Blackfeet, or Piegans, determinedly fought to keep their territory and its contents free from exploitation by foreigners.

The North West Company and the rival HBC merged interests in 1821 and looked for new territories to recover the costs of their former competition. Donald McKenzie resigned to take his "peculiar talents" to St. Louis when the newly reformed HBC intercepted him on the Saskatchewan River and induced him to accept the command of a reinforced trapping brigade that would introduce direct trapping east of the mountains. McKenzie and the HBC designed the Bow River expedition to exploit the beaver reserves of the Piegan Blackfeet that lay across the international border in the American territory—where Ashley-Henry and the MFC were both headed.[85]

The Bow River expedition contained a strong force of 143 boatmen and trappers shivering in a palisaded camp and depot at the mouth of the Red Deer River, near the winter camps of the Blackfeet, Blood, and Gros Ventre. Piegan warriors drifted in bragging about the beating they had recently administrated to the Snake Indians and accused McKenzie of selling arms to those enemies.[86] Big Donald answered that the HBC only came to test the potential of beaver trapping and might even build a trading post for their convenience. But the Indians realized that this trapping brigade meant to exploit their land, and they discouraged several attempts to explore or trap toward the south.

McKenzie learned some Piegans had traded at the MFC's Big Horn post, but he was unaware of the Ashley-Henry effort staging at the mouth of the Yellowstone.[87] When returning Blackfoot raiders told McKenzie on 19 March 1823 that they saw six Americans wintering near the River Crow camp at the Musselshell, he was only aware of Henry's advance camp.[88] He realized, though, that Henry's men were witnesses to British intrusion on the upper Missouri.

An apprehensive winter and frustrated explorations convinced the Bay men that trapping Piegan beaver constituted too great a risk.[89] While Andrew Henry moved up the Missouri in spring 1823, Donald McKenzie fell back down the Bow River and advised the HBC to continue depending upon fixed posts at Rocky Mountain House, Edmonton House, and Fort Carlton. If those surly, uncooperative Piegans wanted to trade, decided McKenzie, they would have to travel 350-400 miles to the nearest British store.

The British traders and invading American entrepreneurs denied that Indians had legitimate territorial interests and the right to reserve what their land contained for themselves. Unfortunately for the expectant capitalists, the buffalo-sufficient Indians of the northern plains could get along without them.[90]

HBC's new governor of the northern department, George Simpson, came to Edmonton in spring 1823 to check the results of his gamble at direct trapping. He learned that the risk and cost exceeded the returns, and his first experiment in increasing production had cost the company around £10,000. To make up the loss Simpson discharged many employees and raised the price of goods sold to those still on the ledgers. He determined to infiltrate the Piegan preserves with "confidential servants." The first of those secret operatives who traveled with the Indians, Edmonton clerk Hugh Munroe, encouraged them to hunt and induced them to bring furs taken in American territory to the HBC.[91]

Governor Simpson's economies worked against his company. After McKenzie resigned from the Snake Brigade the leadership devolved on Michael Bourdon, one of the earliest American hunters of Canadian extraction on the upper Missouri. As the HBC exploited its new monopoly, the Columbia River freemen and Iroquois trappers who made up the Snake Brigade saw themselves sinking into debt bondage. On the eastern side of the Snake Plain fourteen hunters of the 1822 brigade refused to carry their catch to Spokane House.[92] The dissidents buried seven hundred prime pelts in a cache for lack of transport and pretended to return to Fort Walla Walla on the Columbia. Instead they headed east through the Crow country to check the prices the MFC paid at its Big Horn post. This little band of price shoppers spent the winter of 1822-23 with the Mountain Crow in the Wind River valley, just across the mountains from the Weber brigade camp.

The absence of any historically notable disaster indicates that the Danish captain, John H. Weber, succeeded in piloting the Ashley-Henry craft back downriver, and the expedition's trappers produced the furs needed to keep the partnership solvent. In the spring clerk David Jackson brought the welcome news of a good hunt back to Fort Henry along with the less-favorable report that Weber failed to obtain more horses from the Crow. If David repeated the rumor circulating through the Indian grapevine—that a party of wandering British hunters had wintered with the Mountain Crow—that interesting tidbit escaped recording.

Before the thick ice flushed out of the Missouri River Andrew Henry and a party of mounted trappers rode back to the Musselshell advance camp. As a forecast of troubles to come they lost four precious horses to Indian raiders. Two days after the ice broke, on 4 April 1823, Henry moved his hunting brigade up the Missouri.[93]

A month later the boats and mounted parties passed the Great Falls and moved ten or fifteen miles above the mouth of the Smith River. The valley appeared so promising that they set thirty traps in the beautiful clear stream flowing from the Little Belt Mountains. On 4 May the Blackfeet killed four trappers, and Andrew Henry flashed back on the horrors of 1810. Resisting panic, he took the time to cache 172 fine steel traps, intending to return with a stronger party and force a passage.[94] With death at their backs the boatmen took just seven or eight days to return to the central depot where David Jackson brought the only encouragement and an alternative.

Andrew Henry intended to go west of the mountains. The editor of the *St. Louis Enquirer* noted when the major departed that he might "go as far on the other side [of the mountains] as the mouth of the Columbia." Daniel Potts wrote that he left "for the Rocky Mountains and the Columbia for the purpose of hunting and trapping and trading with the Indians."[95] Now Henry had to decide whether to force his way up the Missouri with a properly mounted, reinforced trapping brigade or find a safer approach to the Snake Country along his old return route of 1811.

Even though some British trappers were looking for someone new with whom to trade, they represented a work force already in place and capable of producing plenty of furs. Ashley-Henry, however, had been obliged to import its own hunters, and after those men paid off their initial debts the unruly lot would become independent trappers.

Andrew Henry decided to shift his effort south before heading west over the mountains and avoid the deadly Three Forks. But an overland effort would require more horses, and he had to get a message to Ashley before the resupply boat passed the Arikara herds. For this critical duty the major selected two trustworthy men: his proven clerk, David E. Jackson, and Ashley's new recruit, Jedediah Smith.

Sometime before the middle of May David and Jedediah paddled away in a small pirogue with instructions to meet Ashley, assist him in buying some good livestock, and take a pack train cross-country to meet the Yellowstone brigade on that river. Jedediah, an engaged hand, would return with Ashley's confirmation of the revised plan, and Jackson would guide the overland party. Riding the spring freshet they intercepted Ashley's keelboats, the *Yellow Stone Packet* and the smaller *Rocky Mountains,* just below the Arikara towns before the end of May.[96]

David settled into keelboat life and got to know the new men. The horrendous reports from last year's dropouts had made it difficult for Ashley to recruit a new crew in St. Louis. To get a hundred men Ashley had to offer wages of $200 a year, a serious commitment for a firm already tottering on the edge of bankruptcy. But the general had sunk himself in too deep to back out.[97]

As veterans with a whole year of experience, Jackson and Smith had an attentive audience while Ashley's boat poled its way toward the Arikara towns.

One of the new men, James Clyman, a 31-year-old native of Fauquier County, Virginia, had grown up as a near neighbor of Juliet Jackson's family. During the war Clyman was stationed at Greenville and Jeromesville, Ohio, in the same area where Jackson recruited. After he came to St. Louis to collect his pay as a government surveyor, Ashley hired him and designated him to keep the other recruits penned in a rented house until time to leave. Jim was particularly unimpressed with the boatmen, who he referred to as "St. Louis gumboes."[98]

Jackson's audience also included the six-foot-two William L. Sublette, a raw-boned 23-year-old who matured early from responsibility. His brother Milton was already upriver with the MFC.[99]

Two other notable passengers rode upriver with Jackson and Smith: Thomas Fitzpatrick and Thomas Eddie. Fitzpatrick was a 24-year-old Irishman from County Cavan who still spoke with a thick brogue after seven years in America. Others of the same name lived in Ste. Genevieve County, and Jackson may have recognized Tom from earlier acquaintance.[100] Eddie, a presumptuous Scot associated with the Hunt family of St. Louis, had acquired a farm that he may have been trying to save with the money he would earn trapping.[101]

On 30 May 1823 the two keelboats anchored in the middle of the river opposite the Arikara towns. General Ashley took the skiff to the narrow sandbar beneath the crudely palisaded village to speak with the principal chiefs and arrange a horse trade. To get nineteen or twenty ponies Ashley had to accept two hundred weighty buffalo robes. In return the Indians got twenty-five new guns and a full measurement of William H. Ashley.

Americans often discounted Indian leadership and, at the same time, credited it with too broad of powers. Ashley's ethnocentricity blinded him on two important points. First, in the tribal world an Indian had no obligation to obey anyone else; Indian leadership hinged on the constant demonstration of character, dignity, courage, wisdom, truthfulness, and unrestrained generosity. Chiefs who exemplified those virtues expected the same from others and found Ashley's courthouse and political stump style of delivery transparent and unimpressive. The Arikara orators concluded that the general could be buffaloed.

Ashley's second point of misunderstanding was the Indian justice system, which sought to muffle aberrant impulses with public censure and the threat of ostracism; punitive measures for serious offenses descended into the darkness of revenge and vendetta. A murder-victim's family had the obligation to punish the murderer but did not need to exact punishment from the actual culprit: innocent relatives made acceptable surrogates. Two Arikara braves had been killed in an earlier assault on the MFC's Cedar Fort, and when Ashley gave condolence presents he unknowingly associated himself with his competitors.

General Ashley compounded the dangerous situation by ignoring the warning of the concerned Arikara elders that the people of the lower village intended to attack the whites. He put that off as an expression of band jealousy and left the forty men of his projected overland party camped on the sandbar with the horses while he returned to the boat.

During the evening interpreter Edward Rose convinced Aaron Stephens to accompany him into the village for a brief shore leave with some agreeable Arikara girls. Later that night Rose crashed down the high bank, panting that Stephens had been caught and killed. The men paid an Indian to recover the body, but he returned to report that too few pieces were left to justify the effort. No more sleep tonight.

Whispering to the boats anchored in midstream, the worried men proposed to move across the river. But Ashley, who needed to get more horses, hoped that a bold front would see them through. At dawn the Arikaras began firing from behind the palisades. The men found it impossible to defend the sandbar, and, with terrified horses to protect, they could not make an orderly retreat to the keelboats anchored ninety feet from shore in the strong current. The Indians soon solved the stock problem as the screaming animals started going down under fire. Dragging the bleeding carcasses into a breastwork the hunters hunkered down, loading and firing desperately.

Only seven men, two of them wounded, were willing to go when skiffs came to take them off the beach. Heroic determination broke down when the Indians flanked the breastwork and enfiladed the men. The Arikaras shot some fugitives as they ran for the river; others sank in the current. Shoving his rifle into his belt Jim Clyman bolted for a skiff returning for another load. As the rower, Reed Gibson, pulled the floundering swimmer into the boat, he took a ball in his gut.

In that frantic half hour (Ashley thought it only lasted fifteen minutes) David Jackson saw the action he missed in the war. Years later he told William Waldo that Smith, Sublette, and he stayed behind the horses until

Indians swarmed over the sandbar, then fought their way to the river. The Indians killed eleven men as the perimeter collapsed, but twenty-one survivors made it back to the boats before the men cut the anchor lines and the keelboats drifted out of range. Hunched in the lee of the deckhouse, panting with fear and frustration, Jackson saw Smith praying over the gut-shot Gibson.[102]

After drifting two miles below the Arikara towns, the keelboats took shelter in some timber on the east bank to wait for any stragglers. Ashley's proposal to build breastworks and force a passage was not received enthusiastically.

On 3 June the boats fell downriver another twenty-five miles, to the mouth of the Moreau River, where Ashley convinced Smith and a brave (now anonymous) Frenchman to carry the bad news to Henry. Forty-three heroes resigned the fur trade to see the wounded safely delivered to Fort Atkinson on the *Yellow Stone Packet*. Ashley convinced thirty men to stay with him at the Cheyenne River until Henry arrived with reinforcements.

Nineteen horses valued at $60 a head, thirty-one rifles worth $25 each, a small boat worth $50, and sundry other items worth $300 brought Ashley's total loss to $2,265. And the remaining outfit, now drawing interest compounded daily, he could not get to his customers. The only good point was that some of those expensive $200-a-year men had deserted and others had died.[103]

Fort Henry at the mouth of the Yellowstone lay in ignorance of the deteriorating situation until early June, when Bill Gordon staggered in to report the destruction of the MFC's Three Forks hunting brigade. After wintering at the Big Horn, they followed the road that Immell remembered from 1810 to the Jefferson Fork. Although they saw indications that others had heavily trapped the upper river, they had taken twenty packs of beaver by 18 May. Then an appalling apparition appeared.

The medicine of the Blackfoot Mehkskehme-Sukahs (Iron Shirt) required him to paint his face black and outline his eyes and mouth with vermillion. A Crow painted like that signified a contrary warrior who renounced life and dedicated himself to death in battle. Iron Shirt was leading thirty-eight rustlers against the Snakes when he unexpectedly bumped into the trappers. Instead of allowing his impetuous young men to stage an ambush Iron Shirt approached the Americans waving a letter that the British trader, John Rowand, had given him.[104]

Iron Shirt knew about the two Ashley-Henry keelboats that still lay at the mouth of the Yellowstone and guessed that they would come up as far as the Great Falls of the Missouri. He came by that understanding through the workings of a remarkable Indian intelligence system. If Iron Shirt knew about the recent attack on Henry at Smith's River, he avoided mentioning it.[105]

The MFC traders felt encouraged by previous dealings with Piegans at their Big Horn post. The Piegans had petitioned for a convenient place to trade for twenty-two years, and they had even invited the Americans to establish a store at a more convenient location. When Iron Shirt repeated that offer, the Americans wrote another glowing document for him to include in his diplomatic portfolio.

Loaded with important information for the tribal elders, Iron Shirt called off the Snake raid and hurried back to the bands. Unfortunately, some Bloods also heard of the American offer that would spoil the Bloods' control of goods flowing south from Edmonton House.

Immell, like Henry, remembered the horrors of 1810. Although they parted as friends, he knew the Blackfeet had caught them taking beaver without permission. As soon as the Indians moved out of sight, his party packed up and high-tailed it back toward their Yellowstone base camp. On 31 May the Bloods caught up to them as the brigade was descending the Yellowstone River near the mouth of Pryor Creek. The Indians blew Immell from his saddle as he rode forward to meet them with a truce flag; then they lanced his clerk, Robert Jones, and mowed down five more trappers. The Bloods captured fifty horses and twenty-eight mules loaded with about a thousand pelts (thirty-five packs) for a total loss of around $15,000.[106]

When seventeen intimidated trappers and four wounded men reassembled, Bill Gordon and Charles Keemle returned to the Big Horn post. While Keemle built bullboats to float out thirty-two cached packs, Gordon went ahead with the bad news.

The Blackfeet carried out impressive defensive tactics, molesting only trappers, not traders. Remarkably, the allied but still rival bands—without central authority, an organized army, or an overriding strategy—turned back three assaults upon their heartland. The Bloods also prevented the Piegans from getting a convenient trading post that might have given them an arms advantage in their intertribal rivalry.[107] They even contributed to international harmony by preventing American and British trapping parties from colliding.

The survivors of the Henry and Immell parties on the Three Forks returned to Fort Henry with a sense of impending doom. The boredom of garrison life, latent perversity, or some old insult led boatman Mike Fink to kill his protégé, Bill Carpenter, and get extrajudicially executed by their mutual buddy, Levi Talbot. The men on the upper Missouri already considered themselves at the end of the world when the brazen horns of Armageddon blared the arrival of Smith and the Frenchman with the news that the Arikara had cut off Ashley's keelboats.

Maj. Andrew Henry's operation lay dead in the water. Taking fifty men in a flotilla of pirogues and bullboats, Henry passed the Mandan and Arikara towns without trouble and joined Ashley early in July. If troops came from Fort Atkinson, they would arrive too late to help the traders force the Arikara blockade. Ashley-Henry had to make its own luck.

The ragtag fleet dropped downriver, to the mouth of the Teton (Bad) River, to "purchase as many horses as would enable us to fit out the party inte[n]ded to be sent to the Columbia." The latest trading license issued by Superintendent of Indians William Clark on 12 March 1823 permitted them to trade with the "Ricara, Score, Mandans, Milanawa [Minnataree or Hidatsa], Blackfoot and Crow tribes" within and west of the Rocky Mountains for a period of five years. Ashley-Henry had a new plan to fit out "two hunting parties for the waters of the River Columbia, and one to hunt on this side of the mountains." After riding 120 miles to Fort Brassaux to buy horses from the Sioux Ashley learned that the Army was coming with two hundred men.[108]

Hoping to fend off creditors with the returns Henry brought down with the rescue fleet and with the 202 buffalo robes that he traded from the Arikara,

Ashley wrote to John O'Fallon in St. Louis. He said that the partners were formulating their plans for the next hunt but had already abandoned the hope of reaching the Snake River country this year.

The Indian traders were private businessmen with hired employees. But because they had created the problem with Indians, the Army required their assistance in its military operations against the Arikaras. By the time they finished that campaign it would be too late to get back into the beaver country.

The expedition's leaders organized eighty Ashley-Henry volunteers into two battalions, appointing Jedediah Smith and Hiram Scott company captains, David Jackson and Hiram Allen lieutenants, Edward Rose ensign, Tom Fitzpatrick quartermaster, and Bill Sublette sergeant major. Ashley furnished Colonel Leavenworth, the head of the two hundred men and thirty officers of the Sixth United States Regiment, with a list of his officers, inexplicably misidentifying David as his brother, George, whom Ashley knew from the lead mines. About forty MFC men joined the force, which also found a place for some Cheyenne and Hunkpapa Sioux lusting for Ree horses.[109]

The 10 August attack on the Arikara towns turned into a fiasco of conflicting authority and poorly defined objectives. Sometime during the night before the assault, the Rees (Arikaras) broke camp and left their flea-infested lodges to the torches of the frustrated MFC partisans. A cannon ball killed Grey Eyes, the Arikara leader who had warned Ashley of the danger, but those of the middle river who had attacked Ashley's men went unpunished.

Ashley and Henry planned to abandon the river and proceed as a mounted hunting brigade, a major step in discarding the previous fixation on waterways and beginning the overland process. In the nineteen years since President Jefferson sent Lewis and Clark to discover a portage between the Missouri and the Columbia rivers, traders and trappers had been unable to make a highway out of the rivers. The Missouri became a transcontinental dead end, so Andrew Henry decided to set up interior operations supplied by pack train. Ashley-Henry bought horses from the Fort Kiowa Sioux.

The list of Ashley-Henry creditors now included most of the St. Louis commercial community, making additional funding unlikely until they produced some returns. The partners owed a few of their enlistees for the 1822-23 outfit, and they appealed to them to accept a moratorium on wages. David Jackson's salary as a clerk, around $400 or $500 a year, became an investment in Ashley-Henry, and he had enough extra cash to personally outfit hunter Oliver Wheeler with an advance of $200 against the furs he would take.[110]

In July the eight surviving Columbia freemen staggered into Fort Atkinson. After wintering with the Mountain Crow they headed for the MFC post at the mouth of the Big Horn, but the River Crow intercepted and robbed them. After losing their packs and some of their Indian women, the wanderers were disappointed to find the trading house deserted. Striking east, the small band ran into more trouble in the vicinity of the Black Hills, where Cheyennes killed six.[111]

The deplorable condition of the Columbia freemen drew the sympathy of a visiting European, Prince Paul, Duke of Wurttemburg, and the indignation of Indian Agent O'Fallon. On the first of August O'Fallon wrote to Pilcher that he was sending two of the Iroquois upriver so they could join the expedition that the MFC planned to send to the mountains. They wanted to recover "a squaw and two Children" that the Crows had taken from them.[112]

Those Ishmaels provided grist for the trading community rumor mills with their information on conditions west of the mountains. The difference between the prices that the HBC paid and what an American trader could offer and still make a good profit excited calculating minds. The British paid less than $2 a skin and doubled the price of goods they sold. They used their monopoly to push the captive work force into debt bondage—a hunter had to take 150 skins before he even repaid the cost of his trapping-season outfit. Prices would only get worse as more discharged employees arrived from the upper Saskatchewan.[113]

Henry had an inkling of that valuable information before July, and by 20 August he raced to take advantage of it. Joshua Pilcher also wanted to get into the game and convinced Bill Gordon and Charles Keemle to return to the Indian country with the Iroquois as guides.

To keep his narrowing lead, Henry started inland about the first of September with forty men leading the horses he obtained from the Sioux. He headed toward Fort Henry to pick up the garrison and remaining outfit and march up the Yellowstone. The plainsmen walked up Grand River because their ponies had to carry the outfit.

While hunting ahead, Hugh Glass surprised a grizzly and was horribly mauled. Mountain yarns recalled the paralyzing moments when "Ol' Ephram" reared and the flint dropped out of the gunlock or the primer flashed in the pan. Some yarn spinners fingered impressive scars as they lied about drawing their knife. Henry waited a while to see if Glass would recover, but his prospects looked bleak, so Henry bribed John Fitzgerald and Jim Bridger, the young Virginian, to stay until Glass expired. Soon after the brigade moved on, the lonesome nurses began hearing Rees in the brush. They lost their nerve and abandoned the quivering Glass, who lay unconscious in his agony. But Hugh refused to die and eventually dragged himself back to Fort Kiowa.[114]

A night attack on Henry's camped brigade killed James Anderson and Auguste Neil, and the men answered the assault with shots into the dark. The next morning the men found the bodies of two Mandans, which meant they now had to consider previously friendly tribes as hostile. Were the British responsible for inciting the different tribes against the Americans? Johnson Gardner thought so and never forgave the British for the death of his kinsman in the Arikara fight. David Jackson was learning the reality of field leadership in a hard school.

In late September the pack brigade reached Fort Henry, where the twenty paralyzed guards had cowered behind the palisades and allowed Indians to run off twenty-two precious horses. With winter closing in, Henry had too little time to waste in recriminations. Packing up all the goods he could carry, he cached the rest and started up the Yellowstone.

The brigade ran into some conciliatory Piegans whose leader convinced Henry he was talking to a man of some importance. The pragmatic Henry clothed him in a gaudy trade uniform and treated his companions to token presents of tobacco and ammunition as well as an invitation to bring their beaver to the Mountain Crow country, where the Americans planned to winter.

The Piegans later searched the abandoned fort for caches and opened the graves of Fink and Carpenter. The bodies had ripened too much for the Indians to take the clothing, and the mortal remains of the legendary bull-roarer and half-alligator were left staring up at the deep sky. Instead of heaven, Mink Fink entered American folklore.[115] Ashley-Henry also left at least one of the two keelboats stranded at the fort, and witnesses later saw the steering oar floating past the Mandan towns.

The Piegans hurried back to Marias River to show their new duds to the HBC agent, Hugh Munroe. He took the news of the Americans to Edmonton House in late November, about the same time loot from the Jones and Immell attack showed up. Iron Shirt also mentioned a party of four Americans he discovered coming up the Missouri in two small pirogues at the end of the summer, which apparently confirms the fate of four men—Decharle, Trumble, and two others whose names remain lost—said to have been killed by Gros Ventres on the Yellowstone in 1823.[116]

Freemen from the Snake Brigade of summer 1822 may have trapped the Jefferson Fork ahead of Jones and Immell. After the departure of his fourteen dissidents, Michael Bourdon took his returns to Spokane House and was assigned the winter hunt. The next spring he yielded leadership to Finan McDonald, whose brigade hunted into "the croe Indian cuntre on the rail Spanish [Green] river." On their return across the eastern Snake plain they picked up the cache of seven hundred pelts left by the dissidents and hunted up the Salmon River, where Blackfeet killed Bourdon and four trappers. Just across Lemhi Pass the Indians killed another trapper before McDonald had the opportunity to exact a terrible revenge. Trapping a Piegan war party in a narrow ravine, Finan's men fired the brush and mowed down the singed warriors: ". . . no less than 68 of them that remane in the Planes as Pray for the wolves and those fue that askape our Shotes, they had not Britch Clout to cover themselves. We shoe them wat war was, they will not be so radey to attack People another time." The military disaster brought the Piegans to a council where they promised Finan that "they would not return agane to make ware," and the conquering Snake Brigade went on to the Three Forks. "I sa the Muscourey last fall down as far as the falls, in that Part of the Cuntry is rouint of Beaver by the Americans for they had a fort there fue years agoe about ½ mile beloe Cortais old fort."[117]

McDonald missed connecting with Munroe, who had gone north, but his good trade with the Piegans diverted furs from Saskatchewan House to Spokane House. In addition to chastising the Blackfeet, Finan illegally intruded into United States territory.

The disputed Oregon Country was a bubbling stew of pugnacious trappers, secret agents, desperate traders, and offended Indians. If the Americans saw British North America as a platform for subversive activity, the Bay men saw the incomers jeopardizing a favorable division of the Pacific Northwest. Neither faction considered Indian territorial rights. The United States had no diplomatic relationship with the western tribes and ignored the aboriginal title. The British, too, failed to consider it. Only eastern liberals decried the beaver hunt as an indefensible exploitation of native peoples.

When he returned to St. Louis from an eventful summer on muddy waters, William H. Ashley should have kept a low profile until he paid off his debts. Instead the lieutenant governor set his sights on higher office and began a self-generated public relations campaign to establish himself as the reigning expert on the western fur trade. In the 17 November 1823 *St. Louis Enquirer* he took exception to statements published in the *New York American* "to impress the public mind with the belief that the Indians object to white hunters hunting on their lands."

He felt he must change the impressions of eastern readers that the fur traders meant to exploit the savages: "The idea is erroneous. The Indians make no such objections but rather invite whites to hunt with them."

For a captain whose decks recently ran red with blood, Ashley appeared curiously tolerant: "In waging war upon us, they are not instigated by considerations of that nature; they delight in war, because their other pursuits afford not sufficient employment for their vigorous minds, and because they, like all other men are fond of fame, and war is the only means by which they can acquire it."[118]

6

"They have traversed every part of the country"

WHILE WILLIAM H. ASHLEY cultivated his reputation as a western expert, Andrew Henry and his determined band toiled up the Yellowstone. Subtracting three men lost on the trail and adding those picked up at the depot, the party totaled approximately fifty-seven hunters, most likely including Ezekiel Able, William Bell, Alexander K. Branch, James Bridger, David Cunningham, Thomas Eddie, John S. Fitzgerald, Isaac Galbraith, Johnson Gardner, Caleb Greenwood, George Harris, Moses Harris, Ephraim Logan, Daniel Potts, S. Stone, Stephen Terry, Thomas Virgin, and Oliver Wheeler.

Henry and his men dragged one of the keelboats as far as the fast water above the mouth of the Powder and portaged the lighter pirogues so they could continue to the mouth of the Big Horn. Henry bought forty-seven horses from the River Crow at top dollar, but the small range mustangs were grossly out proportion to their riders.[119]

Americans had packed into Indian country since the days of the colonial frontier. Proud to be horsemen in this tradition, Henry's men had the great spaces open before them—the Big Horn Mountains, already crested with snow, loomed blue in the west. Lacking traditional horse gear, they made do with Indian half-hitch bridles and pad saddles.

Henry broke off Weber's trapping brigade to complete the vacuuming of beaver begun last year on the Powder River.[120] On the second venture up the cloudy stream, Capt. John H. Weber led and petite bourgeois David E. Jackson served as clerk and supercargo—seeing that the outfit was packed, safely carried, and secured at night. Jackson had responsibility for the capital of Ashley-Henry, making sure the goods that rode on packhorses remained safe in case the animals should bolt into the timber at the first whiff of a bear. Having Jackson take care of the mundane chores left Weber free to scout ahead for beaver sign and select camps that allowed them to set traps overnight. If an accident claimed the bourgeois, Jackson was his designated replacement.

When hunters required something from the packs, the traveling store-keeper marked it down in the field ledger against their accounts. While others lolled around the evening fire telling tall tales, the clerk worked out the mathematics that governed their lives. No matter how far they rode or how high the sky soared above them, the mountaineers were inescapably tied to frontier economics.[121]

At the end of the hunting season Weber took the brigade to winter with the Crows in the beautifully austere Wind River valley. Those Indians believed their home was the exact center of the universe. Running generally east between the sheltering Owl Creek Mountains and the Wind River Mountains from its source on the Continental Divide, the Wind River flows first between bluffs sculpted by wind and water to reveal their colorful bands of strata. The groves of cottonwoods and willows lining the river made cozy locations for winter lodges, while bays in the bluffs and open meadows between the trees provided secure horse pastures. Beaver still gnaw on those giant cottonwoods.

The Mountain Crow, whose range stretched as far east as the Tongue River, consisted of two main groups: the Many Lodges and Kicked-in-the-Belly people. Further division reveals six pairs of clans that traced their descent through the mother's side of the family.

Henry continued to the mouth of the Big Horn to build a depot and release his men to scatter and trap in what Potts described as "small hunts." Some may have worked up the Yellowstone as far as Clark's Fork or Pryor's Fork, risking a collision with the dangerous Blackfeet. The Crow, who wanted to discourage trading competition, warned that the Blackfeet were determined to hunt down and destroy all trapping parties.[122]

Beaver ponds overlapped the creekside brush favored by prairie bears, but trappers had to work quietly to avoid alarming the beavers. Grizzlies, when surprised and sensing a threat, become ill-tempered giants fully deserving their scientific name: *Ursus horribilis*. Oliver "Holly" Wheeler, a Massachusetts boy who came west three years earlier to settle his father's estate, signed on with Ashley-Henry to become a real leatherstocking. When poor Holly surprised a snoozing griz he had only one chance to fire his single shot before the bear's knife-like claws and gnashing teeth ended his life. The record mentions his death only because he died owing David Jackson $200, and D. Harris, who took over his possibles, never settled the bill.[123]

Potts and seven other hunters set off from the mouth of the Big Horn to join the brigade on the Wind River. Potts got lost crossing the Owl Creek Mountains late in the season and froze his feet so badly that two toes had to be amputated, sans anesthesia. The Crow family that took him in, dressed his wounds, and cared for him, taught the Pennsylvanian new respect for the natives.[124]

As they planned in July, two of the Ashley-Henry hunting parties were now in place: one on the Columbia and the other hunting east of the Rockies. A third party, under the direction of Jedediah Smith, was late coming to the mountains. The sixteen men who left Fort Kiowa in late September included Jim Clyman, Bill Sublette, Tom Fitzpatrick, and the knavish interpreter, Edward Rose.

Smith unluckily encountered a grizzly and was saved by Arthur Black. His recovery held up the group for ten days.[125] Skirting the Black Hills along the south branch of the Cheyenne River, a Missouri Fur Company (MFC) party from Fort Recovery overtook Smith's party. Goaded by information from the dissident western freemen, Bill Gordon and Charles Keemle were reluctantly returning to the killing grounds. On the Powder River the combined parties met fifteen or sixteen Crows who led them into the Wind River valley and a winter camp near the Popo Agie Fork.[126]

The whites typically held opinions about Indians they had learned from eastern pioneers. But sitting in the honored guests' places around the Crow lodge fires, eating food provided by their generous hosts, and sharing ordinary intimacies with the natives, the bearded strangers began to reexamine their stereotypes. Observant guests learned proper manners and heeded taboos. They became sensitive to where they sat in the lodge and with whom they joked. Straining through the veil of language, David grasped the subtleties and honored the Indians' beliefs and behaviors for much the same reason that the Crow people did—to avoid offending someone or something.[127]

Because so many warriors died, the clans had more women than men and accepted plural marriage, governed by the ability of a hunter to provide for extra wives. The Crows reversed dowries with presents of horses or other valuables given to the bride's parents to reimburse them for the loss of a helper.

The American wild oats sown during the winter produced a crop of half-breeds born long after their fathers drifted on. In that way the Crow people became less Indian and the mountaineers more so. The Crow women provided more than sexual gratification to the men—the blanket companions also served as living libraries of the words necessary to get along in this strange new world and taught the art of being comfortable in the wilderness.

During the winter of 1823-24 the Mountain Crow conducted the first academy of the Rocky Mountains by teaching the raw hunters the lessons that qualified them as "mountain men." To illustrate three-dimensional mountain geography in map form some Indians heaped sand on buffalo robes, indicating particular ranges and passes for Jedediah Smith's party. They also taught the white men that they could find most places by just following the drag trails of Indian lodge poles.

The Crow tribal elders, seeing that the American hunters intended to take their beaver and leave them nothing to trade, slyly suggested that the valley of the Green River was a maze of thickly inhabited beaver streams and the resident Shoshonis were just waiting for someone to come and catch those pesky rodents. Traps were unnecessary; they could simply club a fortune on the head.

Edward Rose, Ashley-Henry's interpreter, became so taken with Crow life that he asked Henry to release him so he could stay with them. Like the Blackfeet and the Arikaras, the astute Crows wanted to control trading in their territory, and Rose saw a bright future with his new friends.

The Ashley-Henry hunters wintering in the Wind River valley split up to avoid straining the Indian hospitality, but, oddly, Clyman, Potts, and Smith failed to recall the presence of their fellow trappers. They must have had exchanges between camps, because Eddie, who apparently came up the Yellowstone with Henry, ended up the next spring with Smith's band.[128]

Henry, camped back at the depot he had built at the mouth of the Big Horn, sent Fitzgerald and the Harrises back to Fort Atkinson. Soon after the men reached the fort on 18 December, William Ashley learned that his partner had taken twenty-five packs, two of which he had traded from the Crow, during the early fall hunt. These would enable the partners to keep their creditors at bay.

Cramped in a shoddy fort, missing his bride, his baby, and his friends, Andrew Henry fell into a black funk. He could not forget the mutilated bodies of the men killed in 1810, the four killed above Smith's River last year, the fifteen slain at the Ree towns, Hugh Glass bubbling his life away, Anderson and Neil killed by the Mandans, and lately, Holly Wheeler torn to pieces by a damn bear. Everything about the fur trade carried a death levy that made the price of felt hats too high.

The appearance of a ghost spoiled a determined Christmas drinking bout. Horribly disfigured by livid scars, Hugh Glass walked in to claim justice for being abandoned to die. After crawling back to Fort Kiowa and healing for a while, he started up the Missouri with some French company bateau men. Just below the Mandan towns Indians ambushed them, and only Glass and the legendary Toussaint Charbonneau escaped. Glass went on trailing Henry's men but found that Fitzgerald had gone downriver. Young Bridger endured the revelation of his cowardice for deserting Glass, but Hugh forgave him. Now Andrew Henry carried an additional burden: he had left a good man on the prairie to die.

The conservative Henry also felt uneasy with Ashley's financial risks. They entered the partnership expecting to recover their investment in the first year, and Henry had borrowed based on that expectation. Now, with his notes coming due, he needed a quick return to salvage the increased stakes.

After the new year began, Henry sent a second message back to Ashley. Before parting in the fall the partners had agreed that Ashley would forward a resupply to the Yellowstone in the following summer. But by late February Major Henry had decided to push his operations farther south and wanted to arrange for the resupply train to come to the upper Big Horn, which would save a long trip up the Missouri and the Yellowstone.

Henry believed that he had the first step of his trapping strategy already underway. Smith was to proceed up the Wind River valley and cross the pass—known since 1811—to tap into the bonanza trapping on the upper Snake River. The major saw the potential of a bonus if Jedediah could find western freemen and trade the cache of seven hundred pelts baymen had buried west of the Tetons two years before; he did not know the HBC recovered those pelts in summer 1823. The major expected Smith and the men with him, all apparently on the Ashley-Henry payroll, to bring in good returns.[129]

Ashley-Henry's original plan to recover its outfitting debts from obligated hunters failed because the trappers never got a good opportunity to work. With their obligations now behind them, the men considered themselves free to sell to the best market, including the Missouri Fur Company, which was already hanging around Wind River hoping to get some of the freemen's packs. Henry's supply of goods was inadequate to monopolize the trading. The problems of debt service and long-distance supply had already cost him two expensive courier-carried letters.

Hugh Glass, E. Moore, A. Chapman, Dutton, and Marsh probably had a bellyful of the skin game by now and left on 28 February 1824 with Henry's second message to Ashley. They followed the Powder River until they could cross to the North Fork of the Platte and build a buffalo-hide bullboat. The mariners had the bad luck to run into the Arikaras, who promptly killed Chapman and Moore while the others ran for their lives. Dutton and Marsh staggered into Fort Atkinson in mid-May, and Glass made it to Fort Kiowa about the first of June. The St. Louis papers reported the news of their disaster on 7 June.[130]

The Missouri Fur Company party trapped down the Big Horn and shipped their returns on the Yellowstone in bullboats. Gordon and Keemle managed to ransom the kidnapped Iroquois wife of the western freemen from the Mountain Crow, but they subsequently lost her to a war party of River Crow. When the MFC men reached Fort Atkinson, about the fourth of July, Charles Keemle was ready to retire from the fur trade to the slightly less dangerous occupation of frontier journalism. Gordon returned to the middle Missouri River trading posts, but the momentum of his earlier adventures escaped him.[131]

Henry trailed up the Big Horn Valley toward Shoshoni country in a desperate search for beaver pelts to salvage his partnership. After a 200-mile ride to oversee the spring hunt, Henry was disappointed to learn that Smith failed to cross the passes because of deep snows. Those eleven hunters in Smith's party came back to cache their excess outfit on the Sweetwater branch of the Platte and head around the end of the Wind River Range, hunting the same streams that Henry hoped to exploit. "As soon as he [Henry] was able to travil Last Spring he came Down a Cross and crossed the Missouri [upper Platte] and went a Course about four hundred miles and there Came on this he speaks of [the Colorado of the West or Green River] and found beavour in abundance and saw no Indians until he returned to the Missouri again."[132]

A 400-mile compass arc from the designated rendezvous at the mouth of Wind River encloses the valley of Green River as far south as the Uinta Range and as far west as the edge of Bear River valley. According to his Missouri friend John Hawkins, Henry rode southwest and "supposes he was last spring on the Colorado of the West that runs into the bay of Callaforny from the best acct. he could get from the Crow Indians." He found "beavour in abundance" and was convinced that "a fortune Could be made was it not for the Difficulty of the Indians. They are Incouraged by British Traders."[133]

Three contemporary records refute the after-the-fact documents used to credit Smith, Fitzpatrick, or even Ashley with the strained "effective" discovery of South Pass.[134] Andrew Henry, a businessman with an important job to do, made no pretense of discovery. His men were disinterested in describing the unknown for the edification of eastern fans. Exploration as a rationale for western discovery overlooks the more practical reasons for why men found out and confirmed the geography of the West.

About two thousand or so Northern Shoshoni lived in the Green River drainage, and the Americans coming down the Big Sandy probably encountered the Kogohues division led by a Comanche-Shoshoni named Ohamagwaga (Yellow Hand). Like the Crows, these horse people were dedicated to hunting buffalo, but they also enjoyed roots and berries.[135] When Smith and Sublette met small groups of hungry Indians during their spring hunt, they gave them naked beaver carcasses to eat. But when eighteen Shoshonis from a camp of six lodges attempted to steal the trappers' horses, the reprisal was pitiless.[136]

The Smith-Fitzpatrick party had a cold, hungry, and thirsty passage, showing signs of disharmony even before they crossed South Pass on 11 March.[137] They decided to split their hunt on the Green River about 19 March, with Smith and six others taking the downstream route while Fitzpatrick, Clyman, Branch, and Stone trapped upstream.[138]

Henry, Weber, and Jackson moved through the Green River valley to the western tributary, known from then on as Henry's Fork of the Green. The major, who may have peeked into the upper end of the Green in 1811, wanted to confirm his geographical guesswork.[139] Indians probably told them that Hudson's Bay trappers had worked the headwaters of the Green River the previous year. Moving slowly along the narrow beaver streams and leaving obvious trails of campfires and skinned carcasses the Ashley-Henry parties may have attempted to contact each other. But Jedediah's band of hunters returned east to their Sweetwater caches without admitting contact with the boss. On 17 or 18 June they met Fitzpatrick, Branch, and Stone, but Jim Clyman was missing.

Expecting to meet General Ashley coming up the Platte with the resupply column, Fitzpatrick and his trapping companions decided to build a bullboat and float out. After a gesture at finding the missing Clyman, Smith rejoined the main body of Henry's hunters gathering on the Popo Agie fork of the Big Horn to celebrate the Fourth of July and greet the new store when it walked in.

Daniel Potts's letter to a Pennsylvania friend extolled the beauty of the country where he had hunted up to the snow line. Potts described the sporting glory of white bear, buffalo, elk, deer, antelope, and mountain sheep, but beaver comprised his principal diet. He earned $350 by wading up icy creeks to avoid leaving a scent that might scare away the beaver, setting his traps near likely points of passage, and securing the stakes and chains in deep water so the animals would drown before they chewed off their own legs. We can only imagine how that water felt to his recently amputated toes.[140]

Major Henry knew he had taken a long chance in sending Glass and the others with new instructions to Ashley and was beginning to suspect that his plan had fallen through. As the first mountain rendezvous failed to develop, Andrew Henry remained mercifully unaware of the real reason.

Henry's message got through, but it cost the lives of Chapman and Moore, and William H. Ashley made no preparations to move supplies into the mountains. He kept himself busy selling off town lots, country tracts, and slaves to pacify creditors, who soon swallowed up the money from the furs that Henry sent down last summer and the $5,000 raised at Fort Kiowa by the distress sale of unused supplies. Even so, Ashley's cold-eyed creditors saw little possibility of recovering their investment.[141]

In the election year of 1824—with Missouri politics dominated by factions instead of real parties, and lacking a nominating system—Ashley had to present himself as a gubernatorial candidate to the electorate by stumping the hustings. He did not have time to conduct his campaign *and* attend to the organization of a resupply column at some isolated place like Council Bluffs.[142]

The information that returned from the mountains with the Missouri Fur Company brigade provided Ashley another out. Gordon and Keemle saw evidence of Indian hostility at the Mandan villages, where Tildon & Company (the latent Columbia Fur Company) had apparently abandoned its post. Ashley rationalized that risking another outfit was foolish.[143]

By 7 July, on the Popo Agie, the trappers realized that Ashley would not come. If Henry's letter failed to get through, the general might be waiting for his partner on the Yellowstone. Henry remembered that Manuel Lisa failed because he tried to be all parts of the trading equation: financier, chairman-of-the-board, administrator, accountant, personnel director, purchasing agent, transporter, field leader, and trader. Henry entered partnership with Ashley to divide the responsibility between them. He did his part, but where was Ashley?

Standing at the doorway to success for the second time after two frustrating years, Andrew Henry realized that he had to go back to St. Louis with as many packs as possible to satisfy the creditors. Without a pack train, he could carry only a portion of the forty-five packs that his trappers had collected during the spring hunt. The remaining hunters needed proper mounts for the long ride across the Green River valley, and to lose trapping time to help a partnership that could not resupply them was more than he could expect from the men.

Henry decided to cache the spring hunt on the Popo Agie and ride back to the mouth of the Big Horn, where he could ship the packs stored there down the Yellowstone in bullboats. With luck he would meet Ashley on the way.

He arranged the fall hunt with his field leaders. "He has left John H. Weber on the missouri when he left there and thirty men with him which was to start Emidiatly after Henry left them a Cross to where henery had been in the spring, there to stay until Next Spring and then Return and come home next fall," reported Hawkins.

Daniel Potts wrote on 7 July: "we are about to embark for the Columbia waters where I expect to remain for two years at least." He recalled passing the Sweetwater headed southwest with Weber's brigade about the middle of July.[144]

The long bullhide-covered canoes left the Big Horn post carrying the twenty-five packs that Henry reported last fall supplemented by the spring hunt of the men who remained on the Yellowstone.[145] Finding his caches at the old depot robbed, and the other keelboat destroyed, Henry continued down the Missouri. Disappointment tempered his relief in finding Tom Fitzpatrick, who had come down the Platte from Smith's party at Fort Atkinson. Arriving there on 13 August, he learned that Fitzpatrick had already sold his furs to the Missouri Fur Company.[146]

The *Arkansas Gazette* reported the return of Andrew Henry on 30 August. The *St. Louis Enquirer* picked up the story on 16 November, and national recognition followed in *Nile's Weekly Register* on 4 December. The stories repeated Henry's statements about "a passage by which loaded wagons can at this time reach the navigable waters of the Columbia River." Linking the Platte River trail to the easy passage of the Green River and Bear River valleys opened a road as far as the Snake River, and demonstrated "the propriety of forming a colony at the mouth of the Columbia, which a few years ago was ridiculed as visionary."[147] Continental thinking had switched from dead-ending rivers to feasible overland emigration in just a year, and rabid expansionists considered the Oregon Trail already laid out.[148]

As late as 21 September Henry's friends in Washington County still expected him to return to the mountains. At the Tracy & Wahrendorff warehouse where the Ashley-Henry returns lay stored, he learned that the "considerable quantity of furs, e&c" he brought from the mountains at such great cost were worth, at best, $10,000. New York buyers colluded to drive down prices on the already depressed fur market, and Henry found the news hard to take. Those 1,500 or more skins represented twenty-eight months of hard work and personal risk—and the lives of thirty-nine good men.[149]

Andrew Henry realized that his sacrifices depended upon unfeeling eastern manipulators who never saw an Indian or risked a griz. That was the bottom line of the fur trade, the rule of ultimate downstream betrayal, which

Frenchmen learned in the first days of the colony of New France and British traders discovered at Grand Portage, Michilimackinac, and Montreal. The major luckily learned the lesson in only two trips out; some fur traders squandered their entire lives. The mountains offered less freedom than the hunters liked to believe. The remorseless laws of economics operated there, too.

Henry faced other pressing problems. He had been away longer than originally planned, and his financial base in Washington County was in deep trouble. In their haste to get on the river in 1822, he and Weber assigned bills to creditors. The debts went sour with the men away and unable to force payment. Opportunists moved in on 22-year-old Mary Henry, inexperienced in business and with a baby daughter to protect. Facing lawsuits brought in October and December 1822, and more court actions in June 1823, Mary sold the Blackwater farm. Although Henry considered it the best property he could ever have acquired, the tradition of his family always held that "he was too proud not to stand up to his wife's bargain."[150]

Because the furs that Henry brought down covered only a portion of the outstanding debts of the partnership, he had no funds to put into a new outfit. To break even, Ashley-Henry needed the packs that remained stored on the Popo Agie.

Henry, having done all the recent field work, asked Ashley to lead the next outfit while he stayed in Missouri to get his affairs in order. This was a risky request because Ashley had twice demonstrated his limitations in the field. The general had selfishly devoted himself to his political career while the men in the mountains waited. After losing his bid for governor, Ashley began angling for William Clark's job as superintendent of western Indians. The skeptical John O'Fallon wrote that Ashley lacked even "a single qualification for that office."[151]

Instead of giving Henry time to settle his affairs, General Ashley, who considered his valuable time a waste in the saddle, made a counterproposal to assume all the debts of the partnership in exchange for Henry's half of the business. Ashley must have thought the proposal would force Henry, who had no income to fall back on, to return to the mountains. In his gamble to force the issue the general mistook his man.

The records that William Ashley failed to preserve tell what took place between the former friends. Cornered in an unfavorable termination deal, Henry renounced all of his efforts. At forty-nine, Andrew Henry withdrew from the business he had twice helped establish and returned to Washington County to dig himself out of debt by working in a lead pit.

After the lead played out around Potosi, Henry moved to Webster (now Palmer) in the southwest corner of the county. By standing surety for the notes of friends, he became responsible for their defaults. Like his less-scrupulous neighbors, he could have transferred his property into his wife's name and avoided losses, but his sense of honor prevented him from stooping to underhandedness.[152]

In giving advice to a young boy Andrew Henry said a lot about himself: Resting on his pick, Henry told the boy that "honor and self-respect were more to be prized than anything else." Friends, neighbors, and Hiram M. Chittenden—the early historian of the fur trade—spoke of Andrew Henry's pride and honor.[153]

Among the first Americans to cross the Continental Divide, Andrew Henry led the pioneer development of the central-mountain fur trade, and first represented the United States in the Pacific drainage. Trappers continued to use his techniques until the skin game ended with the establishment of a trading post just seventy miles south of the place where he had started it all on Henry's Fork of the Snake River.

History is the revelation of human character and its effect upon events. Understanding Andrew Henry shows the development of his protégé, David Jackson. Willing to stand back and observe and judge the other hands in the game before playing his own, Jackson would soon find himself forced out of the shadows.

7

"The grand rendezvous of the persons engaged in that business"

AFTER A GOOD SPRING HUNT and a refreshing celebration of the national birthday, Uncle Sam's tribe marched west. Jedediah Smith's party "in the fall 1824 crossed from the head waters of the Rio Colorado to Lewis' fork of the Columbia and down the same about one hundred miles thence northwardly to Clark's fork of the Columbia."[154]

Capt. John Weber and David Jackson led thirty men around the southeast end of the Wind River Range and through the now familiar South Pass. They may have trailed along the southern foothills of the Wind River Mountains and the eastern slope of the Salt River Range but were too early in the season to take good beaver pelts. When fall came they began working the western tributaries of the Green River toward Black's Fork. Daniel Potts wrote that they "had very good traveling over an inconsiderable ridge and fell on the Bear. . . . [A]s you approach from the head of the river is a small sweet lake, about 120 miles in circumference, with beautiful clear water and when the wind blows has a splendid appearance. There is also to be found in this valley a considerable sour spring near the most northerly swing of the river [Soda Springs]. The valley is scantily supplied with timber, as is the case with most of the low grounds of this country."[155]

Potts was describing Bear Valley, a place that became central to the American hunt. Rising in the south, Bear River flowed north past a large lake that they named after Weber, and disappeared around the north end of the Wasatch Range. Low hills sometimes crowd the river, but in other places the lazy stream meanders through broad flats where willows made perfect beaver habitat. Vividly colored autumn bushes edged the meadows where deer placidly watched the strangers, and startled antelope floated away in marvelous leaps.

George C. Yount, another trapper, observed that Bear Valley created

> the great arena—the Grand Park or Battleground of the blackfeet, Snakes and Crows, famous and foremost of all the Nations of the great central domain. This spot was to them what Kentucky was for a thousand years to the tribes east of the great Mississippi. There those numerous and warlike nations have for Centuries congregated to try their comparative power, and the whole territory is one vast graveyard

of their braves for many miles around. The trappers could hardly have found a more dangerous place for a winter's encampment.[156]

Looking back from California retirement, Yount tried to link the long-hunter traditions to the whitening bones of western warriors. But he missed the point that Bear Valley served as a trading depot for the continental Indian trade network, where shells from the Pacific shore eventually reached middle-Missouri villages and dried salmon from the Columbia Basin was exchanged for Great Plains buffalo meat. The Ashley-Henry traders had located a promising mart.[157]

Friendly exchanges with the Indians induced the trappers to work in efficient teams of two or four men. While two men could set traps and guard each other's backs, four proved more efficient because it allowed two men to guard camp and condition the pelts. Their commitment to self-improvement and a better life was never stronger than in the scrotum-tightening moment before they wetted their moccasins. As they stepped into the ice-rimmed streams and later massaged their bleached shanks beside roasting beaver carcasses, they saw beaver pelts as a fast way to a nice piece of bottomland back home.[158]

The Americans soon swarmed over the Bear River country, taking so many beaver that Potts began to believe he really could earn $600. Captain Weber and Jackson left the trapping to others while they and a few hired hands herded the pack train, which by now included some ponies loaded with Crow buffalo-skin lodges.[159]

Just beyond the marshy area where Bear River turned south, another wall of mountains provided a lookout with a clear view across the widening valley. Old Pierre Tevanitagon and twelve of his Iroquois trappers had been hanging around the upper end of Bear Valley for most of the summer, expecting to meet their brethren who went east two years earlier to look for a better market than the exploitive British monopoly.

Those independently minded trappers made the western fur traders uncomfortable because the far-ranging beaver hunters of the six Iroquois nations already had two hundred years' practice in the skin game. Rival Montreal firms brought them to the Canadian northwest as contract trappers, and they were among the first to cross the Rocky Mountains. When the Nor'westers began the Snake River hunt, Donald McKenzie had trouble with Old Pierre's band. The Iroquois preferred to hunt by themselves, but when he turned them loose they wasted their time and outfits gambling and trading wives with the local Indians.

McKenzie's successor, Mich Bourdon, let fourteen Iroquois slip away to the Americans two years earlier, and the previous June Alexander Ross lost Old Pierre's group from the Snake Brigade.[160] They ran into Snake Indians on the upper Portneuf River and offended their hosts while trading for horses and women. According to Old Pierre's story, the Snakes took 54 steel traps, 27 horses, 5 guns, and nearly all their clothing. Suspiciously, 900 beaver pelts owed in debt to the Hudson's Bay Company were also missing.

The new prices offered by the Americans tempered the Iroquois' disappointment in their friends not being with them. Old Pierre's followers traded for horses, ammunition, an old pistol, looking glasses, buttons, tape, needles, and other odds and ends worth 105 pelts.[161] The new arrivals were pleased to find that their Iroquois friends had a large number of beaver pelts.

Trading a competitor's returns was an old tactic of the skin game. Jedediah Smith had the luck to begin his mountain career with a fishy deal because Weber and Jackson, who carried the company store, had larger commitments; the free hunters who traveled with them depended on the Ashley-Henry outfit for supplies. Ashley's $200-a-year enlistees, still subject to orders, accompanied Smith. Returning west with the Iroquois and pretending to be hunters permitted them to penetrate the HBC system and widen the connection with other dissatisfied British trappers.[162]

After Smith and the Iroquois headed across the Snake River plain, Captain Weber kept his men trapping until winter locked the streams in ice and the beaver in their dens. When the first snow fell, the bone-cold men needed to find shelter, game, dependable pastures, and companionship to ease them through the winter. Weber's brigade trapped down the Bear until they found a promising location that they named Willow Valley. Snow on the heights would soon drive deer and elk down to browse on the willow tips. Potts, the perpetual optimist, reported that "numerous streams fall into this valley which like the others is surrounded by stupendous mountains, which are unrivaled for beauty and serenity of scenery."[163]

The trappers found the Shoshoni almost as hospitable as the Crow. The Shoshoni had learned to tolerate Astorians, Nor'westers, solitary trappers, and Iroquois, but grumbled that Snake Brigade hunters recently killed their tribesmen. Because strangers took their beaver, they lacked the means to buy enough guns. One of their precious North West trade fuzees bore an 1802 stamp.[164] And on those occasions when they might trade arms with willing whites, Blackfeet intervened to prevent the arming of their old enemies.

The Shoshoni, reconciled to changing times, saw the advantage of competing suppliers. They found the liberal Ashley-Henry standard of trade attractive and the exchanges equitable. The trappers were good customers for moccasins, robes, ponies, and women.

Longing for a river that connected to *La Mer de L'ouest*, the Americans inquired closely about the true drainage of the Rio Colorado. Snake descriptions of the yet unnamed Humboldt River sounded less than promising, although the Americans thought it might be the fabled Buenaventura River that flowed into San Francisco Bay. In the spring Jim Bridger and other explorers built a bullboat and floated down the Green to taste the salt of a great inland lake.

After long winter evenings in a cramped leather tent, even Potts's pranks and Bridger's long yarns grew tiresome. While the wind rattled the smoke flap David Jackson kept busy calculating the remaining stores, doling out the dwindling powder and ball, and repeating Major Henry's promise to return next spring with everything they needed. During the brilliant winter days he slipped outside with his thoughts.

When he signed on with Andrew Henry, David planned to be in the mountains for three years. Two years had been wasted on the Missouri, and now, when the hunt had finally broken into the treasure house, he was scheduled to go home. Three years' accumulated clerk's salary added up to roughly $1,000—enough to buy a nice property in the depressed Missouri real estate market. But could Ashley-Henry come up with the cash? He considered returning to his family and settling down to a more substantial and responsible line of work. He couldn't continue to expect his father and his brother Cummins to look after Juliet and the children.[165]

Then again, if the next hunting season proved as lucrative as he expected, he would be foolish to turn away from that golden promise. Individual trappers, limited to the gain from their traps, left the real potential for income to those who used the efforts of others through trading. And David rode with the only organized American effort in the mountains.

When winter eased, the trappers went back to their onerous duty, although the snow still lay deep on the higher drainages. They trapped the lower Cub so closely that the HBC dubbed it the "American branch of the Bear." They secured two caches of pelts from the fall hunt in the hills above Willow Valley.[166] They left Ephraim Logan's name on a tributary while moving south down Bear River, and when the brigade camped near a stream coming out of the Wasatch Mountains they also put Weber's River on the map.

In early May Jedediah Smith and his band of six trappers returned from wintering in Flathead country with intriguing tales about the vulnerability of the HBC. Perhaps it was un-Christian to gloat, but Jed could not resist while telling how Alexander Ross's face formed a perfect picture when Old Pierre told him he had lost nine hundred beaver. Smith told the HBC field leader that he had cached a similar number of skins, and, to rub it in, he added that Major Henry was expected to return "to penetrate the Snake Country at the head of American trappers next season." The appalled Ross remembered Henry "as the same gentleman who wintered on Snake River fifteen years ago."[167]

Because the Oregon Country was under the provisions of the joint occupancy treaty, Ross could not prohibit Smith from following him back to the Flathead Post. Smith cynically offered him the common decency of traveling together for their mutual protection from Blackfeet horse raiders.[168]

At the Flathead Post on Clark's Fork of the Columbia, the Americans watched HBC's Snake Brigade turn in 4,900 "made beaver" (MB) and then take the trade of the Flathead, Kutenai, and Pend d'Oreille Indians.[169] The Bay men collected another 1,183 beaver, 529 muskrats, 14 otters, 8 fishers, 3 minks, 2 foxes, a marten, and 11,072 pounds of dried buffalo meat from the local tribes and freemen.

The American hunters, who had to wade the cold waters to make their catches, thought the HBC trade looked comparatively easy; but the Indian average of only three skins per hunter disgusted Ross. By comparison, the enterprising free trappers took about twenty-six skins per man—still too little to clear their debts.[170]

American suspicions about the HBC taking advantage of the buyer's market turned out to be true. It paid less than a dollar per pound for well-prepared beaver. Smith and company passed the word to the freemen and Iroquois that Ashley-Henry would pay three times that amount for anything it could get.

Smith and his men missed the shock rippling through the HBC's Columbia District that year. Gov. George Simpson traveled west of the mountains on a personal tour of inspection and to set an extensive reorganization in motion. The HBC planned to close Fort George at the mouth of the Columbia and build a new depot inland, near the mouth of the Willamette. A new post near Kettle Falls on the Columbia would replace the old Spokane House, and the company planned to move all other posts north of the Columbia, which they expected to form the boundary between the United States and the British Empire in North America. Chief Factor John McLoughlin, holding up the Rainy Lake end of the HBC's trading frontier, was coming to take charge of the Columbia District. Peter Skene Ogden, a bully young trader of the Nor'wester school, was taking over the Snake Brigade.[171]

Ogden came to finish something that had bothered Governor Simpson since the expensive mistake with the Bow River Expedition. Simpson still wanted to trap the Piegan beaver reserves on the Three Forks of the Missouri and made Ogden's unstated mission to follow up McDonald's accomplishment and exploit the Blackfoot barrier from the west.[172] Ross guessed that the returns from the next Snake Brigade would total 14,000 MB, more than half of the 24,000 MB that Governor Simpson expected from the Columbia District in 1824-25.[173] But the presence of Americans to witness a border violation would jeopardize the Snake Brigade's operation.

Smith's party, trailing the Snake Brigade, left the Flathead Post in mid-winter. The rival groups played cat-and-mouse games as they worked through the mountains. Deep snow on the Blackfoot River forced both parties to backtrack and come up the Portneuf. Jed's boys left the British at Bear River on 26 April, but Ogden decided to teach the intruders a lesson about staying in their own backyard. He planned to outflank the Americans by crossing through the mountain bowl that took his name and get ahead of them before they moved east. Considering the price differential between what the rivals offered for pelts, Ogden knew that staying close to American traders was foolhardy.[174]

Four old Oregon Country hands were finally returning to the West with a party operating out of Santa Fe or Taos. Jack McLeod, Patrick O'Conner, Francois Method, and Lazard Teycateycowige—the last of the freemen who went east in 1822-23—wanted to get back to their mountain friends. The French Trading Company saw them as a passport to the fur bonanza, and they left Taos about the first of August 1824 with Etienne Provost and Francois LeClerc.[175]

Leaving his partner at the base camp near the mouth of the White River, Provost took ten men across the Wasatch Mountains to the Jordan River, where, instead of friendly Utes, they ran into some Bannocks bearing a grudge. These Indians had tangled with HBC hunters the summer before and lost a chief in the quarrel. They recognized Patrick O'Conner as one of that despised breed. Their leader had a physical deformity or some dream medicine that caused the French to call him *Mauvais Gauche*, or Bad Left Hand. The American and British trappers called him Bad Gocha.

Provost fell for Bad Gocha's old line that iron adversely affected his medicine and agreed to have his group leave their guns and knives outside the council circle. When the Taos trappers settled in for a friendly smoke the

Snakes ambushed them with hidden knives. Provost and another scared rabbit ran for their lives, leaving eight trappers and one Indian slaughtered.

Provost's report convinced LeClerc and Antoine Robidoux to return to Taos, but Etienne, made of tougher convictions, decided to continue hunting with a diverse bunch that included a Russian, an old Spaniard, twenty Utah Indians, and the much-traveled western freemen. By mid-May they were coming down the newly named Weber River.[176]

Peter Skene Ogden congratulated himself that the Snake Brigade averaged fifty-eight beaver a day and left a trail of rotting carcasses to disappoint the American hunters. On 18 May 1825 he confided in his journal, "I presume the Americans intended returning this way [to Ogden Valley] but they will be, as we were on Bear River, taken in—they ought to keep home—not infringe on their neighbor's territories."[177]

When the trappers of the Snake Brigade broke over the divide from Ogden's Hole into Weber Canyon they met Jack McLeod and Lazard Teycateycowige, who came up from the south. Other Bay men probably encountered John Weber's men in the brush; trappers who wandered far from base camp sometimes slept out, so Peter Skene Ogden felt little concern when fourteen of his freemen failed to return on the night of 21 May. "M'sieu Pete" would have rested less soundly if he had known that his men were in the American camp getting high on the promise of fabulous prices. When one of Provost's trappers rode down to the American camp, the Ashley field leaders hunkered down for a strategy session.

The damned British intended to cut them off from the beaver streams ahead. As they moved east to meet Major Henry, the American hunters would face empty traps in a country they had already staked out for themselves. If Ogden wanted to play that way, they had to answer him in kind, but without involving the Ashley-Henry management in something that might generate international repercussions. Weber might have wanted to stay out of it entirely, but Jed Smith, David Jackson, and young Bill Sublette saw an opportunity to trade Ogden's returns and teach the Englishman a telling lesson.

The vigilante instinct still smoldered in the Americans who remembered the bloody experiences on the upper Missouri and believed that meddling British brought about those Indian troubles. Johnson Gardner still nourished the hatred he derived from the loss of his kinsman, John S. (or Joseph S.) Gardner, during the Ree fight.[178] He and his companions came to the mountains to earn fortunes and get out as soon as possible, but now the King's men were going out of their way to block them.

As Jeffersonians, the trappers believed they were "taking an inevitable and even heroic step toward righting wrongs from which the rest of the world suffered"; they had a duty to maintain the freedom that people in other countries could only envy and hope to emulate.[179] They could provide asylum for the abused Columbia freemen trying to escape from a ruthless, authoritarian institution.

David Jackson inherited the staunch republicanism of his family, growing up with the dreams for the new nation expressed by his father, his Uncle George, and his cousin the congressman. His brother George had a close call when he came up against British competitors on the upper Mississippi River, and David remembered the Ree fight, too. He now had a good opportunity to repudiate the agreement of joint occupancy in the field.[180]

Without a direct connection to Ashley-Henry, the rabid Anglophobe Johnson Gardner made a fine torpedo. He readily took on the role as spokesman for the simmering mob. The men took out a flag bearing twenty-four stars and thirteen stripes and tied it to a cut sapling. In the dawn of 25 May 1825 twenty-five representatives of democracy and free enterprise rode up Weber Canyon. Eleven men, including the Ashley-Henry field management, stayed in camp.[181]

The Snake Brigade camp spread along the north bank of Weber River just below the mouth of Dry Creek, west of present-day Mountain Green, Utah. The lodges sat snugly on the morning side of a cottonwood grove fronting a wide meadow. Enjoying an unusual second day in the same camp, the women puttered around the campfires or worked pelts while the children tumbled among the piled horse gear. Suzanne Montour had her four-month-old son, Louis Robert, sunning in his cradle board. Marianne Grey, a striking Iroquois mixed-blood woman, traveled with the brigade because her jealous husband loathed leaving her untended at the Flathead Post.

The camp babbled in French, English, and several Indian languages. A sense of expectation underlay the apparent serenity as they awaited the appearance of Provost's hunters. When the fifteen Taos trappers rode in about midday, they informed Ogden that their outfitting base lay fifteen days away.

As the British officer wondered whether he had strayed into Mexican territory, the riders came thundering across the meadow behind an American flag. Ogden's dapper little Canadian clerk, William Kittson, a veteran of the War of 1812, found himself again in the front line to see what the Americans wanted. He guessed that they came under several leaders but listened as the ill-clad, offensive fellow called Johnson Gardner spoke for the group. Intent on revenging his kinsman, Gardner proclaimed "the freedom of the country they were on, being, as he said, American territories, and that whomsoever wished to go with him, they were welcome. No man would dare oppose the measures they would take, he and his party were ready to stand by any that wished to Desert Mr. Ogden, Free or Engaged men were the same in this land of Liberty." If the trappers wanted more than a promise of golden freedom, the Americans were also willing to pay $3.50 a pound for beaver.[182]

While Kittson kept a "Strick watch" and hoped for fair weather, the Americans went into camp only a hundred yards from the British lodges. The next morning Gardner returned with bombastic broadsides about territorial possession and denial of the joint occupancy, ironically an argument conducted on Mexican soil.

Johnson instinctively fixed on the weakest link, the untrustworthy Iroquois John Grey, who informed Ogden that he and his people had wanted to join the Americans for some time. Ogden could say nothing to change their minds. On Grey's signal the freemen began packing under the cover of American rifles. One of the dissidents, Lazard, called on the Americans to fire so they could loot the British outfit. Ogden stared him down, but Kittson and the Blackfoot interpreter, Charles McKay, had to watch the departure of eleven Iroquois families with their furs.[183]

Ogden recovered ten company horses from the freemen by "enduring the most opprobrious terms they could think of, from both the Americans & Iroquois."[184] The former Astorian Alex Carson and Joseph Annance paid off their debts before leaving, but the HBC lost most of the outfits. The hostile camp moved off about half a mile, where mocking laughter echoed from its blazing campfires. Anticipating that the pirates intended to return in the morning to pillage the camp, the Bay men lay on their arms during a long night.

The next morning, as the remaining men were loading the horses, Nicholas Montour, Bazill Prudhomme, and Antoine Clement informed Ogden that they also intended to join the rival camp. Montour, a former North West Company clerk and sometime master at the Kutenais' outpost, was the country son of a founder of the NWCo. After the coalition the HBC turned Montour out of service, reducing him to the life of a common hunter. Charging that the HBC held £260 of his savings on its ledgers without paying him interest, Montour told Ogden to apply those funds to his, and Prudhomme's, debts because he was through being cheated.[185]

As the raging Hudson's Bay officer swung into his saddle, Gardner hit him with a parting shot, bragging that the company could expect to "see us shortly, not only in the Columbia but at the Flatheads and Cootenaies, as we are determined you Shall no longer remain in our territory." He promised that U.S. troops would come in the fall to force the British out.[186]

The shaken handwriting in Ogden's journal preserves his humiliation. The wounds still smarted a month later when he reported the loss of twenty-three trappers and £3,000 worth of furs. M'sieu Pete, still having problems with upper Missouri geography, erroneously dated his letter "East Fork, Missouri" when he was actually on the western branch at the springs of the Beaverhead. That mistake led the HBC gentlemen in London to believe that he had violated the international boundary, leaving them without diplomatic recourse.[187]

The American trappers and the Columbia freemen rode back to the Weber Canyon base camp whooping that the mountains were now theirs. If any liquor remained in the Ashley-Henry packs, David Jackson broke it out, deciding that when Major Henry returned they would all drink high wine.

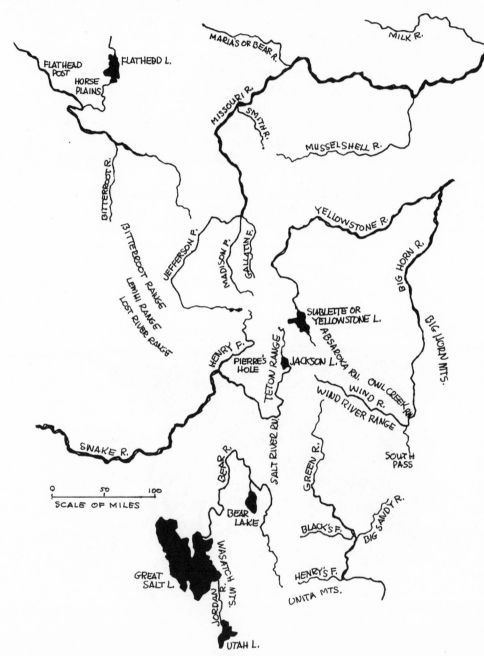

Rocky Mountain fur trading area.

8

"All the men . . . with whom I had concern in the country"

WAKING TO A NEW DAY IN THE ROCKY MOUNTAINS the American camp now included thirty-seven trappers of the combined Weber and Smith parties, fifteen Taos trappers, and sixteen subverted Columbia freemen. The defections reduced Ogden's trapping force by a third and increased the American hunting capability by 41 percent. Counting the three men who returned with Provost and three others who left Ogden later, the converted Hudson's Bay Company trappers totaled twenty-two.[188]

In the immediate wake of the competitive glory few understood what the subversion of the Columbia freemen meant to the newly declared contest for beaver pelts. The Iroquois and métis hunters had worked in the Northwest for more than twenty years. Among them, former North West Company and HBC clerk Nicholas Montour understood the British trade at the field level. The status-ridden HBC could ignore the poor treatment of those workers and brand them disloyal servants, but the mountain air held the breath of independence.

Johnson Gardner and his trapping partner Oliver Williams soon attached themselves to the Iroquois hunters. Williams had previously killed a half-breed named Thomas on the Bear River.[189] Old Pierre Tevanitagon and Ignace Hatchiorauquasha (John Grey) became their associates, but the more sophisticated Nicholas Montour, also of Iroquoian descent, apparently stayed apart.

Henry had promised a resupply, but if a new outfit failed to reach the mountains during the summer, Weber meant to bring the men home in the fall.[190] By the end of May 1825 Indians reported Americans hunting to the east, and Weber started his men toward the branch of the Green that Major Henry had designated as the rendezvous site. David Jackson, perhaps accompanied by Jedediah Smith or Bill Sublette, returned to the Cub River to recover their cached pelts from the fall hunt while the rest of the brigade hunted eastward. They soon met a newcomer named Zacharias Ham and seven trappers working on a branch of Black's Fork of the Green River. Ham said they had left the supply caravan on 20 April and in five or six weeks had taken 450 beaver. Tom Fitzpatrick and Jim Clyman were also out with small trapping parties, but William H. Ashley, not Major Henry, conducted the supply caravan. He had gone off to examine the Green River by boat.[191]

The exasperated mountaineers had waited a year for supplies. They could have told Ashley that Provost and other Taos hunters were already working the Green, but instead he had gone off on a useless "voyage of discovery," leaving them waiting for supplies. Gathering in stray hunters as they drifted east, the mountaineers reassembled in late June in a camp about twenty miles from the appointed rendezvous. They entertained themselves hunting, fishing, target shooting, and running foot races until the general showed up.[192]

A shaken Jim Clyman reported that while he had been hunting about sixty miles to the north, Gros Ventres or Arapahoes attacked his sleeping camp and tomahawked his horse guard. In their stampede away from the Blackfeet, Clyman's party bumped into sixteen of the men Henry had left at the Big Horn post in the fall and who were now working out of a base camp on Willow Creek.[193] Hunting up the Yellowstone they came to Henry's Fork of the Snake River about 12 June. Their knowledge of the rendezvous further substantiates Henry's planning before he left the mountains.[194]

Inhaling Green River water while trying to navigate the rough river convinced explorer Ashley that the Rio Colorado offered no alternative to mountain navigation, and he saw that the Taos trappers had already been in the area. Abandoning his boats near the mouth of the Duchesne River and buying a few horses from the Utah Indians, he luckily met Etienne Provost, who retrieved his cache and guided him to the rendezvous. Opening the mountain store saved Provost a long trip back to Taos and the uncertainties of Mexican customs.

Ashley, thrilled by the expectation of obtaining the furs of the subverted freemen and pleased to learn that Johnson Gardner was herding them to the rendezvous, saw salvation from his debts. The excited general broke off his exploration journal on 27 June, still sixty miles from the rendezvous site on Henry's Fork.[195]

Ashley indicated when he left Missouri early in 1825 that he expected to go to the "spanish country." Henry had described his earlier visit to the Colorado of the West, actually the Green River, which flowed through previously Spanish, now Mexican, territory. Ashley also knew "the place of randavoze for all our parties on or before the 10th July next" when he broke off his trapping parties on 22 April. He then arrived at "Rendezvous Creek," where he made his first cache.[196]

The wording of Ashley's three-year trading license for business with "a band of Snake Indians, west of the Rocky Mountains, at the junction of two large rivers, supposed to be branches of the Buonaventura and the Colorado of the West, within the territory of the United States," proved that Andrew Henry had described this stream, hereafter known as Henry's Fork, and its junction with the Green to his partner.[197] Ashley must have embarked on his profitless adventuring down the Green to find a stream he could use to float furs out of the mountains.

Arriving on Henry's Fork for the rendezvous, Ashley recorded that "all the men in my employ or with whom I had any concern in the Country, together with twenty-nine who had recently withdrawn from the Hudson Bay Company, making in all 120 men were assembled in two camps near each other about twenty miles distant from the place appointed by me as a general rendezvous."[198] New arrival Jim Beckwourth recalled that the general refused to begin trading until everyone was present. That gave the clamoring hunters an equal chance at the supplies and also assured Ashley a seller's market.

Ashley and the trappers apparently conducted the entire trade in a single day on the first of July 1825. Weber, Jackson, Smith, and Sublette helped the inexperienced Ashley appraise, count, and credit the packs that the grinning hunters threw down. Some men turned in as many as a hundred pelts, which Ashley's clerks had to weigh on a balance-beam scale hanging from a tripod. Under the broiling high-country sun the sweating clerks handled four tons of dusty furs while Ashley carefully noted the accounts in his book.[199]

Beaver was the only fur that would repay the cost of transportation, and the best came from the Columbia freemen who understood how to properly skin and scrape a pelt, comb out the sand, and periodically air and dry their packs.[200] The HBC broke down its purchases into large pelts, small pelts, and cuttings, but those technicalities went beyond the capability of the American clerks, who discounted poorly prepared or summer skins and the lighter-colored Southwest pelts that Provost's men contributed. Ashley's clerks allowed the disappointed Taos trappers only $2.50 a pound.[201]

Ashley sold a surprising variety of trade goods at a substantial markup. The hunters needed lead, powder, and blankets for their next outfit, and they purchased tobacco, coffee, and sugar as modest treats. Items for trading with Indians also went into the packs: a few extra knives, some cloth, and rings and beads.

Ashley had a $4,000 performance bond posted on the $8,000 outfit and downplayed references to liquor sales, even in his private business record, because the men traded alcohol directly across the barrelhead, a skin for a pint. Some drunken men might have made fools of themselves, but the traders usually refrained from exploiting that advantage. Men properly equipped and with enough heart to continue producing furs for the next hunt was in their interest. Most of the hunters worked in the mountains to earn money as fast as possible and then return home, so they left their earnings riding as credits on Ashley's book. The purchases recorded at the rendezvous contradict the popular image of an unrestrained mountain frolic.[202]

Practical American hunters could postpone celebrations, but this fair provided the only reward for the Columbia freemen, who knew no other life or home. Nicholas Montour, for example, traded forty-five made beaver and an otter skin, altogether worth $137.50. To reward Suzanne for sticking by him after he lost his position in the HBC, Montour bought beads, rings, ten yards of ribbon, two yards of cloth, four yards of scarlet, and buttons that she could sew in characteristic métis decorations. He needed the two-gallon copper kettle he purchased, but he also treated his family to sugar and coffee. With his remaining credit, Montour took a fire steel and a pistol, which he later returned. The Montour family ended up with a credit of $52.75 for six months of winter camping and bone-chilling labor.[203]

The Iroquois understood private enterprise. Pierre Tevanitagon and his two grown sons laid out their pelts for a modest trading outfit that included eleven gallons of rum to soften up British Indians. They intended to hunt north and trade with their Flathead friends, apparently in cooperation with Johnson Gardner and John Grey. The latter also purchased a black silk handkerchief for his smashing wife, Madame Grey.

When Ashley wrote the name G. Jackson for the hunter who turned in eight prime beaver skins worth $24, he must have meant David Jackson's body servant. Since Jackson handled beaver pelts for Ashley, the general would not have made such a deliberate mistake in identifying his clerk. We know David was present because he entered into the arrangements for the following year's business.[204]

Did Jedediah Smith confine himself to the certainties of his Bible while the impious men around the campfire read from the books in their minds? Men aiming for field leadership needed to know where they stood, especially since the HBC confrontation gave knowledge of western geography new significance. Weber's men shared their recently acquired knowledge of the Bear River drainage and the mountain heartland. Provost added understanding of the Southwest and the enticing proximity of Mexican senoritas and the killer distillation known as "Taos lightning." The hunters who had worked up the Yellowstone and down the upper Henry's Fork caught a glimpse of a beautiful mountain valley that many wanted to see. Even Smith's visit to Clark's Fork was overshadowed by the more complete experience of the Columbia freemen who knew the southern and northern Oregon Country, the entire sweep of the Columbia and Saskatchewan rivers, the northern Rocky Mountains, the upper boundary of the Great Plains, and even the subarctic.

The men put other geographical questions to the nomadic Shoshoni, who sometimes rode animals with Spanish brands. The ruts of their lodge poles led to most of the practical passes. Tribal geographers provided accurate sketch maps to Europeans well before the appearance of Lewis and Clark and continued to advise later discoverers.

During evenings, floating on diluted whiskey and expectation, the Americans came to realize that the real job of developing the mountain resources, and denying British rivals, still lay ahead. William H. Ashley got high on another kind of intoxicant as he calculated the returns that would regain his place in respectable St. Louis society. His investment of less than $8,000 in trade goods, marked up to mountain prices, brought him 8,829 pounds of made beaver; although he purchased these at $3 or less a pound, he could sell them in St. Louis for $5 a pound. If he could get those returns out of the mountains, he would gross $44,145, realizing a profit of about $18,000.[205]

Ashley entered the trade intending to serve as the downstream capitalist for a wintering partner, but his responsibilities had forced him to make two trips to the mountains. His sporting appreciation of the outdoors did little to cushion his thousand-mile ride in a hard saddle and near-drowning in the Green River. A hard bed of rough blankets provided an improper resting place for an aspiring Missouri politician.

Ashley had fallen into a temporary monopoly of supplying the hunters west of the Continental Divide, but the pile of furs outside his tent would surely attract St. Louis competitors. The offended HBC would come back next season with better prices to recapture the dissident Columbia freemen. The recent confrontation with the Bay men might generate an international protest that could damage the general's political future. Ashley was ready to distance himself from mountain competition and step back into his preferred role of a downstream supplier.

Ashley needed a trustworthy wintering partner. He worried that Weber, the proven hunting-brigade leader, had too close a connection to Henry. Ashley liked Smith, "a very intelligent and confidential young man," and was willing to overlook his tendency to make mistakes. He also considered young Sublette promising because he was more mature than his twenty-six years and had already pulled himself up from a trapper to the role of "asst," at a salary left blank in Ashley's account book.[206] And then there was Jackson. At thirty-seven, he fell midway between the old bourgeois who had fallen from grace and the younger men coming up. Ashley knew the mature and quietly confident Jackson was not a man to go off half-cocked. His broad experience as a farmer, soldier, miner, slave overseer, horse trader, lumberman, boatman, and merchant also included some potentially helpful connections in Washington. Jackson's small interest in the business came from three years of accumulated salary that Ashley was unprepared to pay. Ashley thought he could perhaps divert it into a deeper investment. The general's only worry was that Jackson was a little stiff-necked in his principles, but Ashley could keep what had transpired between himself and Henry a secret.

The three potential mountain operators all lacked the capital to buy Ashley's remaining outfit or to pay for the goods he could furnish next year. But a syndicate might work out—if Smith, Jackson, and Sublette would agree to become partners.[207]

As the campfires burned down and the mountain men snored, Ashley thought about how he would get nearly four and a half tons of beaver pelts plus camp gear to the mouth of the Big Horn. He'd need at least fifty pack horses to haul the 140 or so packs of pelts, and he had to pick up another 1,800 beaver skins from the Popo Agie caches. He would have to borrow horses from the mountaineers and convince some of them to escort him through the Green and Big Horn valleys.

The pack caravan left the rendezvous the next day, 2 July, with Smith riding at Ashley's side while Jackson and Sublette kept with the twenty-five men who had volunteered to help bring back the borrowed horses.[208] Provost departed with his men, and Gardner and Williams split off with the Columbia freemen, leaving Captain Weber with a brigade of about twenty-five veteran trappers.

After crossing South Pass Ashley and Sublette took twenty men to recover the caches on the Popo Agie while Jackson and Smith steered the main column on a direct route to the Big Horn. Jed was high on the new arrangement to accompany Ashley back to St. Louis and bring out the next outfit.

David, however, felt more skeptical. He couldn't understand Henry's decision to leave the skin game so soon. He saw how Ashley had won the pot by holding his hand through another raise, and now Ashley's willingness to push back and let someone else sit in smelled of something unrevealed and untrustworthy. David knew that his family would be disappointed if he stayed in the mountains, but he felt compelled to accept this promising opportunity. The letter he sent to Juliet announcing his decision did not survive her reaction.

A courier disrupted David's ponderings when he raced in and announced that sixty Blackfeet hit Ashley's camp the previous morning, driving off all his horses except two. Cutting out enough animals to carry forty-five packs, the rescue party found their friends sheepishly cowering behind an expensive barricade of beaver. Later the combined parties were attacked by opportunistic Crows, but the men fended them off by killing one warrior and wounding another. Trudging alongside overladen horses, the trappers finally reached the old Big Horn post on 7 August 1825.[209]

Using the same boat yard where Henry built last year's fleet, Ashley's men took five days to construct enough bullboats to carry the pelts. In the tradition of French-Canadian voyageurs, they used the old fur press to compact their loose field bundles into ninety-pound packages. After adding the caches left by the sixteen men who had wintered on the Big Horn, the general had about one hundred heavy packs.

During those five days at the Big Horn post Ashley, Jackson, Smith, and Sublette discussed the future course of the trading company. Smith would accompany Ashley and bring out the next outfit. Sublette, wounded by the Blackfeet, and Jackson would winter in the mountains and try to get enough furs to buy into a three-way partnership with Smith. Ashley would retain the rights and potential profits of a downstream supplier.

After the skin canoes floated away, Jackson and Sublette closed up the old place and headed upriver with twenty-five eager hunters.[210] At the mouth of Wind River, Old Caleb Greenwood decided to go home after all and set out by way of the Platte River to Fort Atkinson, where he arrived on 26 November. Greenwood brought the latest news of the projected mountain operations to the rival French company, which immediately hired him.[211]

The trappers rode west, between the colorfully eroded bluffs where the Wind River valley begins to wedge into the Continental Divide. They intended to complete Smith's unsuccessful probe across the Wind River Range and examine the promising valley on the other side. After crossing Togwotee Pass they descended into a broad, flat hole laying in the evening shadow of the Teton Mountains.

Aspen trees shone white against the dark pines, their leaves flickering like golden jewels of autumn. Beaver, innocent of the men's intentions, drew slow lines across mirror ponds, and birds stubbornly resisted the instinct to move south. Bill Sublette, a most pragmatic man, felt moved to set his new partner's name on the lake that reflected the snow-dusted peaks. The next year, David reciprocated by naming the companion lake to the north after Bill. Jackson Lake still carries David's name, but Sublette Lake is now known as Yellowstone Lake.[212]

The braided channels of the upper Snake River made an ideal beaver habitat. After setting their traps the hunters rode over to look at the lake. Despite the serene reflection of the darkening peaks, the late September temperatures had already frozen the summer rain trapped in the cracks of rocks. The ice occasionally levered off slabs of granite that fell unseen; the voice of the growing mountains echoed in the breathless silence. The hunters worked south until the valley started to narrow into the Snake River gorge. They forded the river and climbed a steep Indian trail toward Teton Pass.

To the west, the rolling hills of the Teton Basin masked the distant Snake River plain and the region where Ogden had retreated after his confrontation the previous year with the American hunters. The loss of his hunters during that unhappy episode forced Peter Skene Ogden to head for the Three Forks country in a desperate attempt to refill his packs from the forbidden Piegan reserves. He had gathered 3,000 beaver skins by the time he bumped into some of the HBC confidential servants traveling with the Small Robes Piegans. Jemmy Jock Bird and Hugh Munroe told Ogden that trappers had already cleaned out the headwaters of the Missouri, and Pete's remaining Columbia freemen refused to take the risks inherent in violating Piegan territory. On 16 August most of them cut loose, leaving Ogden with just sixteen men, only seven of whom were trappers.[213]

When the reduced party tried to move east and Indian rustlers harassed them, the exasperated Ogden had the ears of an apprehended Piegan "clipped" to discourage such behavior. The Bay man must have regretted his action two days later when he learned that two hundred tents of Bloods, Gros Ventres, and a few Piegans were camped nearby at the head of the Red Rock branch of the Jefferson Fork. Fed up with the situation, the Snake Brigade killed another Blackfoot horse thief near Monida Pass, then turned west in late September at the beginning of the best trapping season.

When Ogden reached Fort Nez Perces on 12 November 1825 he turned in about 4,000 skins and met Columbia District Chief Factor John McLoughlin. McLoughlin had been waiting since there since the third to confer with Ogden about the American incident and Ogden's involuntary perversion of Governor Simpson's trapping strategy. The chief factor activated two new trapping brigades, one composed of Ogden's veterans and another of twenty-two engaged men led by tough Finan McDonald and the much-feared Thomas McKay. They took four Indians, no women, and only two of the untrustworthy freemen, which suggests that the Snake Brigade prepared itself to fight if necessary.

Both parties intended to make the fall hunt in eastern Oregon, a galling admission that the HBC was abandoning Governor Simpson's offensive to turn the Snake country into a fur desert. Now the HBC was desperately trapping in the west in order to buffer the new Fort Vancouver depot.[214]

The fall hunt in the barren marches of the Oregon desert yielded only 485 made beaver, and the hunters felt lucky to find enough game to keep themselves from starving. In early February 1826 the HBC Snake Brigade gathered itself for another trapping adventure up the Snake River.

The desertion of the western freemen shook the HBC, and they worried that another meeting with the Americans might cost the rest of its trapping force. Taking personal initiative, Chief Factor McLoughlin increased the prices offered to the trappers and reduced the cost of goods advanced to them. But his price of 10 shillings (about $2) per beaver was still less than the Americans paid at their rendezvous.

Ogden's misunderstanding of upper Missouri geography misled London to believe that he had intruded into United States territory and convinced the HBC to forego lodging a formal protest over the Weber Canyon incident. But the HBC's inability to trap the Three Forks stemmed from reasons other than their concern for international law and Ogden's geographical errors.

For the second time in three years the HBC had run into adamant Blackfeet opposition to direct trapping. The Blackfeet excused the HBC for killing horse raiders in the act of stealing, but Ogden's mutilation of the captured horse thief probably incited others to avenge his disfigurement. Hunters with the Snake Brigade again became personae non grata in the Piegan heartland.

By fall 1825 the British were burdened with Indian animosity while the American hunters enjoyed a fresh start. Trappers considered losing horses a normal cost of doing business in the mountains, and, with the exception of the fifty-two horses that Weber apparently lost to Blackfeet, the American hunters seem to have escaped bad experiences with the Indians.[215] The eventful year ran out with the British held at arm's length in barren southeastern Oregon by a combination of Blackfoot territorial insistence and American trade competition.

Jackson and Sublette, unaware of the British plight, led their men down the west slope of Teton Pass. Turning south they came back to the Snake River where it emerged from the gorge into a beautiful valley. Crossing parallel ridges, they reached the Blackfoot River where deep snow had denied them access the previous spring. They trapped until ice forced their retreat to the winter camp in Willow Valley.

That winter snow fell to depths of eight feet. When the ribs of their valuable horses began showing, the mountaineers moved down into the Salt Lake valley and kept separate camps with smaller herds to find adequate forage. Most of Ogden's former freemen, split between Weber's brigade and that of Jackson and Sublette, camped in the valley; the Iroquois, however, wintered far away in the northern Flathead camps, where Johnson Gardner continued to torment the British traders. As many as six hundred Indians— Shoshonis, Bannocks, and Utes—lived around the American trappers in the Salt Lake valley. Bad Gocha, the Snake rustler who robbed indiscriminately whenever the opportunity arose, lurked on the fringes.[216]

That winter David Jackson and Bill Sublette hunkered down in a wind-lashed buffalo-skin lodge to work out a scheme for the spring hunt. The cautious men had reservations about Ashley's offer to capitalize outfits in St. Louis and deliver them to the mountains, but it gave them a chance to pull themselves into the fur trade by their bootstraps. To make the scheme work they would have to keep up trapping production and have an assured market for the outfits they would take on credit. Their profits had to come from the difference between the cost of the outfit and the gain on their resale of the goods; it was a slim opportunity, but they lacked the funds to get started on a more even footing. Come spring they would survey the Snake River valley; if it proved out, they could commit themselves to a deal with Ashley.

Gusts of wind drove the smoke back into the tepee where the two accidental entrepreneurs blinked and rubbed their eyes with dirty paws, ignorant that their fate was being considered in the elegant offices of Whitehall and in the muddy equality of Washington. The effective debate on the disputed Oregon question was conducted in this smoke-cured tent beside a saline lake.[217]

9

"The business of taking furs in the Rocky Mountains"

GOVERNOR GEORGE SIMPSON RETURNED to the company depot on Hudson Bay in early 1826, unaware of the Ogden incident. He sailed for London in the fall of 1825 confident that his few masterful strokes had set things right in the Columbia District. After conferring with Simpson, the committee of the HBC authorized him to inform the government on the measures the company had taken in the interests of the empire. In late December 1825 Simpson enlightened Undersecretary of State Henry Addington about the Pacific Northwest.

The HBC maintained thirteen establishments in the Pacific drainage, and the new Fort Vancouver served as headquarters for the Columbia District. Fort Nez Perces received the trade of the western Snake River valley, Fort Okanogan welcomed pack trains from New Caledonia, and a new inland sub-headquarters at Fort Colvile supported the Flathead and Kootenai outposts. In anticipation of a boundary decision the HBC relocated those places to the north side of the Columbia River or scheduled them for removal.

The HBC guessed the United States would improve its claim to lands south of the Columbia River, and the company, resting its beaver reserves in the areas it expected to remain in British hands, determined to exploit the joint occupancy of Oregon Country by sending hunting parties to trap south of the Columbia. According to Governor Simpson, these operations were "still in their infancy," but the West, including New Caledonia, now produced £30,000-40,000 a year. The company expected substantial increases.

Simpson emphasized that the Columbia River was essential to the HBC transport system and that the company should retain use of it in any future agreements. Simpson left Undersecretary Addington with the distinct impression that Oregon Country problems were entirely diplomatic.[218]

Washington was also considering the Oregon question. The western congressmen who favored expansion went up against New England mercantile interests hungry for West Indian seaports and the Pacific Coast sea-otter trade. Those self-interested Yankees of the trading age felt no need to concern themselves about a handful of scruffy beaver hunters. They endorsed letting the Oregon boundary question run on until developments forced reconsideration of the awkward joint occupancy.[219]

In Cache Valley two smoke-cured entrepreneurs were already working on the next step to discomfort British expectations. The annual cycle of Snake Indian life began with the spring root harvest followed by the summer buffalo hunt, fall salmon fishing, and winter camp near the mouth of the Portneuf River. After a difficult winter, two hundred northern Shoshonis left their camps in February 1826 and stirred their American neighbors into action. John Weber's band of hunters followed the travois tracks toward the upper Snake River. The Jackson-Sublette brigade of about thirty-four Americans and western freemen moved around the dismal north end of the Salt Lake.[220]

Indians warned Jackson and Sublette of saline deserts to the south, so they detached four men to build a bullboat and explore the shoreline for an outlet of the fabled Buenaventura River. That thirsty month-long voyage ended the dream of a Pacific Ocean outlet, and the adventurers returned to Cache Valley to meet the supply caravan.[221]

The trappers found beaver sign on the head of Goose Creek in the wastes of the Raft River Range, but an autumn fire had burned through the country and destroyed the willows, driving the beaver out. Living on a diet of antelope meat, the Americans followed a rocky, hoof-gouging trail on the south side of the Snake River valley.[222] Jackson and Sublette turned northwest across stark ridges and gullies to the Bruneau River in search of beaver. Trappers exploring upstream soon found canyon walls towering 800 feet over their heads, so they turned back. According to the Indians, the nearest beaver were on the next river to the west, a three-day march over sharp rocks. Unwilling to risk such damage to their horses' hooves, the brigade turned down the Bruneau.[223] "Most of what is known of this section of the country has been derived from Mr. Jackson and such Partisans as have traveled through it. Apply this note to the opposite waters of the Lewis [Snake] River and the Owyhee River."[224]

While waiting for the annual run of salmon to return to the rivers, local Indians lived on a diet of ants and grasshoppers. Finding no stomach for bugs, the trappers resorted to eating horseflesh. Sometime after mid-April the Americans crossed the Snake at the mouth of the Bruneau. A dusting of snow set off the pale emerald sagebrush stretching far ahead under heavy clouds that smothered the distant mountaintops and pressed down on the barren wormwood plain. The prospects looked depressing, but the Columbia freemen assured the others that better beaver hunting was just ahead.

The column trudged north until a line of stark trees marked the Boise River. Beyond that lay the Payette River, which curved through a pretty valley. Alex Carson, the former Astorian, said that Alex Ross and the Snake Brigade had trapped a hundred miles of it two years ago and made a good catch.[225] When the Payette headed at a lake surrounded by snowy mountains, the hunters returned downstream and followed an old Indian trail back to the Boise.[226]

Jackson and Sublette were south of and too early for the spring rendezvous of northern Shoshoni and Bannocks at the Camas Prairie root grounds in May and June. The trappers had more interest in contacting the beaver-hunting Flathead Indians who wintered at the lower end of the Bitterroot Valley or on the horse plains near the HBC fort. Johnson Gardner, Williams, and John Grey probably accompanied those hunters, trying to deflect the trade that usually went to the Flathead Post.

The freemen insisted that the nearby Godin's River (the Big Lost River) disappeared into the rocks on the Snake River plain. David assured the freemen that his grandfather had told him of a similar stream that sank into the Shenandoah Valley. The campfire skeptics snorted that the first liar never has a chance.

Last fall, Ogden lacked the men and equipment to do much damage to the beaver population of the area's rivers, and the Americans found good trapping. Continuing east they saw the three distinctive volcanic cinder cones that rose from the plain near Henry's Fork. The distant foothills on the west side of the Teton Mountains looked like billowing waves of a green ocean. Groves of aspens and cottonwoods stood like islands before the dramatic backdrop.

These were the places where Blackfeet came to levy on the Snake horse herds. Ninety Piegans who passed the upper Snake plain at the end of March may have been returning about this time. Their trade with the HBC on the Saskatchewan the previous fall left them resentful of British overbearance, and they were interested in reports that the Americans paid high prices for pelts and asked low prices for goods.[227] David and Bill realized that the mountain business required more than one-sided reliance on trapping—Indians could add a third leg to a fur-supplying tripod that also included Columbia freemen and independent Americans.

The 750-800-mile circumnavigation of the Snake country gave Jackson and Sublette a good survey of their prospects. Although familiar territory to the British, the north side of the Snake River valley still offered the trappers a promising factory of pelts. The Bear and Green rivers south and east of there provided them an ace in the hole beyond British reach. And they felt certain that they had been unable to reach other beaver rivers to the southwest. Encouraged by the investment prospects, they turned south to meet Ashley at the bend of Bear River.[228]

Ashley's last trip to the mountains proved consistent with the level of his previous performances. His parsimony in wintering sixty men in the Pawnee towns cost him twenty-five to thirty enlistees who resigned and went home. Smith's poor choice of a winter camp or slack superintendence of the 160 pack animals resulted in losing about one-third of them to winterkill. The general found twenty-six additional men and bought more expensive animals in the spring, but he still showed himself inept at field operations.[229] David and Bill heard about Ashley's recklessness from Robert Campbell, a young Irishman coming into the mountains for his health.[230]

Campbell described the hilarious Fourth of July celebration in Cache Valley, where the men "partook of a most excellent dinner, after which a number of political toasts were drank." The general traded with sixty-five to seventy hunters and fifteen lodges of Iroquois.[231]

When Ashley met Jackson and Sublette at the bend of Bear River he had 125 field packs worth approximately $32,000 in St. Louis.[232] His residual outfit was valued at $16,000 in mountain prices.[233] On 18 July 1826 Jedediah Smith, David Jackson, and William Sublette agreed to receive the stock of goods. Smith put in the $5,000 that Ashley owed him from their previous arrangement, but Jackson and Sublette could only come up with $4,000 between them. They executed a note to Ashley for $7,821 and agreed to pay it off in good, marketable beaver delivered at the west end of the little lake of Bear River on the first of next July.[234]

Campbell quickly grasped the economics. "Beavers furs cost in the mountains $3 per pound. They brought in the States $5, and upwards and in St. Louis $5.25 to $6.00 per pound, and from $6.00 to $7.00 in New York."[235] Because they lacked the money for a better deal, the partners had to promise to pay Ashley with furs at the price they would pay to obtain them. Their profit had to come from the markup on trade goods.

Looking for a long draw to a small hand, they confidently made preliminary arrangements for another $7,000-15,000 outfit they would confirm on a given date.[236] The new partnership also took over forty-two of Ashley's men hired on eighteen-month contracts and obliged to turn over half of their fall and spring hunts to repay the expense of bringing them to the mountains.[237]

... of agreement made and entered in to this 15th day of ... 1826 by and between William H. Ashley of the first part and Jedediah Smith David E Jackson and Wm L Sublette trading under the firm Smith Jackson & Sublette of the second part witnesseth that whereas the said party of the second part are now engaged in the fur trade and contemplate renewing their stock of merchandise for the ensuing year for the purpose of continuing their said business should their proposals of ... their doing so now Therefore the said party of the first part promises and hereby obliges himself to furnish such an assortment of Merchandise as said party of the second part may require according with an Invoice hereunto annexed reference thereunto will more fully show and for the prices therein mentioned to wit Gunpowder of the first and second quality at one dollar fifty per pound Lead one dollar per pound Shot at ... dollar twenty five cents per pound Three point Blankets at nine dollars each Green ditto at Eleven dollars each Scarlet cloth at six dollars per yard Blue ditto common quality from four to five dollars per yard Butcher Knives at seventy five cents each two and a half point Blankets at seven dollars each North West Fuzils at twenty four dollars each tin Kettles different Sizes at two dollars per pound Sheet Iron Kettles at two dollars twenty five cents per pound Squaw axes at two dollars fifty cents each Beaver Traps at nine dollars each Sugar at one dollar per pound Coffee at one dollar twenty five cents per pound Flour at one dollar per pound Alspice at one dollar fifty cents per pound Raisins at one dollar fifty cents per pound Grey Cloth at common quality at five dollars per yard Flannel common quality at one dollar fifty cents per yard Callicoes assorted at one dollar per yard domestic cotton at one dollar twenty five cents per yard Thread assorted at three dollars per pound ... twine at fifteen dollars per ... finger rings ...

... five dollars per Gross, Beads a[ssor]ted at two fifty cents per pound
Vermillion at three dollars per pound fills a[ssor]ted at at two
dollars fifty cents per pound; fourth proof rum reduced at thirteen
dollars fifty cents per Gallon Bridles a[ssor]ted seven dollars each
Spurs at two dollars per pair Horse shoes and nails at two
dollars per pound tin pans a[ssor]ted at two dollars per pound cents
hand kerchiefs a[ssor]ted at one dollar fifty each, Ribbons a[ssor]ted
at three dollars per bolt Buttons at five dollars per Gross Looking
Glasses at fifty cents each flints at fifty cents per dozen
Powder awls at twenty five cents per dozen Tobacco at one
dollar twenty five cents per pound Copper Kettles at three dollars
per pound Iron Bridles a[ssor]ted at two dollars fifty cents per po[und]
fire steels at two dollars per pound dried fruit at one dollar and fifty
cents per pound Washing soap at one dollar twenty five cents per
pound Shaving soap at two dollars per pound first quality James
River Tobacco at one dollar seventy five cents per pound Steel
Bracelets at one dollar fifty cents per pair Large Brass wire
at two dollars per pound which merchandise is to be by
said Ashley or his agent delivered to said Smith, Jackson
& Sublett or to their agent at or near the west end of the little
lake of Bear river a water of the Pacific Ocean on or
before the first day of July 1827 without some unavoidable
accurrance should prevent. but as it is uncertain whether
the situation of said Smith Jackson & Sublett's business
will justify the proposed purchase of Merchandise as
aforesaid it is understood and agreed between the said
said parties that the said party of the second part shall send
an Express to said Ashley to reach him in St Louis on or
before the first day of March next with orders to forward
the Merchandise as aforesaid, and on its arrival
at its place of destination, that they the said Smith
Jackson & Sublitt will pay him the said Ashley
the amount for Merchandise sold them on this
day for which the said Ashley holds their note
payable the first day of July 1827 for. and it is
further understood that the amount of Merchandise to

be delivered as aforesaid on or before the first of July 1827 — shall not be less than Seven Thousand Dollars nor more than fifteen thousand and if it is in the power of said party of the second part to make further payment in part or in whole for the Merchandise that be delivered that they will do so or if not that they will pay the amount at St Louis on or before the first day of October in the year 1828 but if the said party of the first part receive no Order from said party of the second part to forward said Merchandise as aforesaid or instruction not to forward it by or before the time before mentioned then this article of agreement to be null and void; and it is understood and agreed between the two said parties that so long as the said Ashley continues to furnish said Smith Jackson & Sublett with Merchandise as aforesaid That he will furnish no other company or individuals with merchandise other than those who may be in his immediate service

In presence of —
Robert Campbell
— // —

Wm H Ashley
J S Smith
D E Jackson
Wm L Sublette

Smith, Jackson, and Sublette (SJ&S) took on a large risk. Smith and Sublette were young men with little to lose, but Jackson, a man of substance, had properties subject to foreclosure if the partnership failed. What David lacked in cash he made up for in substance; men would follow him because he had earned their respect by avoiding the mistakes that made for good campfire yarns and lonely graves. He was stepping out of the shadows where men like John Weber and Johnson Gardner remained. Mountaineers valued leadership they could trust.[238]

The SJ&S contract included a provision that designated Ashley as the transporter but reserved for the three partners the option of selling their own furs. In their enthusiasm the new partners overlooked the last paragraph of the supply agreement, which stated "and it is understood and agreed between the two said parties that so long as the said Ashley continues to furnish the said Smith Jackson & Sublette with Merchandize as aforesaid that he will furnish no other company or Individual with Merchandize other than those who may be in his immediate [charge deleted] service."

The partners spent a leisurely two weeks at the big bend of the Bear working out their trapping strategy. The Snake Brigade had passed the mouth of the Bruneau on 25 February, before Jackson and Sublette descended it.[239] The twenty-eight American trappers and western freemen who hunted along the Snake River in early April ran into this reinforced Snake Brigade. Because his men were now hired hands, Ogden dared risk another trial of American prices. To make certain of their loyalty he brought the tough clerk, John Dears, to control them.

During a guardedly amiable meeting the freemen Montour, Prudhomme, and Old Pierre settled their outstanding debts to the company. Two previous deserters, Keyackie Finlay and Jacques Launge, rejoined the HBC, while Antoine Godin left it to go with his father, Thyery. Such acts encouraged Ogden, who recorded that the freemen were already tired of the Americans and the HBC could expect them to return to service at the Flathead Post in the fall.

Montour disproved Ogden's optimistic prediction ten days later by writing a letter to his old friend Henry Fisher, the HBC trader at the Rocky Mountain House. Montour bragged that he had made $2,000 since joining the Americans and expected to earn enough in another season to be able to retire.[240] If Montour failed to fit M'sieu Pete's idea of a disillusioned hunter, then three of Ogden's own men may have; when they tried to leave the brigade to join the Flatheads, Ogden had one of them beaten up.[241]

The Snake Brigade turned around and worked back down the Snake with the intention of circling around and going to the Flathead Post in the fall. Ogden, to his surprise, learned that an American brigade had crossed behind him, and Johnson Gardner and John Grey were among the northern Indians. He urged his superiors to send an officer and outfit with the Flatheads to prevent them from trading with the Americans.[242]

The return of the HBC required some strategic planning, which Jedediah Smith described from the large advantage of hindsight:

> August 7, 1826, at our rendezvous at a place known as the bend of Bear River, my partners Messrs, Jackson & Sublette and myself came to the conclusion that in order to Prosecute our Business advantageously it was necessary that our Company should be divided. We had at that time in all [space left blank for Ashley to fill in] men. It was decided that Messrs. Jackson & Sublette should go north on the waters of Lewis River and the Missouri with men and that I should take the remainder of the men and go to the south.

The practical-minded Jackson and Sublette, aware of their debts, apparently missed Smith's real intention.

> In taking charge of the S western Expedition I followed the bent of my strong inclination to visit this unexplored country and unfold those hidden resources of wealth and bring to light those wonders which I readily imagined a country so extensive might contain. I must confess that I had at that time a full share of the ambition (and perhaps foolish ambition) which is common in a greater or lesser degree in all the active world. I wa(nted) to be the first to view a country on which the eyes of a white man had never gazed and to follow the course of rivers that run through a new land.[243]

Smith and his clerk, Harrison Rogers, picked up an outfit worth about $331 and fifty horses worth about $60 a head, which made a total value of about $3,331.[244] Daniel Potts watched Smith and his fifteen men leaving for places he, too, wanted to see. The disappointed adventurer believed that they planned to explore the country southwest of the Great Salt Lake, winter there, and make a spring hunt toward the mouth of the Columbia. The partners designed the expedition as another attempt at the country Jackson and Sublette were unable to examine the previous spring.[245]

Jackson and Sublette mustered a large brigade of about one hundred men on the Bear River. The group consisted of either twenty-four or twenty-seven engaged men, twenty-eight Columbia freemen, and free mountaineers accompanied by their Indian wives and children. The brigade's strength allowed it to penetrate the Piegan heartland with a large assortment of trading goods. They hoped to strike a balance between trapping and trading acceptable to the Blackfeet.

Fledgling clerk Robert Campbell, contract hunter James Beckwourth, and free trapper Daniel Potts recorded the fall hunt of 1826. Campbell's improved health found him taken by the "bold, dashing life," while the less-aggressive Beckwourth appreciated the leisurely summer as they moved toward "the fall harvest of beaver." Potts, still sulking, wrote, "I took my departure for the Black-foot Country much against my will as I could not make a party for any other rout."

The eastern Snake plains attracted Snakes, Flatheads, Kutenais, and Nez Perces who came to make winter meat and Blackfeet who came to prey on their horses. Bushes along the river, or the islands of trees, sometimes held deadly surprises. The American herd was "daily harassed by the Blackfeet" and Potts lost his hundred-dollar horse.

Jackson and Sublette took the brigade to Henry's old post, where they cached part of the outfit and some early returns. Beckwourth, in his account of the fall hunt, said that several Blackfeet came *to the post to trade*, and "one of their chiefs invited Mr. Sublet to establish a branch post in their country, telling him that they had many people and horses, and plenty of beaver, and if his goods were to be obtained they would trade considerably; his being so far off prevented his people coming to Mr. Sublet's camp."[246]

The poorly armed Blackfeet began making peace overtures to the Flatheads in 1824, and the next summer they crossed the divide to negotiate peaceful access to the Flatheads' trading post. Ogden noticed the Flatheads and Piegans meeting amiably, and one of the confidential servants with the Small Robe Piegans admitted that it was the middle of the summer before he could get them to cross the mountains to hunt beaver.[247] As a consequence of the Blackfeet traveling west, the Saskatchewan trade fell off, forcing the HBC to reopen Rocky Mountain House for their benefit.

Jackson and Sublette faced the dilemma of obtaining trade through arming potential enemies.[248] The SJ&S agreement with Ashley specified the price for a "North West Fuzil at twenty dollars each" but omitted any indication of how many trade guns Ashley brought out the previous summer.

The partners gained new insights into the HBC vulnerability, learning of the Piegans' deep resentment of the long, dangerous ride to trade at the Saskatchewan posts. When the Missouri Fur Company opened a post on the Yellowstone in 1821, Blackfeet soon appeared to trade. They learned of Donald McKenzie's broken promise of a convenient HBC southern trading post and of the company closing Rocky Mountain House. They also found out that the Piegans accepted Finan McDonald's penetration of their domain because they badly needed munitions. But the question of whether the Blackfeet would tolerate a trapping brigade for the trade-off of attractive American prices remained.

Robert Campbell recalled that "Jackson Sublette and myself ascended the Snake River and its tributaries." Potts specified that they went thirty miles up Henry's Fork and crossed a large mountain to the other fork, which they followed to its source. It was there on the top of the world that David named the large lake (Yellowstone) for Sublette.[249]

Moving around the lake they came to an awesome geyser basin, inspiring Potts to produce the first written description of Yellowstone:

> At or near this place head the Luchkadee or Callifom [Green River] Stinking fork Yellow-stone, South fork of Masuri and Henrys Fork all those head at an angular point, that of the Yellow-stone has a large fresh water lake near its head, on the verry top of the Mountain, which is about one hundrid by fourty miles in diameter and as clear as crystal, on the south borders of this lake is a number of hot and boiling springs some of water and others of the most beautiful fine clay and resembles that of a mush pots and throws out particles to the immense height of from twenty to thirty feet in height. The clay is white and of a pink, and water appear fathomless as it appears to be entirely hollow underneath. There is also a number of places where the pure suphor is sent forth in abundance, one of our men Visited one of those wilst taking his recreation, there at an instan the earth began a tremendous trembling and he with difficulty made his escape when an explosion took place resembling that of thunder. During our stay in that quarter I heard it every day.[250]

Leaving Yellowstone the SJ&S brigade circled north around the headwaters of the Madison and descended the Gallatin River toward the forbidden Three Forks. Campbell believed that "twenty or thirty men were considered equal to any emergency," and they made it their habit to have two-thirds of the party trapping while the others took care of camp.

The party was too large for efficient trapping. Men planting up to eight traps each had to spread out to make effective sets, covering a creek for as far as three or four miles. The distance made them vulnerable to ambush when they returned the next day. Dissension also developed when greedy men began meddling with other men's sets; but the danger also encouraged teamwork, and some of the pairings lasted as long as the friends survived.[251]

The junior clerk had the privilege of posting three reliefs of horse guards every night—a duty shared by everyone except the bourgeois. The Iroquois were notoriously poor horse tenders, but Jackson and Sublette maintained strict camp discipline and avoided any major incident. With danger as the justification for strong discipline, the new hands soon recognized the unchallenged authority of the leaders, which was recognized even by men over whom David and Bill had no explicit authority.

After twenty-five years of resisting direct trapping, the Blackfeet now tolerated the hunters' invasion. Jackson and Sublette had fallen into an unusual lull in the war games and decided to put aside their cultural stereotypes; they wanted to buy Piegan furs and keep their expensive hired men busy. In November 1826 the HBC trader at Edmonton House noted that the Assiniboins and Plains Crees had "visited American traders [who] profer assistance to exterminate *our* Piegans." This statement seems a desperate attempt to rationalize the Blackfeet acquiescence of direct trapping by the Americans.[252] Although the Indians needed to trade for munitions, they continued to harass the vulnerable trappers.

Potts and two hunters who pushed ahead of the column in a narrow place bumped into a large party of Blackfeet. Both of the startled parties took to their heels. Another time, while riding point as the group moved down the Gallatin, Campbell and Bridger spotted suspicious smoke ahead. Realizing they had no safe way to approach, Sublette characteristically decided on a reckless charge. They were relieved to find only a backlog still smoldering at a month-old Indian camp. The brigade mocked Sublette by dubbing this exploit "the battle of the burned logs."[253]

Ogden warned headquarters that the Piegans' favorite wintering place on Marias River was "the most suitable spot for a Yankee establishment," and if the Americans carried that out, "we shall lose our Flathead and Cootany trade." If Jim Beckwourth's account is truthful, Jackson and Sublette had already opened commercial activities with the Blackfeet when they passed through the Three Forks. Jim's highly colored yarn has him going with two companions to a Piegan camp at Beaver Creek, about forty miles below the Three Forks, where the Indian leader As-as-to (Heavy Shield) was entertaining some visiting Flatheads. During a stay of twenty days, the Americans traded thirty-nine packs and several splendid horses, after which the Piegans escorted them south in style.[254]

By October 1826 the HBC trader at Rocky Mountain House sat on forty pieces of untraded goods. The Piegan Man-e-cape (The Young Man) brought Montour's propaganda letter, in which he bragged of making $2,000 since joining the Americans, causing Chief Factor John Rowand to observe, "nothing but Americans is with every word those fellows utter and [British secret agent] Mr. Munro was directed how to act in regard to finding out the truth or falsehood of such stories which banter much with the feelings, whether or no the Americans are established upon lands visited or convenient to the Piegans." He directed Henry Fisher to "seek the means of sending paroles for the Piegans to come in there as the Establishment was continued solely on account of them."[255]

As cracks appeared in Saskatchewan District operations, Governor Simpson tried to organize a second Snake Brigade to clean up the beaver before the joint occupancy expired. On 20 August 1826 Simpson wanted a party of forty-five to fifty Red River half-breeds and their families and charged Donald McKenzie, the original Snake Brigade leader and now the governor of Assiniboia, to facilitate their recruitment. The métis leaders Cuthbert Grant and Patrick Small could pretend to lead the group, but Simpson intended to place Chief Trader Simon McGillivray in actual charge.

Simpson planned to send most of those recruits to Edmonton House in the early summer 1827 while others took boats to York Factory to pick up a supply of arms, ammunition, traps, tobacco, and other supplies sufficient to sustain a two-year hunt. Leaving Edmonton in September with 150 horses, they would "make a Fall Hunt in the neighborhood of the mountains and pass the Winter among the Buffalo in the Coutanais plains." Since the most direct route was south along the mountains, they would also sweep through the Three Forks beaver reserves.

Simpson, willing to risk diplomatic offense to get at the Blackfeet beaver, planned to abandon those hunters west of the mountains after four years.[256] But the governor was unaware that Jackson and Sublette were already in the Three Forks country where they could observe, and would surely report, border violations.

The Columbia District, at Flathead Post, also felt American pressure. By mid-August Indians volunteered that Americans were in the Horse Prairie camps just upstream. John Work's Pend d'Oreille informant identified those agents as J. Guy and Jacques (John Grey and Jacques Ostinstericha), renegade Iroquois now associated with the Americans. Jacques in particular disquieted the HBC because of his connections to the Kutenais still free of American infection.

Grey and Jacques bragged that the Americans took 200 horse loads of beaver out of the country last spring and planned to return with 150 loads of attractively priced goods. By then the boundary decision would exclude the

British, and this year was the HBC's last chance to trade with the Flatheads. The two Iroquois also reported five American ships headed for the mouth of the Columbia River and completed the shock by adding that the Americans "were going to build this fall on the upper waters of the Missouri at a place called the Grand (T_____) ."[257]

Giving generous gifts of tobacco and scarlet cloth to influence the Flathead chiefs Gros Pied and Grand Visage, the troublemakers rode off by 24 August, accompanied by a few Flatheads, some Nez Perces, and two visiting Snakes—twenty-two in all, going to visit the American traders.[258]

The appalled Colvile District reacted by sending Chief Trader John Warren Dease to winter in the Flathead country. He spoke French and might be able to convince some of the dissident Columbia freemen to return. Dease wisely refused to take any additional freemen or Iroquois into the Flathead country where they would be susceptible to American influence.[259]

The piddling Flathead summer trade of 267 beaver pelts confirmed the American inroads. The Indians explained that disruptions on the buffalo grounds caused the lack of pelts, but William Kittson at Kutenay House observed that Dease would turn over less than one-third of the previous business because Americans met the Indians at the heads of the Missouri and traded all their furs. His trade held up only because the Kutenai Indians had yet to encounter the Americans.[260]

Dease confirmed the indifferent returns "in consequence of the Indians falling in with the Americans," who sold guns and tobacco at a cheap rate in the summer and took most of their furs. The Flatheads now badgered him about high HBC prices. "To lower our prices at present I am aware would be a bad procedure and it will affect the Nez Perces and Kootenais Posts but it is possible the Indians already mentioned may again meet the Americans, we cannot expect to get their hunts if those they may meet have wherewith to supply them at a cheaper rate."[261]

Far downstream at Fort Vancouver, Chief Factor John McLoughlin also realized that dissident freemen and Iroquois held the key to the western hunt. He risked his job with a unilateral improvement of the price differential in November 1825 that still fell short of the American prices.

Sending out engaged hunters cost the company but prevented more desertions. When Ogden returned to Fort Vancouver via the Willamette River, the company had lost almost half of its free trappers. But McLoughlin's complaints about manpower shortages went unheeded because Governor Simpson had convinced London that his measures to create a fur desert were working, and hiring more men would expose the illusion.[262]

Campbell recalled that the SJ&S brigade hunted across the Three Forks and trapped back to the headwaters of the Columbia. Beckwourth returned to the trading post on Henry's Fork escorted by 250 Piegans and 100 Flatheads. Others calling in probably included Grey, Jacques, and the 22 Flatheads who left John Work in August. Returning to Bear River, the hunters cached their furs and headed for Cache Valley to winter.[263]

Jackson and Sublette could congratulate themselves on cracking the Blackfoot barrier to trapping, something no trader and trapper had accomplished. But they had little time to celebrate—the terms of their resupply contract required them to notify Ashley by the first of March. Because Smith failed to return, Jackson and Sublette had to calculate the status of SJ&S on the basis of their northern hunt, which they felt was good enough to justify further commitment.

Accompanied by the experienced expressman Black Moses Harris, Sublette left the winter camp on New Year's Day 1827. Drifting snow made for difficult traveling, and the lack of game forced them to eat their faithful dog. After considerable suffering Bill reached St. Louis, where he was shocked to learn that the small print in Ashley's contract now threatened the existence of SJ&S.[264]

Soon after returning to St. Louis in September, William H. Ashley opened negotiations with Gen. Bernard Pratte of the French trading company, offering half interest in his enterprise. "The expedition which I propose sending in the spring will consist of about forty Men, one hundred and twenty mules & horses, the merchandize &c. necessary to supply them for twelve months, and that to be furnished to Messrs. Smith, Jackson & Sublette, all of which must be purchased for cash on the best terms."[265]

Ashley proposed sending a trapping outfit into the mountains to compete with his friends because his 1826 returns failed to match what he allowed the St. Louis papers to publish. And until he sold those furs in New York his capital remained tied up and his credit suspect. The man promoting himself as the founder of the mountain fur trade stood ready to fragment it for selfish reasons. Ashley had already finessed Andrew Henry out of the game, and now John Weber claimed that the general had cheated him out of $20,000.

Ashley added the fine print in the resupply agreement drawn on Bear River with SJ&S so he could supply men under his immediate charge, but he deleted that wording and changed it to read "in his service." John Grey's statements to the Flatheads referring to General Ashley as the leader of the American hunt promised that he would return with an extravagant outfit. Did that suggest premeditation even before Ashley left the mountains?

Ashley, taken aback that the French company and Pierre Chouteau, Jr., failed to respond, wrote two more letters during the winter. Pratte and Chouteau were stalling because they sought a merger with the giant American Fur Company and Chouteau was in Philadelphia ironing out the details. Ashley went east to sell his returns. At the old trading town of Lancaster, Pennsylvania, in December he offered to lead the joint venture in person, although he preferred to use two "confidential persons."

The new western department of the American Fur Company evaded a direct refusal with the sly grace of corporate gamesmen, and the French fur company would agree to finance only half of the new SJ&S outfit on condition that their representative, James Bruffe, went along as supercargo and watchdog.

Gossipy St. Louis was a poor place for secrets. Bill Sublette soon understood Ashley's subterfuge, but he may have declined to confront Ashley after the general abandoned his plan to send a competing trapping party to the mountains. Sublette obtained the new trading license on 27 March 1827, authorizing SJ&S to trade for two years at "Camp Defence, on the water of a river supposed to be the Buenaventura, Horse Prairie, on Clark's river of the Columbia, and the mouth of Lewis fork of the Columbia" with a stated capital of $4,335.

When the supply caravan moved out that spring Ashley rode as far as the edge of the Missouri settlements but turned back before Bill and his young brother, Pinckney Sublette, came up.

After the mountain winter broke, David Jackson took Campbell as his clerk and led a spring hunt on Green River. All Campbell could recall about the uneventful trip was an extraneous appreciation of the euphonic Indian name for that stream: Seeds-ke-de-agie.[266] Those waters had rested for two years, providing the party with a rewarding hunt.

Jackson and Sublette met at the south end of Bear Lake, where Bill's characteristic impetuosity placed the tenuous Blackfoot alliance in peril. About 120 Blackfoot horse raiders cut out and butchered an unwary Snake family, sending Snake and Ute warriors out for revenge. The Blackfeet retreated to a small wooded hollow with commanding fields of fire. Sublette and six excited Americans joined the fight. Bill charged, firing his pistols. Sam Tullock got wounded in the wrist. Beckwourth reported 173 Blackfoot scalps, a ridiculous exaggeration of the six raiders who died and others wounded, but more than enough to jeopardize the Piegan relationship.[267]

After trading, Jackson and Sublette took stock of their first year. They had the partnership on the path to solvency without any contribution from Smith.

Jackson and Sublette had opened trade with most of the western Indians, including the Blackfeet, and denied the British a substantial business. If the diplomats were using the disputed Oregon Country as the place to test the comparative effectiveness of democratic institutions against imperialism, Jackson and Sublette had certainly upheld free enterprise.

10

"The Americans have almost resided on these rivers"

HURRAHS AND BACKSLAPS FROM THE HUNTERS greeted the supply caravan as it approached the rendezvous site. But when the partners shook hands, David Jackson noticed the troubled look in Bill Sublette's eyes. Jackson's apprehension turned to disgust when he learned about Ashley's duplicity. The partners' good faith was repaid by the bottom-dealing Ashley, who sent a pair of watchdogs to stand over them. Hiram Scott represented Ashley, and the men pegged James Bruffe as a French company spy. While they chewed on that tough piece of meat, a buckskin disaster staggered in from California.

The emaciated appearance of Jedediah Smith generated some initial sympathy, but the salutes he liked to recall echoing off the high ridge behind Camp Defiance soon turned into the angry explosions of his irate partners. While Jackson and Sublette labored to pay off the start-up costs, Jed had let them down.[268]

Smith led last summer's Southwest expedition into a desert where three experienced hunters refused to go. The Mexican Manuel Eustavan, the métis Robeseau, and the Ojibwa Nipissing "were anxious to go more East which I [Smith] would not consent to do." The high plateau country, where the Sevier, Virgin, Escalante, and Fremont rivers headed, promised better beaver hunting. But Smith cared more for exploring than for following the agreed trapping plan.[269]

When his party reached California Smith got a cool reception from the authorities, who ordered him to exit over the same route he had entered. Ignoring the order, Jed trapped north as far as a tributary of the Sacramento River and wintered. In the spring he left his men and furs in camp and crossed the Sierra Nevadas with two companions, heading for the rendezvous. Jed's description of his suffering in the Nevada desert elicited little sympathy from his partners. They felt angry that he went there in the first place and decided that his innocence and ignorance were unbecoming a leader.

Jackson and Sublette heard Smith's ingenuous recitation with clamped jaws. Angrily, they listened as their partner tried to explain why he ignored the potential of the country south of the Snake and left the returns they needed to pay off Ashley marooned in California.[270]

They needed to take strong measures to make up for Smith's missing returns. Buying beaver at $3 a pound and reselling it to Ashley at the same price meant squeezing profits from the marked-up trade goods. SJ&S decided to increase the price of trade goods by about one-third, which generated howls and hard feelings from the men during the rendezvous.[271]

As disgruntled customers glowered across the barrel head, David Jackson finally realized the fundamental rule of the skin game: The isolation of the hunting-country economy permitted suppliers to dictate the terms. The British had two methods of exploiting their men: the Nor'westers paid high wages and charged high prices for goods; the Bay men paid low wages and sold goods cheaply. When the coalition of 1821 gave the British a monopoly to exploit the most advantageous terms of both methods, prices became so punishing that the Columbia freemen turned to another market.

American traders walked into the picture with better prices for beaver and more liberal charges for goods. Their standard of trade was based on the St. Louis model of relatively economical river transportation. But overland packing increased their expenses and reduced their profit margin. Beaver prices also fell as Ashley's substantial returns of 1825 and 1826 drove down the fiber market. The best price he could get was only $4 a pound.

SJ&S had subsidized the mountain hunters by stabilizing fur prices at a consistent $3 a pound. They marked up their goods to obtain a profit because raising those prices sat better with the hunters than reducing the price they paid for beaver. Dissatisfied hunters had the option of taking their furs to a better market. Jim Clyman and Robert Evens refused to accept the increases and took their furs to St. Louis, which cost them a year of hunting and still left them at the mercy of some uncaring warehouse bookkeeper. Other trappers preferred to swallow their indignation, work harder, reduce expenditures, and live off the land. The most destructive consequence of the 1827 price increases was the erosion of harmony and the potential alienation of the Columbia freemen and Iroquois, the swing element in the western work force.

At the end of the rendezvous SJ&S delivered 7,400.33 pounds of beaver, some castoreum (beaver scent glands used as bait), and a few otter skins to Ashley's new representatives, Bruffe and Scott. The $22,690 value of the whole lot was enough to clear Ashley's note and help the partners pay for a new outfit. They still had some residual goods and counted on Smith's 1,500 pounds of California beaver worth about $4,500 to see them through. During their northern sweep and spring hunt they had taken about 4,485 beaver, 500 of which came from the Flatheads and an undetermined number from the Piegans.[272]

Smith had to go back to California with another outfit, including eighteen engaged men. At that time of critically short manpower, Jedediah took thirty-two hunters away for two years. But, if Smith had given an accurate representation of the excellent trapping he anticipated in northern California, Jackson and Sublette could count on him for a secondary investment. Having seen large herds of horses grazing on California ranches without a market, Smith considered purchasing the animals cheaply and driving them to the mountains, where he could resell them for a handsome profit. The second Southwest expedition departed the rendezvous on 13 July 1827.[273]

The partners assigned Samuel Tullock, wounded in Sublette's recent ill-conceived fight with the Blackfeet, to lead a hunting brigade to the lower Snake River and tap the fur-producing areas that Smith had failed to exploit earlier. Tullock's presence would also keep the Snake Brigade close to home. Tom Fitzpatrick took over Weber's band of independent hunters who liked the Bear River and upper Snake country familiar to them. And Robert Campbell, the sickly greenhorn who had proven himself over the last year, would lead the northern brigade to uphold SJ&S interests against the HBC.

After laying out the plans for the fall hunt, Jackson and Sublette rode down to the States to have it out with Ashley. Jackson had to leave the mountains at a critical time to deal with the threat behind his back, and a long ride in a galling saddle worsened his temper. Passing the recently founded western Missouri town of Independence, they rode to the older outfitting center at Lexington.

When General Ashley came out to meet them, his nervousness caused him to forget to bring the most important document in their relationship, the contract. He faced two grim men who had just ridden 2,000 miles so they could deal with his duplicity. Because Ashley destroyed documents that may have proved embarrassing to him, what took place at the confrontation was lost on the prairie winds. We can see some of the tension in the tone of the nervous quitclaim that Ashley penned on the first of October:

> Whereas Messrs. Smith Jackson & Sublette are under the impression that on a Settlement with them near the grand lake west of the Rocky mountains in the month of July in the year one thousand Eight hundred & twenty six, they gave a note in my favor for the sum of Seven Thousand Eight hundred & twenty one dollars or there abouts which appeared a balance due by them to me now therefore if any such note was given it is to be considered entirely void as they the said Smith Jackson & Sublette have since paid said amount.
>
> Wm. H Ashley October 1st 1827.[274]

The partners made it clear that they were not going to labor in the mountains while Ashley played games behind their backs. After turning over $22,929 in furs, SJ&S took a new outfit worth $22,447.14 and gave Ashley their note for $9,010.04. The French company agent Bruffe wrote out a statement on the same day transferring 87 mules, 6 horses, 14 rifles, 4 fusees, a pair of steelyards, and some kettles to the partners. Jackson and Sublette also took over some of Ashley's caravanners after he paid them $40 for their services to date.

The mountain partners assumed the carrying business, a move calculated to save them up to $1.50 a pound in cartage and eliminate the intrusion of unwelcome observers to their business. They also considered eliminating Ashley as their marketing agent after Robert Campbell sent a letter to his brother in Philadelphia asking him to check on the fur prices in New York, Philadelphia, and Richmond.[275]

Ashley's business representative, Hiram Scott, went back to keep an eye on his master's investment, but the French company had something better cooking. Pierre Chouteau and his people were joining the giant American Fur Company, Astor's old firm. Now operated by Ramsay Crooks, the American Fur Company was moving to take over the Columbia Fur Company, which had built a ladder of trading posts as far inland as the Yellowstone. SJ&S would soon face competition on two fronts.[276]

Western Missouri lay in the dark about the London negotiations concerning the Oregon boundary, an issue complicated by questions about the redefinition of the northeastern border, the right of export on the St. Lawrence River system, and U.S. trading advantages in the West Indies. In the end, Great Britain and the United States agreed to put off an agreement, sidestepping the question with the pusillanimous compromise of allowing the joint occupancy to continue for an indefinite period of time.[277]

The HBC never claimed territory south the Columbia and expected to the U.S. to expel it from those trapping grounds in 1828. But Gov. George Simpson won a reprieve by misleading the British government about company success as an imperial factor. Continuing the compromise gave him more time to exploit the jointly controlled fur grounds, granting the secure reserves time to replenish. Jackson and Sublette went back into the mountains unaware that they had to continue competing with an imperial institution as well as a giant American corporation.

With competition already on the trail and winter closing in, field superintendent Jackson, after six long years in the mountains, could remain on the edge of civilization for only five days. He had too little time even for the few days it would take him to ride to Ste. Genevieve and see his brother.

British claims hinged on their permanent trading posts, but several sources give intriguing references to an American establishment on Bear Lake. Sublette's license referred to Camp Defence (Defiance), and British traders as far away as Edmonton mentioned an American "house" located "near a large lake for the purpose of equipping their trappers." The Mexican secretary of state, writing on 12 April 1828, described "a fort" situated on a lake "four days journey beyond the lake of Timpanagos [Salt Lake]." He based his information on Indian rumors that indicated the presence of a hundred men in the summer of 1827, commanded by a general of the United States who had five wagons and three pieces of artillery. The American officer was promoting treaties of peace between "the Yutas, Timpanagos and Commanches Sozones, and made presents of guns balls, knives &c. to both nations." The Mexican secretary even had an accurate timetable of the May arrival of caravans and their August departure from the fort with one hundred horses loaded with "otter" skins. Smith's expedition also caught his attention. The secretary knew twenty-five men intended to go to California while others would return to the fort in the month of December.[278]

That remarkable demonstration of the accuracy of the Indian grapevine still gives no proof of an actual structure at the south end of Bear Lake. SJ&S built temporary booths at rendezvous and stored their goods in secret caches. What counted was the belief among some British traders that the Americans had a house during a time when Governor Simpson claimed the Americans had no permanent establishments. If they had a post, it would have been in Mexican territory.

The western hunt was left in the iron-fisted grip of Samuel Tullock. Families of that name lived in Washington and St. Francois counties, Missouri, where Tullock later retired, so he probably came into the country with the early Ashley-Henry parties. He rode into the Blackfoot guns beside Bill Sublette and took a wound that left one hand paralyzed. Bill Sublette respected Tullock enough to entrust his young brother, Pinckney, to his tutelage.

Tullock's forty hunters left Bear Lake on 9 July. At the west end of the Snake River valley they split up into four hunting groups to oppose the two columns of the Snake Brigade. Seven American hunters even traveled with Ogden's brigade for a time, which gave the Bay man an opportunity to repossess one Canadian.

In September two Americans, John Johnson and Archibald Goodridge, who had been hunting on the Weiser River, traded one hundred skins to Ogden, who knew they owed substantial debts to SJ&S. Johnson told Ogden that SJ&S had detached six men to trap the Owyhee River while six others hunted toward Fort Nez Perces. Ogden had anticipated an American hunt on the Owyhee and sent Tom McKay with twelve trappers to oppose it.

McKay, who was half Ojibwa, came west with his Astorian father and grew up with the western trade. In 1816, while in the east visiting his mother, Tom got involved in the massacre of the Selkirk colonists. He fled west of the mountains to escape prosecution and never returned. Indians knew McKay as a tough trader and relentless foe. American trappers Ephraim Logan, Jacob O'Hare, William Bell, and James Scott took their chances hunting in McKay's Owyhee River bailiwick, perhaps in the hope of connecting with the brigade Smith was bringing back from California. The four men vanished and their fate has never been determined.[279]

Tullock and six men took an outfit to the annual Indian trade fair in the beautiful Grand Ronde Valley. Sam bought forty-nine Nez Perce ponies for the extravagant price of $50 a head, a price escalation that created considerable discontent at the HBC remount station, Fort Nez Perces.

Sam Tullock was an American partisan with a sense of humor. Unsatisfied with the indirect annoyance of competitors, he composed a sly letter to Chief Factor John McLoughlin on 7 September. Because the Nez Perce worried that the British might take their doing business with Americans as disloyal, Sam sent the Great White Eagle of the Columbia District a twist of American tobacco to appease his anger, saying, "I am preparing to return to the Grand Salt Lake of Bear River with the intention of returning in the spring. I may on my return to this place pay you a visit at Walla Walla."[280]

As his hunters moved eastward Tullock ran into McKay's brigade, and the parties traveled together as far as Day's Defile (Little Lost River). Tullock's fortunes started downhill when the Americans found it difficult to obtain game and had to eat $300 worth of expensive horse meat. McKay bragged that he had taken 500 skins to their 200. After Tullock broke away from McKay on 10 December, the trip across the Snake plain cost him 19 more horses. Tullock found it impossible to avoid the British, running into Ogden and the main Snake Brigade near Blackfoot Hill.

Ogden wintered in the protected bottoms near the mouth of the Portneuf River, where Tullock and his thirsty boys came over to visit on Christmas Eve. In the forgiving glow of HBC rum Tullock excused Johnson Gardner's offensive behavior from three years earlier by attributing it to poor organization SJ&S had since corrected. Overlooking the irony, M'sieu Pete noted the pleasant change in the American attitude.

Ogden and Tullock were men from different planets—one a corporate officer with aristocratic pretensions, the other a frontier democrat brimming with pugnacious patriotism. Since its coalition the HBC had become a paramilitary organization frozen in a ponderous chain of command and dominated by an accountant with delusions of grandeur. Upcoming young clerks who considered themselves gentlemanly representatives of the British Empire blunted the reckless vigor of former Nor'westers like Ogden and McKay.

George Simpson's hirelings preferred to imitate the pukka sahibs of the East India Company, but they had to spend their lives in crowded log cabins, skin lodges, and the demeaning intimacy of canoes. The governor set an example by traveling with a highland laird's tail that even included a hired piper. One of his new clerks reportedly crossed the continent without wetting his boots, requiring the voyageurs to carry him ashore. These men failed to develop a colonial caste system, but their attitudes took the edge off good men.

The British dismissed the seven American trappers who appeared in 1824 as a species of woods ape until the Weber Canyon affair demanded respect for the trouble they could cause. Tullock's openness and honesty charmed Ogden, who overlooked the American's intrusive questions as expressions of interest and loneliness. Ogden and Tullock, both of whom shared the bond of lonely responsibility, discussed international politics while winds rattled the smoke flap. Tullock confidently asserted that the London discussions would decide a boundary favorable to the United States, but Ogden just as surely stated that British diplomats would uphold the interests of the empire.[281]

Governor Simpson's idea of trapping so closely that the lack of pelts would become a barrier to American hunters had not worked out. Tullock's threat to Fort Nez Perces caused the discouraged Ogden to write that "the Americans have almost resided on these rivers for the past eighteen months." The lower Snake, now nearly trapped out, needed at least four years to recover its beaver population. In addition to the pelts they took, the Americans also drove up the price of furs and horses, which reduced a wintering partner's share of profits.[282]

Acquaintance did not alter business, and Ogden concentrated on trading supplies for American furs. By February Tullock's herd had dwindled to only twenty-four animals, a loss of $1,250. When Sam needed to send an express to the Cache Valley camps, his British neighbor slyly deflected his attempts to buy snowshoes or hire a courier. Ogden had the satisfaction of watching several American attempts to travel to Cache Valley flounder in the Portneuf snows.

SJ&S designated Robert Campbell to trap and trade in the north. As his brigade moved into the Flathead country, it met two of the HBC's confidential servants from the Saskatchewan District. Jacques Berger and Louis Brunnais, swayed by a better offer, brought whatever influence they enjoyed with the Piegans to the Americans.

When that news reached Edmonton at the end of November, Chief Trader John Rowand had to leave his comfortable fireside and make a cold trip to Rocky Mountain House. By January 1828 he admitted that "our Piegans, the only plains Indians who give us Beaver, I am sorry to say, have partly given way to the same delusion" and traded with the Americans.[283] The frustrated Bay men complained, "the Indians say the Americans have used their utmost endeavors to depreciate the character of the HBC traders and render them [as] despicable as virulent language and low impressions can impress." Rocky Mountain House, which usually traded 2,000 Piegan beaver, had taken in only 1,100 pelts. Rowand's rationalization that his Flathead Post counterpart had lost the whole of the Flathead hunt to the American party fell flat at corporate headquarters.[284]

The officers took the heat, although Governor Simpson created the problem when he reduced expenses by closing Rocky Mountain House. The corporate good sense in consolidating operations at Edmonton forced the Piegans to travel through the gauntlet of their so-called confederates, the often piratical Bloods and Blackfeet. Simpson's economy backfired and alienated the Piegans at the critical moment when American traders appeared with more liberal prices.

Simpson reopened Rocky Mountain House with Prairie du Chien half-breed Henry Fisher in charge as a temporary winter trader. Fisher's poor education inclined him to "deal in the marvelous," but Rowand thought a métis had a better chance of dealing with the Indians and placating the trapper-traders traveling with them.[285]

At one time Edmonton House Chief Trader Rowand had employed as many as ten confidence men to draw American furs across the border, but the defection of Berger and Brunnais reduced his subversive network to just Hugh Munroe and James Bird, Jr.

Near the end of its fall hunt, Campbell's brigade worked the Hellgate River and waited for the Flathead and Nez Perce buffalo hunters to return with meat. Meanwhile, they had to eat beaver that had browsed on toxic wild parsnip and were ill when the Indians finally arrived with better meat.[286] Campbell's hunt was so good that a freeman who went to the Flathead Post told trader John Warren Dease that the two American parties hunting in the vicinity of the Trois Buttes [eastern Snake plain] averaged seventy to seventy-five skins per man.[287]

Sublette's blunder at the previous summer's rendezvous continued to generate hostility from revenge-minded Blackfeet. "The Blackfeet were always at war with us because we were trading with Indians that they were at war with. They were at war with the Snakes, the Crows, the Flatheads and the neighboring tribes. They had fierce contests and great care was taken to avoid them on their marauding expeditions," reported Campbell.[288]

Campbell's brigade headed toward the winter camp in Cache Valley but bumped into some Blackfeet camped on the Jefferson Fork. When their gestures of friendship failed to get a response, the trappers edged away from the ominous situation. Taking that as an indication of weakness, the Indians began chasing the trappers until they managed to take cover under a cut bank and returned the Blackfeet fire.

A mix of engaged men, free trappers, Iroquois, and Flatheads traveling in tandem formed Campbell's brigade. Campbell watched the Iroquois patriarch, Old Pierre Tevanitagon, become so excited that he ran out into the open to get a better shot and then fell to the Blackfeet bullets. After the battle all that remained of Old Pierre were his mutilated feet in the deserted Blackfoot camp. A beautiful valley on the west side of the Teton Range commemorates the end of the long odyssey of a Six Nations warrior from the St. Lawrence River. His widow was still keening from her husband's death when two unsuspecting Blackfeet suddenly blundered into the camp and Campbell saw his first scalping.[289]

SJ&S's precarious relationship with the Blackfeet deteriorated further when the traders faced the dilemma of providing needed arms to the Blackfeet and denying their enemies. The problem even infected the harmony among the three Blackfeet tribes. In the fall of 1826 the Piegans, desperate for munitions, made peace with their Flathead enemies. The Flatheads sat in the catbird seat between competing British and American interests while getting stronger than the Piegans. That brief truce vanished within a year when the Piegans felt sufficiently rearmed to renew hostilities and continue the balance of terror. Jackson and Sublette, lucky to fall into that lapse in the war games, were seen by the Blackfeet as allies of the Snakes and Flatheads.

The Campbell party's bad experience on the Jefferson gave the freemen and Iroquois trappers an excuse to winter with the Flatheads. Claiming it was too dangerous to return to Cache Valley, they voted to go to winter camps on the Horse Plains. Campbell worried that his trappers would be too close to British influence, but he could do little to dissuade them. While he needed to stay around to prevent them from trading at Flathead Post, Campbell also had to report the results of the fall hunt, get additional supplies, and learn what Jackson and Sublette wanted to do next.

Leaving the brigade camped at a place he identified as Wild Horse Mountain on the Flathead River, Campbell, a Frenchman, and a Flathead crossed the Snake plain to Cache Valley. In open country during a severe winter they experienced the full spectrum of misery only to learn that Jackson and Sublette had not returned to the mountains last fall. Plunging on to the Bear Lake depot through four-foot snow drifts exhausted their horses and stranded the party at Soda Springs. After obtaining a four-dog train and snowshoes from Cache Valley, Campbell glided down the frozen Portneuf to the Tullock-Ogden camp by 17 February 1828.[290]

During the six days he allowed himself to recover, Campbell told Ogden of his successful Flathead operations. Ogden noted sourly that the Americans took about a pack of furs each, as well as trading six packs from the Flatheads and fourteen from the Piegans. In the privacy of his lodge Ogden reflected on the American business:

> Although our trappers have their goods at moderate terms, the price of their beaver is certainly low, compared to the Americans. With them beaver large and small are averaged at five dollars each, with us two dollars for a large and one dollar for a small beaver. Here then is certainly a wide difference. Add to this free liberty to trade with the natives, also it is optional with them to take their furs to St. Louis where they obtain five and a half dollars per lb.; one third of the American trappers follow this plan. It is to be observed goods are sold to them at least 150 per cent dearer than we do, but again they have the advantage of receiving them on the waters of the Snake Country, and an American trapper, from the short distance he has to travel, not obliged to transport provisions, requires only half the number of horses we do, and are also moderate in their advances.[291]

Campbell also loosened up about SJ&S operations. Ogden learned that Ashley cleared $80,000 in three years and retired by selling his goods to

Smith, Jackson, and "Soblitz" at an advance of 150 percent. In their first year of operation, Ogden reported, the new partners gained $20,000 and "finding themselves alone, they sold their goods one third dearer than Ashley did," while holding out the promise of price reductions this year.

This brush with private enterprise discouraged the corporate man. Sandwiched between Tullock's brash optimism and Campbell's innocent enthusiasm, Ogden felt "wretched and unhappy."

"What a contrast between these young men and myself. They have been only six years in the country and without a doubt in as many more will be independent men." Odgen consoled himself by acquiring another fifty skins before the groups parted.[292]

Sam Tullock learned from Campbell that Jackson and Sublette were not in the mountains, and planning the spring hunt sat on their shoulders. After Campbell left on 23 February, Ogden guessed that the American partisans meant to trap toward the forks of the Missouri with a large party.

Ogden thought the snow was still too deep for horses when Tullock and his five remaining men left for Bear River on 26 March. A day after Tullock's departure two couriers finally arrived from Salt Lake, letting slip that so many of the American horses died during the winter that those hunters refused to join Tullock. After they hurried on, Ogden had the impression that the Americans now intended to hunt toward the Utah country in the spring.[293]

The Blackfeet may have marked Sam for revenge for the fight at the 1827 rendezvous. After three or four days on the trail to Bear River, and still within twenty miles of Ogden's camp, thirty or forty Blackfeet struck Tullock's party. The Indians killed three of Sam's men and stampeded forty-seven horses loaded with $4,000 worth of furs.[294]

The circumstances appeared incriminating, but Ogden was apparently innocent of inciting the Indians. His only intention was to use the Americans to screen his horse herd from Blackfeet rustlers while he trapped up the Portneuf. He sent Antoine Sylvaille and six men to trap the Sickly (Malade) River and turned up the Snake River to meet Tom McKay and the detachment that had wintered on the forks of the Salmon River.

McKay finally showed up near the mouth of the Blackfoot River on 8 May. Two days later the HBC ran into a party of Snakes enjoying a rare triumph. They had intercepted some Blackfeet driving thirty horses; they killed two of the herders and captured fifteen animals, some of which carried packs and property bearing American markings. After briefly considering returning the packs, discretion caused the Snakes to cut the ropes and leave perhaps 800 valuable beaver skins on the plain.[295]

The Flathead brigade spent a pleasant winter dining on young colts with wild onions as a condiment. By the end of spring Campbell and his party were near the north end of Bear Lake and heading for the rendezvous. As they broke camp on the last morning, Blackfeet attacked. Campbell ran for a handy willow grove, but after a four-hour fight the trappers' defense slackened. Guessing the trappers were running out of ammunition, the attackers risked a charge, which cost four warriors. Campbell and a brave Spaniard charged through the circle and scampered out for help. By the time the buckskin cavalry galloped to the rescue the Blackfeet had withdrawn with half a dozen horses.[296]

Marooned by the severe weather somewhere between Lexington and the Green River, Jackson and Sublette endured a frustrating winter. Having blunted Ashley's ambitions, they now faced new competition in an old suit of clothes. The old Missouri Fur Company had finally folded, but Joshua Pilcher had assembled some of his friends—Andrew Drips, Lucien Fontenelle, William H. Vanderburgh, and young Charles Bent—into a new trading association. With Johnson Gardner as a guide, Pilcher left the Council Bluffs in September leading forty-five men and one hundred horses, putting him well on the road before Jackson and Sublette cleared Lexington in early October. If Pilcher could beat them to the rendezvous, he might claim the trade of the independent hunters.

Snow was already falling when Pilcher reached the Sweetwater River, where he learned his first lesson in Crow gamesmanship. "Here I had to make a depot of merchandise & property, which is done by burying it in the ground, the [Crow] Indians having completed their designs upon our horses by stealing the last of them." Bucking through deep snow, Pilcher crossed South Pass to winter on Green River.[297]

Whipping their mules, Jackson and Sublette still ceded Pilcher a head start of a couple hundred miles and more than a week. Winter snows pinned them down on the Platte. The HBC reported some Gros Ventres who had been visiting the Arapahos for the past two years returned to Saskatchewan in early January, "well supplied with American goods." Had they traded with Jackson and Sublette on the Platte? As soon as the weather permitted, Jackson and Sublette went on, meeting Pilcher's men coming back to retrieve his caches. They were still in the game.[298]

The south end of Bear Lake was frozen when their caravan arrived in May. The chill deepened when Tullock came forward to tell Bill that his young brother had been killed by the Blackfeet. Sublette brought fifteen-year-old Pinckney out the previous year to make a man of him; now he felt responsible for his death.[299]

The grim reports continued with the mysterious disappearance of the four men who went to trap the Owyhee River. Either dead or gone over to the British, they failed to return to the winter camp.

The competitive web tightened as opposition efforts, some backed by the American Fur Company, came into the field from Taos, the middle Missouri, and from the upper Missouri. Ignorant of the HBC's efforts to field another Snake Brigade, Jackson and Sublette knew the Columbia District was adjusting prices to match theirs.

Pilcher's outfit, a moldy mess ruined by leaky caches, arrived too late to trade, and his salvage bought him only sixteen or eighteen packs of furs. Too smart to go down with a sinking ship, his associates gave up and headed back to cut a deal with the American Fur Company. As a last hope, Pilcher convinced nine men to go trapping with him. He still had Johnson Gardner, with his previous connections to the Iroquois, as a hole card. Joshua later wrote that he decided on "a tour of the northwest, with a view of exploring the Columbia river to ascertain the attractions and capabilities for trade." Gardner would try to bring John Grey back under his spell and pick up the Flathead trade. The torpedo that sank Ogden three years earlier was circling around again, this time aimed at SJ&S.

Gardner, a classic spoiler, exploited trappers' dissatisfactions with the mountain prices. Taking his old friend Hugh Glass aside, Gardner advised him to go down to the new American Fur post being built on the Yellowstone to see what Kenneth McKenzie was willing to do.

Sublette planned to take east some seventy packs of beaver, which weighed 7,107.5 pounds and, at $5 a pound, would yield $35,537.50. The partners also held a tidy surplus of untraded goods.

Campbell thought that the improvement that mountain life made in his health could too easily be undone by the flash of a Blackfoot gun, so he elected to go home while he still carried his scalp. Jackson and Sublette convinced him to take Jim Bridger as his "partner," with twelve engaged men to stiffen up a brigade of around thirty hunters. They could travel east with the returning caravan and break off to trap the Powder River, well removed from the Blackfeet but in need of being cleaned out before the American Fur Company appeared.[300]

Because Pilcher and that damned Gardner were headed for the Flathead country, David had to ensure the Indians who traded with Campbell last year stayed with SJ&S. Where in the hell was Smith when they needed to meet so much opposition on so many fronts?

11

"For a cause in which they are not concerned"

As WITH MUCH OF HIS MOUNTAIN EXPERIENCE, David Jackson left a frustratingly cold trail for historians as he traveled through the Flathead country in fall 1828. Robert Campbell, who briefed him, neglected to mention in his narrative that Jackson went there; Joshua Pilcher did not elaborate on his final embarrassment there; and Jedediah Smith evaded a detailed description of his reunion with Jackson. The only clues to his actions come from Jackson's British competitors.

Tom Fitzpatrick accompanied Jackson as clerk; trapping partners Nicholas Montour and Bazil Prudhomme, both Columbia freemen, went along to their old haunts; and John Grey had inherited Old Pierre's leadership of the Iroquois. Like the tribe of the Snake Brigade, the bearded Americans drove a pony herd, trailed travois, and convoyed wives and children.

After leaving Bear Lake the brigade passed along the east end of the Snake River valley to Henry's Fork, where Jackson traded with any Indians who came—Flatheads, Nez Perces, and Blackfeet—and cached those pelts before continuing northward.

Trade with the Blackfeet that fall disappointed David because their warriors killed a Flathead chief the previous spring and now battled their Snake, Crow, Assiniboin, and Flathead neighbors on many fronts. Under the encouragement of the traveling secret agents Hugh Munroe and Jemmy Jock Bird (James Bird, Jr.), Chief Parflesh Pasant took his people to Rocky Mountain House to turn in their beaver.

After working the Big Hole streams Jackson's brigade followed the Flathead Indians through the dangerous Hellgate defile and north to their usual winter camps along the Flathead River. In late November 1828 they arrived at the aptly named Horse Plains—three natural pockets of grass surrounded by mountains high enough to intercept snow-laden clouds. About the first of December, when some Flatheads went to the British post to trade, Jackson, Pilcher (who had arrived independently of Jackson but wintered nearby), and forty Americans trailed along.

The Hudson's Bay Company's old Flathead Post had burned in the summer, and when John Warren Dease arrived on 28 November, he decided to rebuild it a few leagues lower, nearer better sources of wood and game.

Living in a smoky tent and bothered by Indians with a different sense of privacy, Dease pushed the soggy lodge flap aside on the third of December and saw men who had little respect for the empire.[301]

The appalled Bay man met "the following traders, one Major Pilcher, Gardner, Jackson and FitzPatrick," who had "very little property among them with the exception of some Cloth, tobacco and Ironworks, having expended whatever else they have had in the purchase of Horses and a few Furs." He was given to understand that they had "mustered as they came along . . . four or five packs, including their own hunts."[302]

The Flathead Post journal that recorded the details of this interesting visit is lost, and Dease's report gives only a condensed account. Dease found Jackson—as an Englishman might put it—"backstanding," while Pilcher claimed the British officer's attention by volunteering that the Americans had divided into several parties, "some going back to the Missouri, and others to try and pass their winter around Flatheads Lake," and that last year's Snake hunt yielded only forty packs. He provided misleading business intelligence or downplayed the SJ&S returns to make himself look better.

Dease found a few Pend d'Oreille Indians waiting to trade when he arrived. He sent messages inviting the Flatheads in anticipation of receiving the summer trade that his predecessor, John Work, missed due to the delay of the outfit from Fort Vancouver. Work reported "that they have hidden their Furs which will be recovered in the Fall and probably little loss sustained."[303]

But Dease took in only 600 skins, and half of those he obtained from the American trappers "for Rum, Sugar, Coffee and a few other articles." The 300 pelts supplied by the Flatheads fell far short of the post's average returns of 1,477 beaver, which meant that the untraded outfit would sit as an unrealized investment for another year. The discouraged trader wrote, "it is impossible the trade can turn out to be a profitable one, as a kind of Barrier it may do to keep it up." Luckily, William Kittson had reached the Kutenais in time, "for had it been otherwise the whole of those Indians must have thrown in with the Americans."[304]

Dease had the satisfaction of telling Jackson some bad news he heard at Edmonton House; apparently Indians had killed some Americans in the Snake country. Rumors that Indians had massacred an entire party of eighteen American trappers in southern Oregon reached Fort Colvile in early October, and the information soon made its way to Edmonton House and Dease. From the lips of his competitor David learned that Jedediah Smith had made another costly error.[305]

After a taste of HBC rum and a few traded treats the Americans went off to camp with the Flatheads, who promised Dease they would return in March. Indians did not hunt beaver during the winter, and Dease expected little additional business; however, Montour and Prudhomme approached him about returning to company service, which indicated to him that the other freemen might also feel dissatisfied with the Americans.

Before SJ&S committed to another outfit, Jackson had to let Sublette know what he'd heard about Smith's disaster. Tom Fitzpatrick inherited the dangerous duty of carrying the news to Robert Campbell in the Crow country. Despite having to cross the Rocky Mountains in mid-winter, he left immediately.

Jackson saw that Flathead Post sat at the deprived heart of arterial streams that ran too high and too fast to provide a home for beavers. The discriminating bark eaters would not gnaw the pines and bushes that dominated these stream banks. Jackson felt he had made a mistake coming here to deny Pilcher, which left the Snake country open to Ogden and put the freeman hunters within reach of British propaganda.

A self-reliant frontiersman, Jackson had little grasp of how troubled the HBC found itself when trying to recover its dissident freemen. In looking out for themselves the hunters rejected the submissive traditions of their British heritage, challenging the corporation and the Crown.

Two years before, Chief Factor John McLoughlin raised beaver prices and lowered supply costs to entice the dissident trappers, but his unilateral price reduction still left his trade goods costlier and the price he offered for pelts lower than the Americans'. Until the previous year, Ogden had recovered only a couple of men but lost an equal number more. Then the HBC sent the French-speaking Dease to Flathead Post to see if he could recapture lost loyalties.[306] By March 1828 McLoughlin even considered a form of profit sharing. The shortage of trappers prevented "our endeavor to hunt as much as we can the Southside of the Columbia."[307]

Governor Simpson encouraged his officers to continuing soliciting the freemen while he worked up another plan to bring additional half-breed hunters into Oregon Country from the Red River Settlement (Winnipeg). In March 1827 McLoughlin recommended limiting the party to fifty men—more might prove unwieldy, allowing them to get their own way.

> If such a party is sent they should go direct to Trois Tetons and hunt up that place, then turn north and hunt all the head branches of the Missouris in the vicinity of where Mr. Ogden was in the summer 1825, in three years they would do this which would destroy the inducements

the American trappers from the other side have to push to the Headwaters of the Columbia and by hunting the Head branches of the Missouris where I state, diminish the inducements the Americans have to equip hunters from the other side of the mountains and to interfere with our Saskatchewan trade sooner than they otherwise would.[308]

Simpson failed to get his plan in gear for the 1827-28 outfit because the métis refused his terms.[309] When Simpson renewed the York Factory plan for a Snake hunting expedition in 1828-29, McLoughlin asked that Cuthbert Grant, the métis leader, be equipped and sent "to Join Mr. Ogden in the vicinity of Black foot tribes." On 31 August 1828 he added, "if Grant goes in by way of the Flathead Post . . . he ought without loss of time to proceed to Black Foot Hill say about fifteen miles below on Portneufs river by the 5th January."[310]

The western chief continued his recommendations unaware that Governor Simpson had once again abandoned the plan in July, stating, "we have been again disappointed in the party of half breed recruits expected from Red River Settlement; they would not engage unless large advances were made to them last autumn . . . on the whole I think we are well clear of this band, they would have been exceedingly troublesome, and novelty possesses such charms to them that they could not be depended on within reach of opposition."[311]

At the York Factory council of summer 1828 Dease inherited the onerous duty of going to the Flathead Post to undermine the American influence over the western freemen. Governor Simpson intended to visit the Columbia District that winter, and on Christmas Day Dease received a letter that Simpson sent from Fort Vancouver.

Simpson penned his letter to Dease on 17 November after learning of Jedediah Smith's disaster. The governor wrote that the Clark's Fork trade required superior management in order to recover the lost trappers. "The Freemen require to be skillfully dealt with, we are anxious that they should join Mr. Ogden or Mr. McLeod's party and for that purpose that they should find their way here where they can be well equipped next Summer." Simpson wanted them to deliver their catches to the Flathead postmaster and then come down to be reoutfitted from Fort Vancouver.

They need not be apprehensive of harsh treatment from us as we shall deal liberally with them as regards their old debts—sell them supplies cheap—say at servants prices & give them large prices for their furs. Their savings will be paid by [us] either in England or Canada as they choose, in short we can afford and are disposed to give them the most advantageous terms, so advantageous that any Saving in [undecipherable word] may be clear from £60 to £[?] per annum. . . . if they have any desire to see me on this Subject & if they conceive they would be more secure by treating with me personally than in any other way, I shall be ready to confer with them at Colvile on my way out.[312]

Dease, feigning Christmas hospitality, poured generous drinks and convinced Nicholas Montour and Bazil Prudhomme to meet the governor in the spring. In July 1829 the HBC rehired Montour to travel with the Flatheads as a representative of the company "watching the Americans," and in October he could resume his old position as clerk at Kutenai Post. Montour could thank the Americans for forcing the company to reinstate him.[313]

John Warren Dease, who came from a long line of skin gamesmen, saw through Joshua Pilcher and got him to reveal much about the Americans' plans. But the Bay man failed to grasp the distinct separation of American interests because Jackson played his cards close to his vest. Having lost his chance to break into the mountain trade at the rendezvous, Pilcher had good reason to resent the dominance of SJ&S. But he betrayed the interests of the United States in the plan he developed and pitched to Dease. Pilcher presented himself as "desirous of entering into the service" of the HBC. His plan went so far beyond Dease's responsibility that the Bay man could only forward it to Governor Simpson at Fort Vancouver.

On New Year's Eve Pilcher submitted a scheme to serve as an HBC front man by posing as the leader of a company-financed trapping brigade. These hunters would sweep through the forbidden Blackfoot hunting grounds east of the Continental Divide to reap the sort of returns that put SJ&S on their feet two years earlier. Because the current boundary lines forbade the British from entering that area, Pilcher was offering to betray the territorial integrity of the United States.[314]

Pilcher's proposal justified the cost of an express, and Dease offered Jackson the opportunity to send a letter to his distressed partner Smith. Realizing that every Bay man between the Flathead Post and Fort Vancouver would read it, David wrote an innocuous general statement that he left unsealed to show he excused the company's indulgence. An expressman left on 17 January carrying the letter and Dease's observations, both of which reached Fort Colvile by 28 January and Fort Vancouver by the middle of February.[315]

Discouraged by the inroads Dease made among his hunters, and Pilcher's ambivalence, David rode back to the American camp, which had by then moved about forty miles to Flathead Lake. The bay at the south end of the lake, near fuel supplies and good horse pastures, offered the most logical location for this base camp. Snow did not fall until the middle of January, but a seven-day downpour raised the rivers and made their skin lodges soggy.[316]

During the long period of boring inactivity, the lonely fur trader had time to think about his neighbors. David had known the Grey family since the 1825 rendezvous. Madame Grey, Marianne Neketickon, was a striking, three-quarters French woman who radiated the confidence of a Mohawk matriarch. Her beauty remained intact after coming west as a girl and giving birth to a couple of sons and perhaps as many daughters. She wore a métis costume that included a calf-length dress of dark strouding decorated in floral patterns with ribbons and beadwork, leggings, moccasins, and silver jewelry. David found her imperfect command of English charming.[317]

Her Iroquois husband, John Grey, had a reputation as a difficult and dangerous man whom other trappers alternately cursed as a "turbulent blackguard, a damned rascal," and admired as "a herculean grizzly-bear fighter." He later cut up Bill Sublette's brother Milton "on account of some indignity, real or fancied, which had been offered to the [Rockaway] chief's daughter."[318] After the 1825 rendezvous Grey went off with Johnson Gardner and Old Pierre.

David's relationship with Marianne dangles on the thin evidence that he remembered her in the years after he withdrew from the mountains. Jackson & Sublette ledgers list accounts for the education of her son in Missouri. And, at a later time when he had to deal with some difficult and pressing affairs, David thought to send a gift to Madame Grey, who remained in the mountains.[319] The relationship between Grey and Gardner, and Gardner and Pilcher, overlapped Johnson's previous Anglophobia and Pilcher's newly discovered internationalism.

Jackson was playing a long-distance poker game with a man he never met. Gov. George Simpson held the other hand at Fort Vancouver, and the joker was the distressed Jedediah Smith. After an exhilarating trip through the whirlpools of the Fraser River gorge, George Simpson, the ultimate corporate supervisor, was convinced that the Fraser's boiling water offered an unsuitable alternative to Columbia River navigation.[320] When he arrived at the Fort Vancouver depot in November 1828, the dyspepsia of his disappointment sweetened because a partner of the major American opposition, Jedediah Smith, was in his grasp as a defeated supplicant.

Smith, once again, was a complete buckskin disaster. His second trip to California followed the trail of his previous year's trek. Smith's party fell in with some Mojave Indians, who slaughtered ten of them when the group separated to ford the Colorado River. Jedediah and eight survivors scattered the SJ&S outfit on the sand to distract their pursuers and fled into the desert. When they staggered into the San Bernardino Valley, unsympathetic Mexican authorities slapped Smith into the calaboose until some American and British ship captains secured his release.

Rejoining the men he left north of San Francisco Bay the previous spring, Jedediah sold 1,568 pounds of beaver to the ships for $3,920. On the recommendation of California sea trader and settler Capt. John B. Cooper, Jed bought 250 horses and mules at $10 a head, expecting to resell them in the mountains at $50 or more per head. The California party already had 65 horses, so the total herd swelled to 315 animals.

The party that headed north in November included ten men from the 1826 outfit and seven survivors of the 1827 outfit. They also picked up Louis Pombert and an English wanderer named Robert Leland.[321] Starting with only 47 traps, they worked the upper Sacramento Valley and made good returns until 22 February 1828, when they were down to less than two traps per man.

Deciding to drive the horses to the mountains, Smith, for some reason, rejected the Indian trails leading northeast from the Mount Shasta area and veered toward the coast. They passed the mouth of the Klamath River in May, then the Rogue, and came to the Umpqua tidewater in mid-July.

Leaving the brigade in camp, Smith took John Turner and Robert Leland in a canoe to scout for a crossing. They paddled back just in time to see Indians killing their comrades across the river. Unable to halt the killing, Smith and the two men headed north toward Fort Vancouver, the only sanctuary on this inhospitable coast.[322]

With his fifteen comrades dead, Arthur Black alone escaped into the salal, and staggered to Fort Vancouver on 8 August, two days before Smith's group arrived. John McLoughlin received the refugees sympathetically and directed trader Alexander Norman McLeod to assist in the recovery of Smith's property. McLeod absorbed some of Smith's hysteria as they traveled south to confront the killers—the Bay man found an excuse to discontinue plans to hunt in California and left the southern hunting brigade camped on the Umpqua while he returned to Fort Vancouver in mid-December.[323]

Smith had his origins in the burned-over religious pastures of western New York and eastern Ohio, where fundamentalists preached guilt and sin, and crazy prophets invented new sects. Smith's conscience festered because his mistakes led men to their deaths. During that dark winter at Fort Vancouver Jedediah was a deeply burdened man. The Columbia District offered Smith a poor place to restore his bruised soul, because hell had come in the form of the intermediate fever, malaria. Indians abandoned whole villages to the dead, and the inescapable stench of decay underscored the chilling silence.

Smith made plans to move up the Columbia as far as Fort Nez Perces and follow the Snake River to the mountain rendezvous. Governor Simpson, the past master of boardroom politics and "suave dissimulation," recognized Smith's desperate state and convinced Jed that for him to pass through that country with so few men was too dangerous. He would do better to sell his furs to the HBC and travel east with the spring express. Simpson, smugly aware that a long, circuitous trip would take the HBC competitor out of action for almost a year, offered $3 a pound for Smith's poor furs. Although Simpson made a generous offer, when he presented Smith with a note on 29 December, Jed hesitated.[324]

Peter Skene Ogden, at Fort Vancouver on 10 August 1828 when Smith staggered in, left soon after to join the Snake Brigade. He took those hunters into southeastern Oregon and northern Nevada, the area that Smith had failed to trap, and worked the virgin desert rivers and sinks. That year the Snake Brigade took the best returns since the Americans first appeared—4,000 beaver, clearing £3,141.7.10. Working up the Humboldt River, Ogden went as far east as Bear River and Cache Valley, where he found the old haunts of the mountain men deserted. Local Indians told them that all the Americans had gone off toward the Flathead country.[325]

George Simpson and John McLoughlin carefully put their exchanges with Smith in writing. To soften Smith, the governor implied that it cost the company a potential return of a £1,000 for McLeod to muck around helping Jed instead of hunting. He was less forthcoming in telling Smith that the cost of obtaining beaver in the Columbia District had increased over 50 percent since Americans appeared.

The dispatch that McLoughlin rushed to Dease on 5 January 1828 arrived at Fort Colvile on 29 January and probably reached Dease's hands by mid-February.[326] About the same time Governor Simpson began composing a lengthy dispatch to London. He believed Smith would accept his offer and take the long way home. But sometime before 17 February the express from Flathead Post arrived, and Jackson's open letter to Smith spoiled everything. On 9 March Jedediah accepted the HBC offer for his furs by taking a bill of exchange for £486.18.5 sterling, equivalent to $2,369.60. Three days later Smith and Arthur Black left with the upriver boat brigade for Fort Colvile.[327]

Smith's two outfits cleared only $2,369.60, less even than he had accumulated in California before investing in the horses. Counting the 275 lost horses, with a potential worth of $13,750, he had cost SJ&S $11,380. In addition to denying the partnership his services, he denied them critically needed capital.

The express that brought Jackson's open letter also brought Pilcher's letter proposing an illegal exploitation of the Three Forks beaver reserves. In light of two failures to field a Red River hunting brigade, the HBC took an interest but lacked the manpower until they could recover the freemen.

From this glimpse of two obvious losers Governor Simpson felt no need to make any deals with the Americans. On 17 February 1829 he sent instructions to Dease on how to deal with David Jackson:

> I am favored with your communication of the 7th December and the 17th January and hope this will reach you before your departure from the Flathead Post.
>
> You must be aware that every particular connected with the past, present and contemplated operations of our opponents in trade is interesting to us, but I regret that your letters do not convey that information which I could have wished or expected, the strength of their parties, the description of the people of which they are composed, their recent hunting Grounds, their successes or reverses, their resources, their prospects, in short everything relating to them would have been satisfactory intelligence to us at present, or which to form our plans, but on all points you are silent—The Americans as far as I am able to judge are on their last legs, and from Mr. Pilcher's Letter to you I should infer that they will withdraw from this side of the Mountains after the expiration of the current year—Their attentions will then in all probability be directed to the Blackfoot Country into which they cannot venture without a large & well organized Expedition—To us it is highly important that they should not succeed in that enterprise as it would be cutting off the principal resources of our Establishments in the Saskatchewan and the most effective way in which we can defeat their plans is to withdraw our late deserters from them which would weaken them so much that without a reinforcement from the States they would not keep their ground among those Warlike Indians and after having passed Four Years to no purpose in the Snake Country lost half their people and ruined themselves, it is not probable that they would get another party at St. Louis to follow them—By my letter to Mr. Work you would have seen my anxiety to withdraw all the Freemen, say Montour's Party from the Flatheads had I been aware that the Americans would have been in, I should have urged the same in regard to the other Deserters, but it does not appear that you have

spoken to them at all on the subject—I am well aware of your influence with and talent in managing those people, and therefore beg that you will exert both in not only getting their Skins / for which you may give any reasonable price / but in withdrawing them from the Americans—Do not commit me by making any distinct promises, but let them understand the *desperate state of their present leaders*, point out to them *the great loss of life that has taken place in their Camps from mismanagement*, the high prices they pay for everything, the dangerous grounds to which they are not about to conduct them, in short make their prospects as dismal as you can paint them, and then on the other hand point out our importance, respectability, cheap prices and liberality, in regard to their former offenses, let them understand that if they return to their duty they will find us indulgent, and you can inform them moreover that we have rich countries to work up, and that their former comrades are under the late arrangements making fortunes with us, you must not appear to court them but let it be perfectly understood that if they have any regard for their own interests they will not allow the present opportunity of making their peace with us to escape—all this I leave to your good management. *The Americans appear to be in distress* and if you play your Cards well I think you should get nearly all their Skins, do not spare yourself, move from Camp to Camp, hold out every [point?] you can think of which is likely to take a Skin, every Skin taken from the Americans is worth 10 got in any other way—Pray do not allow your opponents to get anything from the Iroquois at Bitter Root River—Spirits to them is irresistible—Let the Coutanais be well watched so that Sibbet, or Jackson may not do any thing in that quarter, and while a Skin is to be had do not quite your post or allow Kittson to leave his charge—I am glad you have been attentive to the American traders, civility costs us little or nothing, and it always commands its value if discreetly administered in opposition—Yes justifiable. I shall leave this place before the 1st April & I shall expect the pleasure of either seeing or hearing from you at Colvile. You can assure Montour as if from yourself that if he behaves well, his money will be safe & that by trusting us he is sure of a firm support which none can provide him in the Indian country except ourselves—I've had this Season an opportunity of shewing your address among Indians, Freemen and Rival traders—pray make good use of it, as it will resound as much to your own credit as the Hon<u>ble</u> Coy interests, I remain Dear Sir your humble obts,Ser e&c

[signed] George Simpson.

P.S. Have the goodness to forward the inclosed Letters to Major Pilcher & Mr. Jackson, G.S.[328]

147

Simpson responded directly to Pilcher at Flathead Lake by letter, dating it Fort Vancouver, 18 February 1829. In responding to the proposal of 30 December the governor fell back on principle, telling Pilcher, "we as British Subjects cannot infringe openly, and although the protecting services of your Government might be successfully evaded by the plan you suggest still I do not think it would be respectable of the Hon<u>ble</u> Hudson's Bay Coy to make use of indirect means to acquire possession of a Trade to which it has no just claim."[329]

Simpson gleaned from Smith that the Americans represented two rival interests, and Pilcher's American competitors were potentially hostile witnesses. Spurned by the HBC, Joshua Pilcher's bad luck was complete.

Simpson failed to copy his letter to Jackson into his correspondence book or preserve it in HBC records. Beyond regrets and good wishes, he had little to say because Smith would arrive at the same time as the letter. Simpson and his invisible opponent never came closer than that. Like generals conducting a military campaign at long distance, they hoped to discover some exploitable weakness as their armies converged on a collision course.

The two men had contrasting characters: Jackson, an independent man who ignored his public image to a fault, thought of himself as a fur trader doing necessary work; Governor Simpson reveled in flattering titles and the perks and bonuses that followed his full devotion to the institution. Jackson used his frontier experience and natural ability to hold to a linear line of action; Simpson had a wide range of diverse responsibilities. Jackson knew his origin and heritage; the illegitimate Simpson hoped to achieve English respectability. Jackson followed his track anonymously; Simpson performed for an audience of superiors. Jackson, a man of action, took the

surprises as they came and reacted out of self-interest with a smidgen of national purpose; Simpson, a pre-Victorian man transplanted into an alien land, intended to remodel it to fit his Old World expectations. One belonged to the West; the other was like a visitor from another planet.

Working within an imperially designated monopoly, Simpson believed that private businessmen would fail in the western fur trade unless "the all grasping policy of the American government should induce it to embark some of its National Wealth."[330] Subsidy was a foreign word to Jackson as he rowed and bailed the leaky little partnership. He faced the problems of capitalization, transport, supply, trading, and defense with minimum capital resources. SJ&S began business with about $9,000 in capital, soon reduced to $5,000. Audacity, combined with careful stewardship, allowed the partnership to persevere against the giant corporation.

Pilcher fell somewhere between those extremes, a man of flexible ethics who was still trying to get on board after being beaten by one rival and ready to surrender to another. After Pilcher indicated his intent to trade with the Kutenais, Dease warned Kittson to get those Indians out of the way and induce them to discourage American trapping. Dease's desire that the Kutenais "will not allow them" translated into death for Pilcher's man, E. Marlow, and the disappearance of horses sometime in February.[331]

Jackson also hunted northward. After wintering at the big bay on Flathead Lake, he could have taken his brigade along the well-used Indian trail running beside the Fisher River to an old Indian camping site on Kootenai River, near the place where the Astorians and Nor'westers competed in 1811.[332]

Jackson may have pushed as far north as the Tobacco plains, straddling the still undefined border where Indians also liked to congregate, but he found that the Bay man, Kittson, had already traded their beaver. By now he saw clearly that the Kutenai country had poor trapping, and the residents discourteously received whites who came to take their most valuable resource.

The SJ&S hunters fell in with Pilcher's dispirited men. Pilcher, who had yet to receive Simpson's letter, had already abandoned them, leaving his henchman Johnson Gardner with few alternatives. With "no ultimate prospects sufficiently brilliant to bear them up under the present hardships," they joined Jackson's brigade, and Jackson applied the coup de grâce by purchasing Pilcher's traps for $200.[333]

Jackson lost several hunters who preferred to join the Flatheads. Many years later Jesuit missionaries learned that Big Ignace La Mousse, Little

Ignace, Peter (Gaucher?), Gabriel Prudhomme, and Jean Baptiste Gervais joined the Flatheads in 1828.[334]

Smith and Black left Fort Vancouver on 12 March with the early boats commanded by Donald Ross.[335] Because he could catch up in a fast canoe, Governor Simpson allowed Smith a two-week head start and caught up with him at Fort Colvile. Everyone reached Fort Colvile about the end of April to find Dease waiting with the disappointing Flathead returns that included 693 pelts surrendered by Pilcher.

The other posts also showed low production. In the Colvile report John Work explained that the intrusion of the Americans since 1826 had materially injured the Flathead trade, "and had not their own necessities compelled them to retrade a good many beaver in 1827 and 1828 the returns would have been very low indeed."[336]

The HBC strategy for its 1829 outfit was well in place before it allowed Smith to continue to Flathead Post, guided by the expressman who carried the response to Pilcher and Simpson's note to Jackson.

Shocked by Simpson's cold rejection, Pilcher spent the summer wandering and finally appeared at Fort Colvile on 31 August. The company shipped him out of the country by the same detour planned to divert Smith. Work added the arch comment, "from the attention shewn Mr. Smith, another American, by Governor Simpson and Mr. Chief Factor McLoughlin, any attention shewn Mr. Pilcher or facilities offered to him to prosecute his intention of quitting the country will no doubt not only be sanctioned but highly approved by the Governor."[337]

Jackson and Smith had a less joyful wilderness reunion than Smith's biographers claim—Jed returned a loser, and David had the habit of telling the truth as he saw it, no matter who got hurt.

Governor Simpson sent a circumspect 1829 dispatch to London dealing with Columbia affairs. He portrayed the Americans on the point of total collapse and disparaged the partners as "the Genls.[Ashley's] late conductors; men who had formerly been practical Trappers, but who all at once promoted themselves to the Travelling title of Captains." After carefully reciting the circumstantial aid given to Smith, which "may become a subject of future misrepresentation and inquiry," Simpson concluded, "it will appear that there is a probability of our being relieved from Opposition in the Snake Country for a time. That Country has never been rich for its extent, and is now much exhausted."[338] Nevertheless he instructed the Flathead trader to "sell to the Indians at the American tariff; also to have on hand a larger stock of luxuries than usual to meet the demands of the American trappers, with such little necessaries as they are likely to be deficient in: in that way a considerable part of their hunts can likewise be secured."[339] He continued, "if Americans cast up in your quarter let them not trade a skin that you can purchase at any price but if they offer Furs for sale you can receive them at the rate of four dollars Halifax currency for each large Beaver skin."[340]

In September Chief Factor McLoughlin told Work to offer the same bartering terms that had worked on Pilcher to any Americans who showed up, but, he added, "it is not in our interest to induce men to remain about the Flatheads." Later he bragged, "I broke up the American party in the Snake country and I did this simply by underselling them. Ogden's outfit 1828 cleared about £5,000—had this price to the Freemen been adopted at the first starting of the Snake expedition, would so many of our men had deserted— and if I had not adopted the present tariff would not the American party have pushed to this place and got their supplies by sea and spread themselves all over this side of the mountains."[341]

McLoughlin used Ogden's unopposed 1828-29 hunt to prove his figures, but the roll of the 1830 Snake Brigade shows Alex Carson and Louis Kanota as the only former deserters back in HBC service. Pilcher served the company better by drawing Jackson away and leaving Ogden with an unopposed entry from the west.

In late May 1829 Smith and Jackson followed the familiar trail from the Flathead country. Jed carried a piece of British paper worth $2,369.60 as all he had to show for two outfits, and some unresolved settlements with the heirs of dead trappers. David packed an unspecified number of skins—both taken by his hunters and traded from the Flatheads—and picked up his caches from the previous fall. The adventure in the Flathead country wound up disappointing, and Jackson would not return. Operating at will in the HBC backyard and maintaining an American presence in the disputed Oregon Country, like Smith's exploring, returned nothing that he could put in the bank.

12

"An acceptable service to the administration"

AFTER RETURNING TO THE CACHES HE LEFT at Henry's Fork the previous fall, David parted company with Smith and crossed the mountains to meet Sublette. He was loafing in the shadow of the Tetons when the pack train trotted in and Bill stepped down to bring him up to date. Among the fifty-four packers accompanying Sublette, David saw several fresh faces: George W. Ebberts, Caleb Wilkins, William Craig, Robert Newell, Joseph L. Meek, and Samuel Parkman, an educated young man who the partners hoped would develop into a clerk to replace Campbell. In Joe Meek the mountains finally found a historian to replace Potts and a raconteur to equal Beckwourth.[342]

Campbell dutifully waited for Sublette at the mouth of Wind River. His brigade made a fall hunt on the Powder, Tongue, Yellowstone, and Big Horn rivers before coming to winter with the Mountain Crows. After four years without a resident trader, the Crows again were generous hosts, although some of their young men, tempted by Campbell's caches, caused trouble until their great chief let down his long pony tail and rode around camp proclaiming he would not eat until the culprits returned the stolen furs.[343]

Fitzpatrick walked into the winter camp as casually as a country squire on an afternoon ramble after crossing the Flathead country, the dangerous east end of the Snake plain, Jackson's Hole, and Togwotee or Union Pass into the Wind River valley. During the high-country winter, with most places locked in pristine solitude and almost devoid of game, Tom saw his journey as just another chore.

Campbell, Fitzpatrick, and five other (probably engaged) men made a spring hunt while Sam Tullock led the others to scour the Yellowstone country. Tullock lost four of his men during the spring hunt, and the Blackfeet got most of his horses before his trapping party returned to Wind River to wait for Sublette.

When the rendezvous started, the trappers broke out the liquor. Soon an argument developed between Tullock and a drunken Frenchman named Bray, who blamed Sam for the lost horses. Bray refused to let up. When Tullock could no longer tolerate the abuse, he struck the Frenchman with the hand that had been wounded in the 1827 fight with the Blackfeet; the hand had petrified into a clubbed fist, and his blow killed Bray. The other Frenchmen broke into general uproar, and Sublette turned off the liquor tap to avoid creating any more malcontents; Glass and Berger had already leaked away to the American Fur Company.[344]

Sublette sent Campbell, adamant about leaving the mountains this year, down to the States with forty-five packs, then assigned his tough brother, Milton Sublette, along with Henry Fraeb and Jean Baptiste Gervais, to lead the forty Yellowstone hunters.

After resting a few days on the shore of the lake, Jackson and Sublette pushed on across Teton Pass into Pierre's Hole. Fitzpatrick broke off to round up any hunters still hanging around Bear River. The pack train continued to Henry's Fork, where, on 5 August, they found Smith. Robert Newell recalled 175 men met at the meeting in Pierre's Hole on 20 August. At its peak the SJ&S employed 120 men, but they still attracted the largest body of independent hunters.[345]

For the first time since summer 1827 the three partners came together to assess their business and plan their future. Sublette left $16,000 on Ashley's ledger and sent back $2,470 with Campbell. Jedediah had that note on the Hudson's Bay Company, and Jackson had the returns of the winter and spring hunts. But the SJ&S notes to trappers for furs, wages to engaged men, and claims for men killed in the West all reduced the partners' capital.

As the afternoon sun caught the tops of the Tetons the three skin gamesmen recognized that the time had come to cash in their chips. Jackson and Sublette also had some compelling reasons to free themselves of the burdensome Smith.

In early October Smith and Sublette headed out with a combination hunting brigade and pack train to recover Jackson's caches on Henry's Fork and continue on through the high Yellowstone country. Robert (Doc) Newell recalled in his terse style that "we went up henryes fork of Snake river on to Lewises fork crossed the mountain on to the waters of missouri." Joe Meek recalled that the Blackfeet picked off two men, but the casualty list reports no such loss. A little before Christmas this brigade joined the Yellowstone hunters at the winter camp on Wind River.[346]

After leaving Smith and Sublette, Jackson and Fitzpatrick took hunters through the south end of Jackson's Hole and up the Hoback River to the headwaters of Green River. The beleaguered beavers on those streams had been replenishing their numbers for two years. George (Squire) Ebberts, who did not accompany the men, recalled that they went down into the Digger country before coming to the winter camp on Wind River "with plenty of beaver."[347]

Sublette delivered letters to Jackson that announced the death of his father last Christmas Day. Now the conversations that fathers and sons too seldom have would never take place. David lost his chance to describe for the colonel the endless mountains and plains that seemed to go on forever.

The death of Edward Jackson created a legal problem. The colonel preplanned his estate through gifts or deeds and died deliberately intestate. But something went awry in the deed to David's children. Edward had purchased that land in 1807 with notes owed him by third parties. The seller failed to catch up to collect, and twenty-one years later sued the colonel's estate. If David, on behalf of his children, had to sell the property to satisfy the claim, it would involve complex matters he could not handle through yearly letters from the Rocky Mountains.[348]

David also learned that his brother George Jackson, his anchor in Ste. Genevieve, was in declining health through a combination of Missouri bottom fevers, discouragement, and intemperance. George's wife, Catharine, sent desperate letters to David, calling him home, while his own wife, Juliet, remained silent.

During the winter camp the partners considered withdrawing from the trade. The letter "Smith, Jackson & Sublette, Indian traders on the East & West of the R. Mountains," addressed to Gen. William Clark in the hope of claiming reparations from the government for their losses to the Indians, suggests their preplanning.

The letter also casts doubt on the suggestion that Smith made an agreement with the HBC to withdraw from the western country, stating, "until British interlopers are dismissed from off our territory, Americans will never be respected or acknowledged as patrons by the Indians on the west side of the Rocky Mountains. Further, the British influence is gaining ground every day, which our loses and sad disasters can easily show and account for."[349]

The partners listed losses of $43,500 against a total gain to date of $87,000.[350] The lives of forty-two lost men were not so easily calculated.

After deducting the original investment and the cost of the last outfit, they added Jackson's Flathead returns, two fall hunts, and the spring hunt of 1830, but these gains remained uncertain until they successfully hauled the furs 1,100 miles to a St. Louis warehouse, transported them another 1,500 miles to the eastern buyers, and sold them in a favorable market.

Their list of potential successors was as thin as their pocketbooks. Tom Fitzpatrick logically formed the nucleus of a new organization that might include Jim Bridger, Henry Fraeb, and Jean Baptiste Gervais for the French connection. Bill wanted his brother Milton included so they would have someone to keep an eye on the loan necessary to get those expectant capitalists in business.[351]

Jedediah Smith's letters home revealed a bruised ego, homesickness, and a heavy conscience. He had to balance his initiative in reporting his explorations to Superintendent of Indians William Clark against the accompanying casualty list. The ghosts of twenty-five dead men howled in the prairie winds as Jed wrestled with "the perversities of his wicked heart" and tried to convince himself that he did it for higher goals.[352]

Viewing the American operations through British eyes suffers from too many missing letters: Montour's 1826 torpedo, Jackson's open letter to Smith, and Simpson's note to Jackson are examples of tantalizing documents in omission.

Another ghost image lies buried in the half-inch-thick sheaf of Governor Simpson's 1830 report to the Board of Governors in London, which he completed at Norway House on 31 July 1830. The dispatch reported the operations of outfit 1829-30, and depreciated the American competitors, "some of whom, under the direction of our old opponents Smith Jackson & Siblet, are still straying about in the Snake Country, but I think will attach themselves to us in the course of the present year, *as by a letter from Smith* their principal conductor, who benefitted by our hospitality at Vancouver in the winter 1828/29, I find he is to withdraw from the business this ensuing fall—to retire to St. Louis, *and would readily enter the Honble Company's service.*"[353]

Smith wrote to Governor Simpson sometime in late 1829 or early 1830. His last opportunity to send a letter outside came when Sublette returned to the States after Christmas 1829. If sent with

Sublette, a letter to Simpson would have traveled up the Mississippi to the Red River colony and awaited Simpson's return from England in June on the lower Saskatchewan River. Smith could also have reached Simpson by sending his letter across the border with an obliging Indian going to an HBC post. If the letter passed in the fall 1829, or during Smith's 1830 spring hunt on the Musselshell, the surviving post journals betray no clues.

Simpson's comments suggest that Smith asked out of something more than gratitude for hospitality at Fort Vancouver. Jed passed the important business intelligence to British rivals that the withdrawal of their major American opposition left the disputed Oregon Country open to exploitation. Smith's offer to enter British service was valueless in territory where the HBC already operated with experienced brigade leaders. Like Pilcher, Smith was selling disguised entry into the forbidden territory across the international border, into Piegan country where beaver furs were otherwise denied to the HBC.

If, as Smith's biographer Dale Morgan concluded, his letters from the winter camp give insight into his mind and heart, then does this suggest deeper pragmatism behind the sanctimony? Smith conceived the idea when his partners, who had good reason to complain about his contribution, were preparing to divide their interest, and when he was looking for new alternatives. If he could tie the deaths of some trappers to British influence, as Smith himself wrote, then he had entangled himself "altogether too much in the things of time."[354]

On the day after Christmas Sublette and Black Moses Harris, a man who seemed to love walking, strapped on snowshoes and started their dog team. Those hard winter trips gave the partners the advantage over the HBC of operating on interior lines. They could order and receive their outfits in one season. In contrast, the company on the coast required three or four years to turn over an outfit.

As unrelenting winter winds scoured the camp, and the horses grazed the grass down to dirt, the trappers had to gamble between losing their animals where they stood and killing them on a winter march. The camp moved 150 miles to the Powder River, where by mid-January they were peeling cottonwood bark in a sheltered site and beating hungry buffalo away from the shavings.[355] The shank of the winter passed in a happy, noisy camp, where the Indian wives of the old trappers gossiped between campfires and the half-breed children played around the lodges. Under their long hair, preposterous beards, and beaded buckskins the mountain men were still boys a long way from home.

Joe Meek termed the worn copies of the Bible and Shakespeare that circulated around camp as textbooks of "The Rocky Mountain College." Those winter-bound hunters read *The Scottish Chiefs* with the same enthusiasm that Missouri Fur Company trappers had for *The Arabian Nights*, before the Gros Ventre killed them. Meek was a cocky young feller who called the boss "Davy"; his trapping partner, Squire Ebberts, could not even recall Jackson's first name.

Reaching St. Louis by 11 February 1830 Sublette learned that the western department of the American Fur Company was finally on the move. Pilcher's former associates, Lucien Fontenelle and Andrew Drips, and the experienced southwest trader, Joseph Robidoux, were taking an expedition to the mountains this month. If they reached the rendezvous before Sublette, SJ&S could end up with an unsalable outfit. Nevertheless he planned to experiment with wagons instead of packing.

After kicking his new-fangled caravan loose from St. Louis on 10 April, Sublette waited four more days before he could pick up the new license. This document described the area they dominated and planned to pass on to their inheritors: "Camp Defiance, Horse Prairie, mouth of Lewis' fork of the Columbia, junction of the Little Horn with the Big Horn, and at the Quamash flats of Lewis' fork of the Columbia." SJ&S received a three-year license to trade with the Indians and capitalized for a modest $8,205, plus other items better overlooked, including liquor.[356]

Sublette took a heavy train of ten wagons pulled by five-mule teams into the mountains for the first time. The outfit also included two light dearborns pulled by one mule each. The partners needed wagons to bring out two years' worth of collected returns.

Bill also invested in another kind of trail gear. In the SJ&S accounts is his note for $1,050.87 to "T. Grimsly for Sadling." Mexican saddles from Santa Fe, with high horns and substantial cantles that gave support on a long ride, had been showing up in Missouri. During the 1820s St. Louis saddler Thornton Grimsley started adapting the improvements to the English-type saddles still used on the American frontier. Convinced after trying the new models in 1829, Bill Sublette placed a substantial order.[357]

After the Powder River winter camp broke up, Smith and Tullock led the Yellowstone hunters on a long swing around the east side of the Big Horn Mountains to trap the upper parts of the Powder, Tongue, Little Big Horn, and Big Horn. Meek recalled that Smith's attempt to cross Bovey's (Beauvais) Fork of the Big Horn during the snow runoff lost 30 horses and 300 traps, "a serious loss in the business of hunting beaver." Of the 480 animals lost during SJ&S operations, Smith accounted for three-quarters.[358]

Trapping the Musselshell and Judith rivers left slim pickings for the brigade of the upper Missouri outfit that came from Fort Union. When William Henry Vanderburg tried to cross Bozeman Pass to trap the Madison, the Piegans killed one of his men, wounded two others, and destroyed so many horses that he had to retreat to the Powder River and wait for remounts from Fort Tecumseh.[359]

Jackson met thirty Taos trappers in Bear Valley on his last hunt. After wintering on Sweetwater Lake and getting "out on their legitimate employment" by the first of April, George Yount and his companions were returning to their caches when they bumped into Jackson and Milton Sublette's party.[360] David Jackson was giving Milton a tour of the area he would inherit as a principal in the new concern.[361]

Yount latched on to Smith's former associate, Arthur Black, who had much to say about the golden land of California. Yount invented a gold-discovery yarn, but the bonanza of livestock stirred his interest. According to his biographer, Charles Camp,

> After some trading between individuals of the two parties and *some transactions of importance between companies*, in consideration of the information now obtained secretly from Black, Yount proceeded to gather his caches and turn his course homeward—He pressed his march without further delay to trap, having conceived the project of availing himself of the money he had in the concern at New Mexico and to start speedily for California, to purchase mules, and drive them across to Missouri, a speculation which then held out a large, lucrative promise.[362]

Jackson drove his men three hundred miles across the Green River valley in a month, intending to take the trade of the Snake Indians, the residual free trappers, the Flatheads, and any Piegans who might show up on Henry's Fork. Montour, now traveling with the Flatheads in the HBC interest, admitted that those tribesmen made contact with Americans in spring 1830.[363]

Evidence disproves Governor Simpson's claim that the western freemen had returned to the HBC. In spring 1830 ten of the surviving Iroquois hunters still traveled with the American brigades. Comparing the list of 1825 dissidents with the company brigade rosters of 1829 shows few of those names back in the company. The Snake Brigade contained engaged men whose wages added to the cost of creating Simpson's fictitious fur desert.[364]

Leaving the familiar Snake plain through Jackson Hole, David took his last look at that beautiful place and led the laden pack train into the Wind River valley.

Following Jackson's cold trail, the American Fur Company trading outfit from St. Louis went astray in the Green River valley and missed the trappers who went to Wind River. Sublette, however, leading the wagons and a beef herd that included a milk cow to the rendezvous, properly astonished the gathered trappers.

On 4 August the Rocky Mountain Fur Company came into existence when the new partners accepted the residual of the SJ&S outfit, worth $16,000, which they would pay off in marketable beaver valued at $3 a pound if delivered in the mountains, or $4.25 a pound if turned over at St. Louis. The new entrepreneurs had until 15 June in the mountains, or 1 November at St. Louis, to make payment. If they wanted a new outfit, they had to notify St. Louis by the first of March. The agreement duplicated the Ashley-SJ&S contract with the deletion of the clause allowing a competitive outfit.[365]

The townsfolk of Columbia, in the Missouri Booneslick country, turned out on 5 October to gawk at the dusty cavalcade of fifty "hardy and sunburnt mountaineers" who rode beside the ten wagons on the St. Louis road. A gullible reporter for the *Missouri Intelligencer* swallowed the exaggeration that the wagons carried $150,000 worth of beaver. His boisterous informants "who had been so long excluded from the pleasures of society exhibited great demonstrations of satisfaction at their near approach to their families and friends." Four surviving beeves and the footsore milk cow limped home, their food value unnecessary in the buffalo country.[366]

Charles Keemle, the survivor of the Jones and Immell massacre, appreciated anyone's survival on the anvil of the mountain. Now a reporter for the *St. Louis Beacon*, his story ran in St. Louis on 11 October, and the *Cincinnati Commercial Advertiser* soon picked it up. By 4 November the *Alexandria Virginia Gazette* printed it, and the same information appeared in the 26 November edition of the *Philadelphia National Gazette*.[367]

Keemle gave a shot in the arm to the expansionists. The wagons of SJ&S had not actually crossed the mountains, but "there was nothing to prevent their crossing or going on to the mouth of the Columbia." The ease of the accomplishment disproved the idea that the Rocky Mountains formed "a barrier to stop the westward march of the American people."

Disregarding the spreading impact of their accomplishment, the partners made a general settlement with Ashley three days after they returned. Because he could provide them with pocket cash, they retained the general as their business agent to dispose of the furs. On 15 October he advanced them $23,314.60.

After pocketing $7,771.38, and taking four days to acquire a new suit of clothes and a satisfactory hangover, David left for Ste. Genevieve to see his ailing brother, avoiding a potentially painful meeting with the administrator of David Cunningham, one of the trappers killed on the Colorado River. His brother, Joseph W. Cunningham, who went up the Missouri with the first Ashley-Henry party, must have asked Smith some embarrassing questions.[368]

Jackson returned to St. Louis by 28 October to assist in the preparation of a final statement about the SJ&S business and the western situation. They addressed their letter to Secretary of War Eaton on 29 October 1830:

> This was the first time that wagons ever went to the Rocky Mountains; and the ease and safety with which it was done proves the facility of communicating overland with the Pacific ocean. The route from the *Southern Pass*, where the wagons stopped, to the Great Falls of the Columbia, being easier and better than on this side of the mountains, with grass enough for horses and mules, but a scarcity of game for the support of the men.

Bill Sublette tested the wagon road almost to South Pass, and the partners knew the country beyond that landmark was open through the Snake River plain to the mouth of the Columbia. Smith described the HBC post at Fort Vancouver, including its armaments, business, and success in western farming. "At Fort Vancouver the goods for the Indian trade are imported from London, and enter the territories of the United States, paying no duties." With an annual export of about 30,000 beaver skins, besides otter skins and small furs, at New York prices the HBC grossed about $250,000. Observing that the HBC did all its trapping south of the 49th parallel, the partners warned that the territory was nearly exhausted, and the United States would be left with no place where trappers could obtain beaver fur in any quantity.

> The inequality of the convention with Great Britain in 1818 is most glaring and apparent, and its continuance is a great and manifest injury to the United States. The privileges granted by it have enabled the British to take possession of the Columbia river, and spread over the country south of it; while no Americans have ever gone, or can venture to go on the British side. The interest of the United States and her citizens engaged in the fur trade requires that the convention of 1818 should be terminated, and each nation confined to its own territories. By this commercial interest there are other considerations requiring the

same result. These are, the influence which the British have already acquired over the Indians in that quarter, and the prospect of a British colony, and a military or naval station on the Columbia. Their influence over the Indians is now decisive. Of this the Americans have constant and striking proofs, in the preference which they give to the British in every particular.

Smith added that Governor Simpson had treated him with kindness and hospitality at Fort Vancouver, but the theme of the foreign threat returned at the end of the letter.

As to the injury which must happen to the United States from the British getting control of all the Indians beyond the mountains, building or repairing ships in the tide water region of the Columbia, and having a station there for their privateers and vessels of war, is too obvious to need a recapitulation. The object of this communication being to state *facts* to the Government, and to show the facility of crossing the continent to the Great Falls of the Columbia with wagons, the ease of supporting any number of men by driving cattle to supply them where there was no buffalo, and also to show the true nature of the British establishments on the Columbia, and the unequal operation of the convention of 1818.

These *facts* being communicated to the Government, they consider that they have complied with their duty, and rendered an acceptable service to the administration; and respectfully request you, sir, to lay it before President Jackson.

> We have the honor to be sir,
> Yours respectfully,
>
> *Jedediah S. Smith*
> *David E. Jackson*
> *W. L. Sublette*

To the Hon. John H. Eaton, Secretary of War.[369]

Like other Americans of their time Smith, Jackson, and Sublette saw themselves as recipients rather than dependents of the federal government. They hoped to claim reparations for their losses and wanted to protect the investment they left in the mountains. Their expectations had validity because SJ&S provided the only effective American representation in the disputed Oregon Country for the last four years, and through their aggressive competition they discouraged the imperial pretensions expressed through the HBC.

President Andrew Jackson had the letter published as one of four documents supporting his January 1831 message to the U.S. Senate. The other documents concerned the Indian Department and Great Lakes region trade. President Jackson attributed to British competition a cost of $500,000 and the deaths of five hundred men. The message enlightened Congress and refocused public attention on the Pacific Northwest.

The map showing the travels of Jedediah Smith, which apparently accompanied the letter, survived in the War Department until at least 1849-51.[370] Smith's admirers, including this 1832 *Illinois Magazine* eulogizer, attributed it to their hero:

> convinced as Smith was, of the inaccuracy of all the maps of the country, and of the little value they would be to hunters and travelers, he has, with the assistance of his partners, Sublitt and Jackson, and of Mr. S. Parkman, made a new, large, and beautiful map: in which are embodied all that is correct of preceding maps, and known tracks of former travelers, his own extensive travels, the situation and number of the various Indian tribes, and much other valuable information. This map is now probably the best extant, of the Rocky Mountains, and the country on both sides, from the States to the Pacific.[371]

The map contained this notation relating to the Snake River valley: "most of what is known of this section of country had been derived from Mr. Jackson and such Partisans as have traveled through it. Apply this note to the opposite waters of Lewis river and the Owyhee river."[372]

Writers were also reinventing the mountain legends to fit popular expectations. Timothy Flint, capitalizing on the success of James Fenimore Cooper's Leatherstocking stories, published a romantic novel entitled *The Shoshonee Valley*. Mountain men, whom he divided into two classes, appeared for the first time as characters. On one hand were the hopelessly insensitive and deliberately vulgar, "strange, fearless and adamantine men" who renounced society and became "inaccessible to passions and wants, and as sufficient to themselves, as the trees or the rocks with which they were conversant." In contrast he offered potentially virtuous characters capable of experiencing in the mountain landscape "a certain half-chill of the awful and sublime," which the author presented as a state of rudimentary nobility.[373]

By November Jedediah, working out his future, had the clerk Samuel Parkman arranging his notes and journals for publication.[374] He left the missing facts and details for Ashley to fill in. The general may have helped start it on toward the press. On 19 July 1834 Hugh Campbell of Philadelphia wrote to his brother Robert that the account was still in the hands of Ira Smith, who had gone to Santa Fe and left the manuscript with a third party, perhaps the western journalist Alophonzo Wetmore.

Washington Irving, then working on his book *Astoria*, later appropriated the faulty Bonneville manuscript. His editing skewed historical perception of the western events. Actual first-person accounts, like the Potts letters, found publication only after many years. And in those fragmented and often garbled accounts, it was easy to lose sight of a shadow.

13

"The earnest pursuit of wealth"

THE MEN WHO ONCE TRUSTED THEIR FURS to a hole in the ground quickly put their fortunes into land. After sending some money to his brother to buy a farm in Ohio, Jedediah Smith purchased a St. Louis house and slaves for his younger brothers. William Sublette bought 779 rolling acres on Riviere des Peres, six miles west of St. Louis, which he named Sulphur Springs.[375] David Jackson located 160 hilly, wooded acres in St. Francois County, Missouri, and applied for a federal land grant.[376]

David's announcement of his return from the mountains and his withdrawal from the fur trade showed his readiness to make up to his wife, Juliet, for the lost eight years they spent apart. By acquiring the Missouri property he could bring his family together again. Most of his capital, though, he required for reinvestment.

Neither hero nor genius, David Jackson possessed steadiness under fire and quiet resolution. In the mountains he was the rock others depended upon, while Juliet raised their two sons and twin daughters almost single-handedly. Whatever the wound between them, David did not go back to western Virginia immediately, and Juliet did not ask him to return.

Jedediah Smith held a close hand until February 1831, when he asked Congressman Ashley about a passport for the Santa Fe trade. Meanwhile, Jackson and Sublette were busy assembling the outfit to resupply the Rocky Mountain Fur Company. When the first of March passed without confirmation from the mountains, they envisioned themselves stuck with a stock of trade goods. On 23 March Sublette also forwarded a request to the State Department for a Santa Fe passport. He planned to accompany Smith to a certain point and "thence they would take different directions." Sublette requested Missouri Gov. John Miller, David's former commanding officer, to provide introductions to the governors of Santa Fe, Chihuahua, Sonora, and "such other of the Mexican republics" as Bill might visit.[377]

David Jackson stayed in the background. His brother was dying and the Jackson family had gathered to arrange George's property. On 25 March George Jackson sold three slaves to his younger brother, Cummins E. Jackson, for $1,500. Cummins immediately resold them to David at the same price. The transfer protected the farm hands from creditors while keeping them available to George's wife, Catharine. The next day George gathered his last strength and signed deeds transferring his real property to David. They buried the old lead miner and miller in a quiet, private section of his farm.[378]

By 9 April, after a brief mourning period, David arrived in St. Louis, where he gave lawyer Joseph Grafton the power of attorney to act in matters relating to George's estate. E. S. Minter, a Ste. Genevieve neighbor hired by Jackson as his clerk, witnessed the document.[379]

On 10 April the caravan left for Santa Fe. Of the twenty-three wagons assembled at Lexington, Missouri, on the first of May, ten belonged to Jackson and Sublette, nine to Jedediah Smith, one to Samuel Flournoy of Independence, and one to the St. Louis supply firm of Wells & Chadwick. The last, a mutually financed wagon, mounted a cannon on a set of detachable wheels.[380] The eighty-three men who agreed to undertake the adventure included the three principals: Minter, Sam Parkman, and a greenhorn from Connecticut named Jonathan Trumbull Warner. Smith had intimations of mortality and made a will at Independence.[381]

At this critical moment Tom Fitzpatrick finally appeared to explain that he had run into trouble while coming down the Yellowstone in a bullboat. Too late to change plans with the wagons loaded, the crews hired, and the caravan ready to roll, Tom would have to come along and take his outfit into the mountains from Taos.[382]

On 4 May 1831 the big wagons headed across the hills of what is now eastern Kansas at the dawdling pace of about eighteen miles a day. Minter lasted only as far as the Pawnee Fork of the Arkansas. Indians, watching when he wandered off to hunt antelope, casually picked him off. That night David took his turn staring into the embers and feeling the guilt that burdened Andrew Henry and oppressed Jedediah Smith.[383]

Rumors of the killing got back to John O'Fallon, who passed them on to Robert Campbell on 30 June. O'Fallon heard that the caravan had arrived somewhere "NW of the Pawnee, without accident except for the report that Jackson had been killed while separated from his party, by the Pawnees, a report that needs confirmation & which Gen'l Ashley does not believe." David's friends had to wait over six months before they learned the truth.[384]

To shorten the distance between the Arkansas and Cimarron rivers the travelers took a two-day shortcut across the arid sand hills, hauling their drinking water in barrels. Riding ahead to locate water, Smith and Fitzpatrick found the Cimarron just a sandy bottom snaking around the low hills. They separated to look for a waterhole, and when Jed failed to reappear, Fitzpatrick rode back to the wagons alone.[385]

Scouts tried to follow Smith's trail the next morning, but the shots they fired as signals from the hilltops were answered only by silence. The party had to drive its thirsty mules on before the animals balked. When Jed did not ride in on the back trail, David, the tribal elder, drew the duty of telling young Peter and Austin Smith that their older brother probably would not return.

The next morning the appearance of 1,500 Indians thrilled the greenhorn Warner while the more pessimistic drivers began scooping rifle pits under their wagons. Jackson and Sublette recognized the Gros Ventres of the northern plains, allies of the Piegans. Their leader, wearing a distinctive long red woolen capot in the broiling sun, rode forward to say that his people had traveled south to visit their Arapaho relatives and planned to stay awhile. After smoking and distributing a few minor bribes to secure the peace, the caravan proceeded.[386]

Between the landmark Rabbit Ear Peak and the Sangre de Cristo Mountains rising in the west the wagons crawled over long, rolling hills. The Mexican officer named Blas de Hinojoes who met the caravan on 11 June looked like a *cibolero,* a buffalo hunter, in his heavy leather jacket and pants as thick as armor plate. He shaded his eyes with a large, flat straw hat and decorated his weapons with parti-colored tassels.

A band of hunter-traders solved the mystery of Jedediah's disappearance as they traded a brace of pistols from Comanches baffled by the new percussion caps. The Comanches told the Mexicans that fifteen or twenty Indian hunters, hiding near a spring where the buffalo came to drink, surprised an unsuspecting horseman who rode up and dismounted to drink. Finding the opportunity to overpower the lone white man irresistible, they sprang out flapping blankets to spook his horse. The desperate trader got off only one shot before falling under their lances.

At Rio de Ocate, where the prairie travelers first saw pine trees, astute traders had learned to cache goods to evade Mexican customs. Coming out in person to interdict the smuggling, Gov. Santiago Abreu caught Sam Parkman digging and confiscated Smith's estate until the men made an inventory and *aduana* (a customs report).[387]

The stern trail discipline began breaking down after the caravan reached San Miguel on the Pecos River and *avant coureurs* rode ahead to buy provisions, line up storehouses, and refine understandings with the customs officers. David and Bill exercised their prerogative as proprietors to get an advance taste of the famous dust cutter made from cactus. Feeling burned out by the Mexican welcome, they saw no reason to lead the parade into town.

The freighters, as vain as voyageurs, combed their long hair and trimmed their shaggy beards at the last camp. The wagon drivers tied new crackers on their long bullwhips. At dawn on the Fourth of July the little cannon saluted Santa Fe and brought its residents out to watch the wagons roll down the hill and into the square. Dating from 1610, the Palace of the Governors on the north side of the square was one of the oldest structures on the continent.

The tough overlanders, astonished and excited by the senoritas' short skirts and loose blouses, shouted appalling suggestions as their parade rolled past. Some women even smoked little cigarros.[388] The men off-loaded the wagons at the customs warehouse and locked up the cargo. Like sailors on shore leave, they hoped to find understanding senoritas who would make them forget two dusty months on the trail.

Translating the customs manifest of "Jackon y Soblett" into Spanish took four days, but preplanning ensured official understanding; the authorities opened only those bales listed on the manifest. The *derechos de arancel* (tariff imposts) averaged 100 percent of U.S. costs for certain cotton goods, but the inspectors willingly compromised the official rates to encourage the trade. Baffled by the incomprehensible language and ridiculous formalities, the traders were skeptical about the southwestern way of doing business.[389]

During the ten days following 9 July Jackson and Sublette traded that part of their outfit not reserved for the Rocky Mountain Fur Company. They skimmed the cream from the boom year in which a million dollars worth of American goods flowed south, then hurried on to Taos to pick up pelts brought in by western trappers.[390]

The Camino Real (Royal Road) ran along the fertile valley of Rio del Norte (Rio Grande). The rich red soil, irrigated by an ingenious system of open ditches, produced fields of wheat and corn, orchards of apples, peaches, and apricots, and some struggling vineyards. Accepting the invitation of a generous ranchero, the sons of the log-cabin frontier stopped in the cool comfort of an adobe farmhouse to refresh themselves with goat milk and a snack of curdled cheese.[391]

Towering red mountains enclosed the adjacent valley. The communities of Rancho de Taos and San Fernando de Taos had become the favorite sporting places of the mountain men. San Fernando's low adobe houses focused on the treeless plaza, where two church towers confronted the raw materialism of traders' houses and public buildings. Rich in trees, water, and a sense of sanctuary, Taos formed a snug retreat where the morning sun slanted golden over the purple peaks. The light cast intricate shadow patterns through weathered lattices onto the softly contoured adobe walls, and the songs of birds echoed.

Bleary from being struck by "Taos lightning" the night before, local trappers brought Jackson and Sublette up to date on the latest mountain gossip. David recognized some of the men he had seen with Yount the previous year and learned that Yount had headed west with William Wolfskill in September. The trappers who made a spring hunt on the Platte smuggled in about 120 pelts without declaring them to the customs officials. Jackson & Sublette purchased those packs without regard for Mexican law, deciding the furs were taken in U.S. territory and they were only trans-shipping them back.[392]

Tom Fitzpatrick finally took delivery on $6,000 worth of mountain goods. He also accepted $2,800 in "mulas" or untradable goods from the leftover stock of Austin and Peter Smith.[393]

While the men packed the mules, David took Tom aside and asked him to carry a remembrance to Madame Grey. He dared send only three yards of blue cloth and four yards of ribbon to a woman with a jealous husband; but he included a message saying she could send her son down to Missouri next year to go to school, and Jackson & Sublette would pick up the charge.[394]

A trapper named Ewing Young also sold $2,484.22 worth of southwestern beaver to Jackson & Sublette. In California the year before with Wolfskill, Young was run out of Los Angeles after a drunken brawl. After trapping on the Gila River without a license, he could not risk taking his catch to Santa Fe unless he wanted to visit its *calabozo*; he found a more understanding market at Taos. By the first of August Young felt ready for a new adventure, and Jackson saw a candidate for something he had in mind.[395]

David Waldo, a former western Virginia neighbor of Jackson's, had established himself among the Mexicans. Waldo grew up in Lewis County, near Jackson's Mill, and came west with his brothers John and Daniel about the time Jackson went to Ste. Genevieve. Settling in Gasconade County, Missouri, the Waldos performed the same kind of work David did for a while—cutting logs and floating them to a mill. After a year of medical education at Transylvania College in Kentucky, David Waldo made doctoring another facet of a career that included the offices of clerk of the circuit court, justice of the peace, acting coroner, and deputy sheriff of Gasconade County. When he visited Santa Fe in 1830, Waldo saw the possibilities of the trade and even had himself baptized so he could obtain Mexican citizenship.

Jackson found young Waldo a bundle of entrepreneurial energy dedicated to "the earnest pursuit of wealth," and he felt comfortable dealing with men he knew.[396]

Jackson decided to pick up on the California horse and mule trade that Smith had tried to exploit in 1828 and may have been contemplating again before he was killed. Yount and Wolfskill tried it the previous year, and Parkman and one of the Smith brothers were going into Chihuahua on a similar quest. If Jackson could obtain California animals cheaply, he could drive them east to the boom market in Louisiana or the southern cotton plantations.

Waldo had watched the Missouri mule market grow since summer 1823, when Stephen Cooper drove four hundred jacks and jennies back from Santa Fe. Although would-be entrepreneurs lost a herd of one thousand animals on the Cimarron cutoff five years later, the traders went back the next year for a herd of two thousand that redeemed their losses. New Mexican buyers now traveled as far as Chihuahua or Sonora to assemble the herds.[397]

After buying big, strong California mules for $12-$15 a head, Antonio Armijo sent them on to the profitable Missouri market. Jackson appreciated the profit possibilities because SJ&S had bought its pack animals in Missouri at high prices. He planned to go to California and buy a herd of about a thousand animals, which he would drive through Texas to the Louisiana cotton mills.

Sublette still saw his future in supplying the mountaineers and pulled out for Missouri on 28 August with fifty-five packs of beaver and eight hundred buffalo robes. Austin Smith and Waldo's younger brother William—intent on ordering an outfit from the supply firm of Scott & Rule with a $3,377 note from Jackson & Sublette—accompanied him. Taking a cash advance from Sublette for his share of the returns of Jackson & Sublette, David gave his partner a note for $14,945, which he expected the furs would more than cover.[398]

David Waldo's New Mexican connections facilitated the legal technicalities and ensured logistical support when Jackson returned. The third leg of this transcontinental scheme depended on Young, who would take thirty-six trappers on a swing through the mountains and come into California the next spring in time to assist in driving the livestock east. They expected the furs they took to cover the expenses of getting a trustworthy crew of drovers where Jackson needed them. Jackson & Waldo provided the outfit and Young financed some individual trappers.[399]

Ewing Young's bad reputation precluded a legitimate trapping license, but Waldo and Antoine Robidoux obtained permission on 19 September to send twenty-six Mexicans and five foreigners to trap in the north. Robidoux used the license for that purpose, but they also made a copy to cover Young's group, which outfitted at Taos and departed in October.[400]

The plan had no new individual parts, but it had an imaginative scope. The associates meant to drive a herd of valuable animals halfway across the continent, through the war grounds of the Pimas, the Apaches, and the Comanches who dominated the Texas plains.

14

"The facility of crossing the continent"

BEFORE HE LEFT SANTA FE David Jackson paid off an old debt. A traveler named Henry Hook came to him with a note on SJ&S that Jedediah Smith had given to trapper Isaac Galbraith in California. Hook bought planks from the expatriate entrepreneur Capt. John Cooper and shipped the lumber to Guaymas, Mexico, before coming to Santa Fe. Unhappy about turning over $202.50 for furs he never saw, Jackson managed to receive something of value for his trouble. Hook gave him a Masonic letter of introduction to Captain Cooper.[401]

Buying a thousand horses and mules in California at $8-$10 a head would require a great deal of cash. David converted the note from Sublette into Mexican silver coins, which he had sewn into wet rawhide bags. The rawhide dried and compressed the loose coins into almost solid ingots. With typical self-assurance, Jackson hired ten men at $25 a month to help guard his fortune. He may have employed Antoine Leroux as one of his two guides, and the others were just the sort of men one might expect to find on a loose frontier. David still had Jim, his mountain companion and long-time family slave, to guard his back, and he could probably trust the Connecticut man named Warner he had hired as his clerk. The men rode mules and led seven more animals packing the silver.[402]

Although Santa Fe marked the end of the trail for most Americans, it actually served as the northern hub for a network of rough roads and trails reaching far into Mexico.[403] Jackson's party rode down the Camino Real as far as Valverde before it crossed the Rio Grande, then it turned west toward the Santa Rita copper mines that perched on the southern end of the Mogollon and Minbres mountains. A year earlier a St. Louis Irishman named Robert McKnight started improving the old Spanish mining system. The mine owners hired another Missouri adventurer, James Kirker, to provide security for the ore caravans traveling to the smelters in Corralitos, Chihuahua. Kirker organized a private army and refined fighting Apaches into such a specialty that Mexican authorities eventually contracted with him to protect the copper trail. The Apaches had already begun the first convulsions of what became known as the Janos rebellion, adding some spice to Jackson's trip.[404]

From the mines the Janos trail led to Oro de Vaca (Cow Springs) and on to the abandoned mission of San Xavier de Bac. Passing from water hole to water hole, Jackson's troop entered an increasingly outlandish landscape. Every living thing had to stand on its own in this unforgiving world; even the plants were knife-edged, spiked, and armored. Like giants in a moonscape, immense saguaro cacti loomed over the evening campfires.

Baking under his sombrero, Jackson took note of the watering and feeding places his herd would need on the return trip. Meanwhile, his parched men reconsidered the wisdom of signing on with a rider whose ass seemed to be made of iron. By October the party had followed the old Spanish trail into Tucson, where David planned to hire a guide for the next leg of the trip to the Colorado River. The residents warned that the Apaches had been calling the Coyoteros and Pinals to join in a general war.[405]

The undaunted party headed toward the Pima villages on the Gila River across broad, flat valleys accentuated by spectacularly eroded rocks. Casa Grande, a landmark of prehistoric farmers, was slowly melting back into the earth; the descendants of those early agriculturalists now lived along the Gila under the generalized name of Pima. Jackson traded with these gentle people for corn or squash. Remembering Smith's error with the Mojaves, he kept his men under tight rein and avoided creating resentment among the natives that might jeopardize their return.

Crossing the great Rio Colorado six miles below the mouth of the Gila produced some anxious moments for Jackson, especially when the fate of his heavy silver reaching the far bank depended upon the buoyancy of reed rafts. Beyond lay sand dunes and appalling deserts where mirages danced across the flat pans under a dazzling sun. Riding past First Wells (Cook's Wells), the water hole of Alamo Mocho, the future site of Calexico, and up Carrizo Creek to Vallecito, they finally broke over a divide and dropped into the valley that later bore Warner's name. Groves of oaks softened the harsh landscape as they came to the Indian village of Temecula and the nearby *assistencia* (an outpost station) of Mission San Antonio de Pala.

Pala—surrounded by irrigated fields of wheat, corn, and beans, as well as a vineyard and orchards of olive and fruit trees—had served the Catholic God's Indians since 1816. The church, dwellings, granaries, and campanile exuded a sense of eternity. After crossing the desert, the sight of this oasis invited the weary troop.

The proud padre showed Jackson the long, narrow chapel supported by rough-hewn cedar beams that had been brought down from nearby Mount

Palomar. Stooping in the cool sanctuary where candles softly flickered, David perused the primitive Indian paintings in the shadows and decided that religion, like California mission politics, did not concern a mule buyer.[406]

The padre told David that to buy the number of mules he wanted would require him to visit most of the twenty missions that lay scattered like jewels of faith between San Luis Rey and the bay of San Francisco. The nearest place Jackson could obtain that cooperation was at San Luis Rey on the coast. The party pushed on through the dry canyons until they saw a glittering emerald expanse stretching to the horizon. They rode down a bushy barranca to the white sands. Yes, by God, the water tasted of salt, but less acrid than the Great Salt Lake.

Fr. Antonio Peyr had shepherded his Indian converts at the San Luis Rey mission for thirty-six years, but the contest for power between Gen. Comdt. José María Encheandia and Mexico City's new appointee, Col. Manuel Victoria, threatened his dedication. To keep himself in power Encheandia pandered to the cadets of old California families and the dangerous faction of opportunistic *estrangeros* with proposals to appropriate and redistribute mission holdings.

In November David went south to San Diego to buy animals and try to connect with Captain Cooper. While he was there some exiled rebels seduced the garrison and on 29 November seized the presidio. Sensing the time had come to get out, Jackson drove his stock north toward the pueblo of Los Angeles. The rebel army also marched north to a comic-opera confrontation where thirty loyalist troops scattered the 150 rebels. The victory left Colonel Victoria wounded and so discouraged by the lack of support that he left Mission San Gabriel on 20 December to return to Mexico City.[407]

Four days later Jackson wrote to Captain Cooper from the same place: "there has been something said of my taking part in the Late Dispute in government. That is fals."[408] In confirming that his only concern was with business, David continued: "Dr. Sir, I call on you as a friend unknown to act as an ageant for me in send Down and up the coast and Engage all the Mules from 3 year up at $8 Not to Exceed one thousand. Expence I will pay on Sight." As an afterthought he added in the margin, "Sir, the Least Delay is a Loss from Day to Day," and to encourage a man he had yet to meet, he included a reference to their Masonic fraternity.[409]

Leaving Warner and another man in Los Angeles to look after the herd, Jackson started up the ladder of Catholicism and colonialism along the Camino Real. He went from San Fernando Rey to San Buenaventura and on to Santa Barbara, where a small community of American trappers lived and hunted the offshore islands for sea otters. Yount was not around to advise the mule buyer, but one of his associates, Lewis T. Burton, loved to talk, and David was familiar with Isaac Galbraith and Zacharias Ham from the mountains. He also met Love Hardesty, Jean Louis Braun, Joseph Gibson, and a fellow named John Rhea, or Ray, who hailed from Henry County, Tennessee.[410]

Riding into Monterey David finally presented his letters of introduction to Captain Cooper, who felt pleased to see someone going ahead with his stock-buying idea. They understood business, but California politics stumped them.

The foreign community of this port of entry distrusted General Commandant Encheandia, as they did his rival, Pio Pico. Garrison commander Capt. Agustín V. Zamorano, probably trying to undermine the governor's shaky hold, formed the *compania estranjera* to defend the town. Among those forty-four foreign militiamen were three of Jedediah Smith's former trappers: Daniel Ferguson, James Reed, and Louis Pombert.[411] Another unlikely recruit, English scientific traveler Thomas Coulter, arrived in California by sea after exploring in Sonora. When Coulter published his travel notes in *The Journal of the London Geographic Society*, in 1835, he indicated that he made a trip from Monterey via San Gabriel to the Rio Colorado sometime between March and July 1832; perhaps he traveled with Jackson's party.

Another of Smith's trappers who escaped the northern disaster hauled Jackson into court to answer the lawsuit. "[John] Wilson brought suit for wages allegedly due by Smith, Jackson & Sublette, and won a judgment in the California courts for $100."[412]

Glad to escape the simmering politics and relentless legalities of Monterey, Jackson rode to Santa Clara Mission at the south end of San Francisco Bay. A four-mile-long alameda of black willow trees connected the mission to the pueblo of San Jose. David introduced himself to Fr. José Viadar, a large, well-built man whose forty years of missionary work were also threatened by secularization. As the parent of a large Indian family and the supervisor of a huge complex, Viadar was assisted by Mayordomo Don Ygnacio Aluiso.[413]

After morning prayers and singing the "Santo Dios," the neophytes lined up for breakfast. Seeing a thousand people fed impressed the mountaineer, whose greatest logistical culinary responsibility had been cutting a willow stick to broil his buffalo steak. Some of the congregation worked as artisans and the *mayordomo de campo* had 25 vaqueros herding 3,000 cattle, 30,000 sheep, 1,500 horses, 500 mules, and a band of burros.[414]

Jackson continued to Mission San Jose on the east side of the bay where Father Duran welcomed him. David picked up a gray mare branded with the mission 'J' on her neck.[415] The mission records reflect Jackson's purchases, showing a reduction of 50 animals. The 1831-32 accounts for other missions also reveal lowered numbers of the horse and mule herds: Santa Clara by 23 animals; Le Soledad by 80; and San Miguel by 200. Excluding natural factors, Jackson's acquisitions reflect the most significant exchanges of that year. But the 350 animals he bought from missions left him well short of the 1,000-head herd he hoped to assemble, so Jackson also bought stock from private ranches. Prices ran higher than he expected, resulting in a final herd of only about 700 horses and mules.[416]

Going as far north as Mission San Jose meant Jackson had covered 2,500 miles in the past year. Few Americans could match his understanding of western geography.

Heavy rains in the Salinas Valley almost wrecked Mission Soledad and disrupted Jackson's mule drive when some of his stock escaped across the swollen river. While David waited for a break in the weather for thirteen frustrating days, he suspected the corporal of the mission guard of hiding a dun mule and two mares. Fr. Vincente Francisco de Sarria must have shared that suspicion, since he gave David replacements from the mission stock. The persistent drover authorized Captain Cooper to recover the animals if he found them in possession of anyone except the priest.[417]

The "Sailor," Fr. Juan Cabot, presided over Mission San Miguel at the head of the Salinas Valley. Jackson wrote from the flea-infested place on 22 February to warn Cooper that "Gen. Hendea is in full command in Calliforney and Signs his Name officially as Geon comendant of Calliforney."

By late March the drovers met Ewing Young's trapping party at the Sierra Ranch on the Santa Ana River.[418] Those beaver hunters had worked the Salt and Gila rivers in the desert Southwest, fought some Apaches, and killed one of their own, which gave Young an excuse to bring Turkey Green to the Mexican authorities. Ten men who quit trapping early arrived at Los Angeles about 10 February while the more dedicated hunters came in on 14 March.

Six and a half packs containing fewer than 500 light-colored Southwest beaver pelts averaged only about a dozen skins per hunter. Jackson was disgusted with the meager returns. He had expected Young to enter California in the north and work the rich streams that the HBC brigades from Fort Vancouver were exploiting.[419]

Retracing their trail across the Southwest, this time heading east, Jackson's party arrived at the Colorado River in June to find it flooding nearly bank full. It took the men twelve days to get the animals across the swollen stream at Lower Yuma Crossing.[420]

Since the herd was smaller than Jackson expected, he ended up with a surplus of drovers and decided to leave Young, Warner, Job Dye, Moses Carson, and two others to continue trapping. When they parted at the ford, Jackson gave Young an outfit of arms, ammunition, tobacco, steel traps, and other goods valued at about $7,000, plus $3,000 in cash to purchase more mules and follow later. Young and his five trappers returned to Los Angeles.

The thirty drovers included Jackson's slave Jim, Joseph Gale, Isaac Galbraith, Pauline Weaver, an Englishman named Irving, and five New Mexicans: José García, Manuel García, Manuel Leal, José Manuel Ortega, and José Manuel Sevie. Others who may have returned with Jackson include Love Hardesty, John Rhea, David Keller, Blas Griego, Manuel Mondragon, José Archelete, Branch, Francisco Laforet, Baptiste St. Germain, Buatista Guerra, Sidney Cooper, Benjamin Day, William Day, Joseph Defit, John Huggins, Thomas Low, Julien Vargas, Santiago Cordero, Francisco Arguell, and José Taforia.[421]

The drive across the hot southwestern desert began in June when water was scarce. A traveler passing through the area a decade later commented that the area between the Gila River and Tucson "is said to have been an extraordinary drought . . . for several years. A Mr. Jackson once lost many of a small drove of mules he took through in an imprudent manner in July."[422]

Another undocumented account held that "just beyond the Colorado a Mojave attack relieved Jackson of more than half his animals and he reached Santa Fe with only two hundred head."[423]

As they passed Casa Grande, Pauline Weaver, who preferred simply to be called Paul, rode over to the crumbling adobe and carved his name in the structure, thus committing one of the first documentable acts of tourist vandalism.[424]

During the winter the Janos Apaches had drawn Pinal, Santa Cruz, and Tucson warriors into their rebellion. The battle with the Mexicans, which took place in the Santa Rita Mountains on 23 May 1832, left warriors roaming in the vicinity of Jackson's route. While he probably lost some animals to Indian depredation, thirst and heat remained his real enemies.[425]

By the first week of July, as the drovers drew near Santa Fe, Jackson faced the problem of bringing in the six and a half packs of furs from Ewing Young's trappers without a license. His only authorization for possessing furs was the copy of the license issued to Waldo and Robidoux last October. If those hunters returned, it could expose the ruse of Young's copy. Reluctant to risk his stock for a mere $1,750 worth of beaver, Jackson buried the pelts at a stopping place on the El Paso road known as the *Conadero*.

Unfortunately, herder José Manuel Ortega hurried to the second alcalde of Santa Fe and told Commissoria Agustín Duran about the concealed furs. Duran ordered the furs confiscated and hauled Jackson into court. Claiming ignorance of Mexican law as his first line of defense, Jackson explained that he was only transporting the furs and he did not know where they were taken. Jackson said he believed the pelts belonged to Waldo, a Mexican citizen. When the investigators insisted that the furs belonged to Young, Jackson risked showing the dubious license. To his surprise, the board of inquiry accepted the license as proof that Young worked for Waldo. The New Mexicans fixed so strongly on implicating Young that they apparently missed the connection between Jackson, Waldo, and Young, and the inquiry subsided without penalties.[426]

Waldo was appalled to see his carefully constructed reputation tarnished in court. In Missouri his irascible older brother, Daniel, balked at any more investments that returned only 10 percent. The Waldos' supplier, William K. Rule, advised the Santa Fe trader to come home and settle with Daniel, who seemed bent on preventing "any goods being sent to you and Jackson."

Rule's letter also contained discouraging news about the mule trade: "Jacks (Proof fole getter)—raised sufficiently far North to Stand our Cold winters will do well if bought low. . . . a few large Ginnys to raise stock from would sell well. . . . I fear the Success of your mule Speculation as the general introduction of Steam in the Sugar Mills, Cotton Press &c is greatly Curtailing the Southern demand for animal power."[427] In mid-January, however, Peter Smith and Sam Parkman brought fifty animals from Chihuahua and Janos, which Ira G. Smith drove back to Missouri and sold for $1,645.[428]

Jackson's difficulties did little to discourage the California mule rush. In September 1831 two traders, Archibald Stevenson and Juan Purcel (John Poisel), took out a license to bring in California mules. In October 1832 another American group obtained passports for Chihuahua and Sonora but went to California instead. The 1833 parties resorted to rustling and gave the Santa Fe business a bad name.[429]

When he learned the Comanches were rampaging on the Llano Estacado (Staked Plains), Jackson gave up the idea of crossing Texas to the Louisiana cotton mills. After selling all but 250 head of his stock in Santa Fe he set out along the Santa Fe trail at the end of July, intending eventually to head for the Arkansas frontier. Two Arkansas trappers and young William Waldo accompanied him, as did Love Hardesty and Pleasant Armstrong.

Pushing along at fifteen to eighteen miles a day, they expected to reach Arkansas in less than a month. But on the Arkansas River David ran into more bad luck. The 1825 Osage Indian treaty provided a fifty-mile-wide strip extending west from the then Mexican border to allow the Indians an outlet to hunt buffalo. The Santa Fe trail was a poorly marked corridor, and those who got off the road were on their own. Accustomed to ranging over half the continent, Jackson struck east toward the Osage reservations on the Neoshu and Vertigras rivers. Skirting north of the Comanche threat brought his herd into rustling range of the Osages, who drove off eighty-two of his animals. Jackson apparently wrote off the loss, but his partner, David Waldo, continued to press for compensation until 1844, when the government finally denied restitution on grounds that the mule drovers were trespassing on Osage territory.[430]

Since 1821 the cantonment at Fort Gibson, at the head of Arkansas River navigation, had earned its reputation as "the Hellhole of the Southwest." The garrison had the impossible task of protecting the relocated Cherokees from the outraged Osages, and both tribes from white exploiters. A stockade enclosed hand-hewn log cabins, the best of which served as the private boarding house that catered to the post officers and their families. When Jackson and his drovers went into the sutlers to refresh themselves, David learned that an officer who previously served here, Capt. Benjamin Louis

Eulalie de Bonneville, had recently entered the Rocky Mountain fur trade. Envious rumors held that he had the backing of eastern capitalists close to John Jacob Astor.[431]

Jackson took the problem of his lost stock to Captain Bean and Lieutenant Pentecoste, who were trying to organize a regiment of mounted rangers to "enter the Indian country and range the frontier to preserve peace and order." The unit that became the First Regiment of Mounted Dragoons, the first plains-ranging cavalry, had an unimpressive beginning as an unruly gang, poorly clad in ill-cut green capots and buckskins, who amused themselves by drinking, fighting, and gambling with the seven licensed sharpers who milked the garrison. Because the Army required officers to furnish their own mounts, Lt. James W. Hamilton bought a good California horse from Jackson for $100.[432]

David Jackson maintained his anonymity at Fort Gibson, escaping the notice of four visitors who wrote detailed accounts of life there. One, Washington Irving, penned *A Tour of the Prairies*, which established him as a writer and led to his being chosen to varnish over the Columbia adventure in *Astoria*. Irving later appropriated Captain Bonneville's imperfect manuscript and drew a skewed view of the Rocky Mountain fur trade. His interpretations would have benefitted from an interview with one of the founders, but the dusty plainsman slipped through the crossroads unnoticed.[433]

After working out customs problems with U.S. Marshal Elias Rector, Jackson trailed his herd down the Arkansas River as far as Fort Smith, where he arranged winter pasturage in the upper end of Crawford County and left William Waldo to keep an eye on the stock. When herding dulled, Waldo began courting Miss Vaill, the daughter of the Osage missionary.[434]

After riding 5,000 miles in Grimsley's saddle, David indulged in the pure luxury of lolling on the hurricane deck of a river steamer, drink in hand, watching the landscape slide by. Leaving the boat at the mouth of the Arkansas, David scouted sales prospects across the Mississippi River where the Army was expelling the Choctaw Indians, bringing about a speculative land boom. David struck up an acquaintance with Capt. John Ray and David Jones of Paris, Tennessee.

Jackson brought a report of an Indian attack on a party of Missouri travelers who left Santa Fe in December. The item published in the *St. Louis Times* on 2 March 1833 called Jackson "well known as an enterprising Indian Trader" who had recently returned from Santa Fe.[435]

15

"Should my case be favored by feelings"

THE RIVERBOAT THAT NOSED INTO THE SLOUGH below Petite Rocher dropped a trail-worn, slightly overhung traveler on shore. David Jackson followed the Gabbourie Creek road into Ste. Genevieve, where he hired a horse and rode out to his late brother's farm to complete some unfinished business.

David had left for Santa Fe immediately after arranging the administration of George's estate, and now the time had come to turn the farm over to fifteen-year-old Edward Jackson. Edward's sisters, Helen, Lydia, and Mary Virginia, fussed over their uncle, and before long David started paying sister-in-law Catharine's store bills or buying material so she could sew him a new shirt.[436]

Although sixteen years had passed since David last saw his wife, Juliet, other Virginia family connections had persisted. On 16 May 1833 his sister Rebecca acknowledged his safe return by naming her son David Jackson White. When they learned of his return, David's younger brothers, Cummins and Return Meigs, and David's 22-year-old son, William Pitt, set out for Missouri to meet him.

In his father's absence, William Pitt Jackson's mother and both grandfathers tried to guide the boy through childhood. After his grandfather the colonel's death, Cummins became the male role model for William Pitt, as he did for the two orphaned sons of his brother Jonathan Jackson. One of Jonathan's sons, Thomas J. "Stonewall" Jackson, the Confederate military genius, always acknowledged his appreciation of his Uncle Cummins. But Cummins lived the life of a confirmed bachelor, having a reputation for racing horses on Sunday and drinking cider from the bung. And William Pitt showed signs of a nature that required a tougher mentor, his father.[437]

On 1 May 1833 the patent was signed for the 160 acres of land David had claimed earlier in St. Francois County. The boundaries ran along the east side of the southwest quarter and the west half of the southeast half of section 20, township 38 north, range 5 west, near the northern boundary of the county and just south of the Valle lead mines. David put his son William Pitt and younger brother Return Meigs to work on the land digging lead.[438]

With the last of his Mexican dollars evaporating, David went to St. Louis to seek a settlement of the SJ&S partnership with Bill Sublette. Bill had recently returned from a four-month business trip in the East and professed to be "up to his knees in Business." After a drink at Eddie's Green Tree Tavern, Jackson's Calliforny and Arkansas yarns came up a little lame against Bill's elaboration of the previous summer's battle with the Blackfeet at Pierre's Hole and his recent ride on a steam railway.

Sublette, now in partnership with Robert Campbell, intended to confound the American Fur Company; he would have preferred to get that operation underway before dealing with the debts of the previous partnership, but David approached him on 29 March asking for $1,567.87 as his share of the outstanding Rocky Mountain Fur Company notes. Sublette still supplied the RMFCo., but mountain competition had become so tight that he felt uncertain whether they would ever collect. The Jackson & Sublette accounts and the remainder of SJ&S would have to wait until fur sales produced cash. David agreed to accept half of his share and leave the rest as a reserve against the lawsuits brought by the heirs of men who died in their service.[439] He came away from the meeting with only $783.93.[440]

Jackson & Waldo settled the business accounts of their brief partnership without leaving any known records. Apparently David found the arrangement satisfactory because Waldo escaped notice in Jackson's last letter.

David watched from the levee on 10 April when the steamer *Yellowstone* departed for the upper Missouri with the American Fur Company's 1833-34 outfit. Kenneth McKenzie and his associates had used former Bay man Jacques Bergier and the HBC confidential servant Jemmy Jock Bird (James Bird, Jr.) to gain access to the trade of the Piegan Indians. Another former associate, Joshua Pilcher, was returning upriver as one of the three U.S. Indian agents whom the AMFCo. appeared to have in its pocket. Traveling as tourists were Pierre Chouteau and his daughters and visiting German scientist Prince Maximillian of Weid-Neuweid, who wanted to observe wild animals and wild Indians.

Cummins Jackson warned David that William Pitt wanted to get his hands on his father's money. But a letter young W. P. wrote to Grandfather Norris expressed a sincere desire to learn from and prove himself to his father.[441] W. P. and Return Meigs devoted themselves to the pick and shovel until July, when David took his son on a trip. Leaving St. Louis on 14 September, the pair paused four days in Ste. Genevieve before steaming into the Ohio. At Paducah the boats turned up the Tennessee River to Pittsburgh Landing, the nearest point to Memphis. The two travelers completed their 450-mile trip on horseback.

After spending a week in Memphis, W. P. rode another 150 miles to Fort Smith to reclaim the mules William Waldo was herding. He received 147 animals but had only 133 by the time he reached the Mississippi. Fourteen mules were either sold in Arkansas or lost in the struggle through the White River swamps and the Mississippi river bottoms.

David kept forty animals in Memphis and sent the boy on toward the stock-hungry cotton plantations. At Somerville, thirty-six miles beyond Memphis, Capt. John Ray agreed to buy the herd if W. P. would deliver it to Huntington or Paris while he met with David Jackson and arranged payment.[442]

The large loss of stock cut deep into the initial investment of between $5,600 and $7,000, plus expenses. Selling 133 animals at $60 a head recovered the investment but failed to adequately compensate David for his risks and a long year on the trail. And David now had his capital tied up in notes from strangers.

Jackson's experiment demonstrated the feasibility of transcontinental commerce at a time when some eastern conservatives still believed the continent was too large for any kind of unity. Eight years earlier even Thomas Hart Benton, the great proponent of western expansion, viewed the ridge of the Rocky Mountains as the natural and everlasting boundary where "the Western limit of the republic should be drawn." By successfully operating in the disputed Oregon Country and by freely traveling to California, men like Jackson disproved those doubts. David's stock drive, one of the longest yet undertaken, demonstrated more than far-western commercial potential, because it gave Jacksonian frontiersmen an irresistible new goal.

While he waited for his father to rejoin him in Paris, Tennessee, W. P. believed that they would return to St. Louis and start for Santa Fe, or the mountains, in spring 1834. But Sublette & Campbell, up against the corporate wall, agreed to what was called "the partition of Poland," a competitive truce that gave the Rocky Mountain Fur Company time to repay its debts.[443]

Although the military adventurer Captain Bonneville and the New England entrepreneur Nathaniel Wyeth mucked about in the mountain fur trade, most knowledgeable mountaineers were already convinced that the bonanza beaver trapping was finished.[444] The American Fur Company on the upper Missouri had already shifted to the buffalo-robe trade.

David put W. P. and Return Meigs back to digging lead on his St. Francois property, and he worked with them. William Pitt Jackson's letter to the folks at home from the Valle mines on 1 February 1835 reported that his father was away to the Mississippi Indian land sales. Two months later David called upon his son to take over a mercantile investment at Pototoc, Mississippi.[445]

William Pitt Jackson and a man named Parlow got into a scrape with a mob of rough miners. Young Jackson professed to misunderstand the cause but bragged that he had published his enemies as "the most degenerated cowards and swindlers," which they did not resent "as they feared the shot." Five days after the young gunman arrived in Pototoc he accidentally shot himself in the knee with his own pistol. The ball, "45 to the pound," lodged in his knee joint and had to be agonizingly extracted with his own gun screw.[446]

The typical frontier boom town of Pototoc was conceived by Thomas C. McMachin on 26 April 1836, but David Jackson's unlikely investment in the combination store and saloon preceded the incorporation. Perhaps it represented the collection of a debt rather than a new interest in mercantilism.

Standing six-foot-seven and bursting with strength, Return Meigs Jackson, an impressive frontiersman, could not resist showing off during the celebration of the glorious Fourth of July 1835. He strained himself by leaping as high as his own head and died two days later, probably from a strangulated hernia.

The unfathomable waste brought David to the consideration of his own mortality. The death of his mentor, Andrew Henry, two years earlier left little in Washington County to mark his passage. As Missouri bottom fevers weakened him, David remembered the mountains and despised the future.

A good coat, a handmade flannel shirt, and store-bought pants replaced the romantic buckskins and Indian beadwork. Working in the lead pits required tough jeans that David tucked into the top of his boots and held up with suspenders. The cotton handkerchief that protected his sunburned neck also wiped his brow. In his pockets he carried a pocket book, a burning glass, a comb, chewing tobacco, and a dirk for self-defense.[447]

Jackson made a working arrangement with neighbor Robert Chapman to purchase two lots on the main lead of the Merimack Mines for $300 in hand and $400 to be paid from the value of the mineral taken out. David gave Chapman $500 to get started and authorized him to purchase supplies, tools, and blasting powder in his name. But the men neglected to inspect the lots, and when digging began they discovered the property was smaller than the stated size and lay away from the main lead. When Jackson refused to complete payment Elias Gibson took him to the Franklin County Court.[448]

Jackson and Chapman shifted to a tract of the Virginia Mining Company held by the Inge family. In early 1836 the Inges sued Jackson & Chapman for $300, an action that became entangled with another filed by Nathaniel P. Hibard. The lawsuits in two counties dragged on through the rest of the year while the legal costs eroded David's cash. His appeal of an unfavorable judgment failed in December, and the final indignity came in Franklin County when Jackson's friend Stephen Compton attached the slave Moses to satisfy a $150 promissory note. Three days later Jackson was obliged to pay $339.80 to satisfy the Gibson judgment.[449]

With legal harpies circling, Jackson ordered his son to close the Pototoc store and come back to Missouri by the end of the year. David's declining fortunes resulted from more than bad judgment. The government had created another panic similar to the one of 1819, which drove him into the fur trade. Another speculative frenzy followed the opening of the southern Indian lands. From his concern that those flush times were getting out of hand, President Andrew Jackson ordered federal land officers to require hard cash for land purchases, a restriction that sent prices plummeting. The action wiped out those who had speculated beyond the real value. County sheriffs lay buried under foreclosures as the wildcat banks crashed and the frontier toppled into another depression.

David needed to collect his debts in Tennessee, but he considered William Pitt too inexperienced (or too hotheaded) to squeeze desperate men. Weak with fever, David left Missouri sometime after 25 January 1837.

By western standards twelve-year-old Paris, Tennessee, was a well-established place, boasting a population of eight hundred, including twelve lawyers, twelve doctors, and two clergymen. Exhausted by the trying two-week journey, David Jackson stayed at the home of his debtor. The family was infected with typhus, and in his weakened state David contracted the disease. A medical book of the time described the terrible symptoms:

> Typhus Fever: This first comes on with great weakness, low spirits, excessive weariness and general soreness, with pains in the head, back and extremities, succeeded by shiverings; the eyes appear full, yellow-ish and often a little inflamed; the arteries of the temple throb violently, the tongue is dry and parched, breathing laborious, interrupted by deep sighing; the breath is hot and offensive, urine pale, bowls costive.[450]

David's doctor treated his bilious vomiting with emetics. David's servant Jim gave him vinegar washes and tepid baths to assist sweating, a well-intended treatment that weakened a body struggling to throw off a deadly disease. And calling in a doctor did not always offer the best solution, as this telling portrait of frontier medicine indicates:

> . . . some unscrupulous horse doctor will set up his sign as "Physician and Surgeon" and draw his lancet on you, or fire a box of pills into your bowels, with a vague chance of hitting some disease unknown to him, but with a better prospect of killing the patient, who or whose administrator, he charged some ten dollars a trial for his marksmanship.[451]

Ironically, Jackson's doctor doubled as clerk of the probate court.

Typhus fever usually lasted about a week in warm climates, and David soon recovered enough to move to the tavern operated by John Atkins and Major Brown. In April he learned that his son William Pitt had died on 30 March. Joe Meek later recalled the hard rules that mountain men lived by: "If a man gets in trouble he is only laughed at; let him keep out; let him have better luck is what we say."[452]

Day after day David lay on a musty straw tick covered by flea-infested blankets and stared at the cobwebs in the rafters. Sometimes he thought he could still see the shining mountains, the high valleys fringed with trees, the deserts shimmering in the heat, but the corn-liquor drunks stomping and laughing in the tavern below broke those dreams. Sometimes strangers came up to gawk at the dying mountain man.

The letters that David wrote between those tortured dreams show he maintained hope. But by the end of November he made an admission to himself and sent Jim to fetch the county clerk. From his bed he executed a deed giving his nieces the old Francois Valle Spanish land grant on the Establishment River, the land he faithfully held for them.

His time running out, he had to contact his oldest son. Edward J. "Ned" Jackson had stayed at home looking after the West Fork farm and his mother. What he thought about his absentee father no longer mattered, because the two men had the business of a dying parent and an heir to conclude. On 12 December David began writing with remarkable clarity of purpose and mind as he systematically laid out the details that Ned would need to know to close out his business. The list of eighteen names reached back fourteen years and included men whom David had trusted but were sometimes unworthy of it.

Paris 12th December 1837 Western Tenasee

Dr Son

I have been here Since January last I have written you Since that time but not Received any answer I announced the Death of your Brother W. P. Jackson that I gave no detail of for I have never had any Perticulars from Mo my Self and knows the least how my business stands there of any Person that is interested.

I have been Sick all the last year and a great part of it confined so that I was not able to attend to any thing I have been here for the purpose of making Collections but had bad suckess and I think it advisable for you to come to Tenasee (Henry County Paris) where you will find me if you can come soon at the Tavern of Messrs Brown and Atkins or any remaining Papers with Dr Porter Clerk of the cty Court and my Phesician.

As there is Several of my Claims that is left in a very awkward situation, one on Kimp Holand too Hundred and upward of dolars the note was put into the hands of a lawyer for colection and I cant hear from lawyer nor Debtor 150 on Whartun Rector and I hold the Receipt of Captn Wm. Burch of Cooper Cty Mo Rector lives at Little Rock Arkansas $100 loaned to James Hamilton 1st Lieut of Dragoons in the fall 32 he was stationed at fourt Gibson Cherokee Lands and he says that he gave a Note to Wiliam Waldo in my favor and Waldo says he did not give said note you will have to call on Waldo for the facts you will find among some old Receipts of My advanceing for him and Charles Lee in Debt a balance of 8 dolars he lives in St. Louis and a conection of one of the wealthy houses of that place Colo W. B. Ayres holds a Note of mine for $15 and there ought to be a credit on it by Wawson for 10 the other five is to be paid.

Wm Waldo lives on the Osage River and can give you information pertaing considerable to my Business as he was Near 2 year in the Employ Love Hardisty is indebt a Mule and 50 dols that I paid a security not for that Waldo can act for and is in arrears him Self you will find amoungst papers his act by Self W. L. Subletts 5000 Hundred that I think I hold the note of [word crossed out]

Watkin Young I left on Red River of the west with three thousand Dolars in cash of My Money for to buy Mules and follow me and a Large outfit of Armes Amunition and tobacco Steel traps and &c belonging jointly to Jackson Waldo and Young for the purpose of catching beaver and I have not heard anything of him since and see book in Mo the amount of stock that I put in with D Waldo and I Expect that all the cance of geting any thing to do with him will be to watch him in St. Louis and bring him Up to Settlement

D Harris is by asumpact for oliver Wheeler $200 and there is a Large Settlement to make with Robt Chapman of a partnership business in Mining and in the first Purchase I advanced $500 and Chapman Some thing like 25 and had done More than a share of labor and you will get a bill from the Houses where I delt and they will show what part he has to pay for Powder and tools for blowing Rocky and call on Stephen Cumpton for infermation and a gentleman that will do all he can to assist you and he will tell ["him" crossed out] you where William Beers is I loaned him five Dolars that he had not paid and I dont know where you will find my mine book but likely at Runlletts vile My St afee Books is at your cousin Genings I have a claim against the Estate of Geo E. Jackson ["estate" crossed out] in the hands of Colo Grafton of a considerable amount that if the court grants me that I wish laid out in the purchase of the two Negroes for the use of the children, for Should my Case be favored by feelings it is tolerable Desperate and bring it to a close Give my Respects to your sisters and friend from

> Father with Due Respects
> D E Jackson

E J Jackson[453]

For a man who refused to leave a written record, he penned a good, workmanlike letter. The shadow on the Tetons had waited until the last possible moment to reveal himself, and he modified nothing by self-pity or apology. Two weeks later, on Christmas Eve, he died.

Epilogue

GUESSING THE CHARACTER of invisible men is risky. What kind of man would abandon his wife, family, and prospects to run off into the mountains for eight years? David's relationship with Juliet may appear as abandonment, but the evidence shows that he acted responsibly toward his family and tried to make the best of apparent incompatibility. At the time "pulling out" offered the solution to an impossible relationship, an escape the husband of one of David's daughters also followed. His sad letters home reveal the sense of guilt and loss.

Before coming to Missouri William Pitt Jackson apparently found his way to Williamson County, Tennessee, where he married Mary Ann Norman. They had a son born on 3 March 1832, and three years later Mary Ann died. The boy was taken to western Virginia to be raised by his grandmother, Juliet Jackson.[454]

With a list of strangers to run down instead of a proper will, David's son Edward ("Ned") faced some large problems with his father's estate. He had not seen his father since he was seven and only knew him through the reports of his uncles and the memories of a bitter mother.

Accompanied by his friend Joe Mitchell, Ned Jackson arrived in Paris, Tennessee, on 2 April 1838 to find that sympathetic Masonic brothers had buried the fur trader. When the probate court accepted Ned as his father's administrator, two local men, perhaps from the same fraternal loyalty, secured the $8,000 bond.

Ned and Mitchell raced to Missouri, where the news of Jackson's death arrived in February and by 11 April sent the harpies circling. The opportunists were disappointed to learn the estate inventory listed only the Negro man named Moses, who was already under legal attachment in Franklin County; the pistol that wounded William Pitt; and the land claim in St. Francois County. The deed executed at the last moment in Tennessee excluded the attractive Establishment Tract.

At the end of June Ned had himself declared defendant to address the claims, petitions, attachments, and suits by creditors. Inge obtained attachments and a judgment of $250 plus damages of $56.50. Hibbard inflated his claim against the estate to $1,000, which he said he paid to Jackson on 25 May

1837, a date when David was in Paris. The probate court allowed him only $575.14.[455]

During the summer Ned returned to Henry County, Tennessee, where he obtained 640 acres from David Jones at an additional cost of $960 and then resold it to him on 3 November for $1,500. He returned to Paris again in January 1839 and brought suit against John Ray for the overdue payment on the mules. They settled the matter out of court, denying history the final figure on the transcontinental stock drive.

One of the bondsmen protested Ned's petition to the Ste. Genevieve court for permission to sell his father's land to pay the debts of the estate, and the homestead was retained until July 1844, when a Ste. Genevieve lawyer named Ammoureaux finally disposed of it for $325. No evidence exists to indicate that Ned tried to recover any of the personal loans his father listed in his last letter.[456]

This pioneer cabin was relocated at Jackson's Mill State Park. The old man seated in the doorway is Edward J. Jackson, David's only surviving son.
—McWhorter Collection, Washington State University Archives

By 1840 the trail to Oregon was gaining reputation as the way to a new beginning. Tom Fitzpatrick guided the first significant party of emigrants in 1841. Jim Clyman, Black Moses Harris, and many other former mountaineers also shepherded pilgrims across the continent. David's younger brother John E. Jackson became an early plains traveler. Four cousins also made the trek to Oregon, where the influx of pioneers finally forced the resolution of the boundary question in 1846. During the California Gold Rush, Cummins Jackson, Ned, and eleven cousins and kinsmen rode among the first forty-niners. Several died chasing the elusive dream.

The tenacious Waldos remembered Ewing Young, who had drifted into Oregon in 1834 to reestablish himself as a rancher. When Young died intestate five years later, the community of retired mountaineers and Methodist missionaries had to deal with the disposal of his property, constituting the first step in the organization of the provisional Oregon government. Tough old Daniel Waldo, who came to Oregon in 1843, soon brought before the provisional government the matter of $3,000 in cash and $7,000 in equipment that Waldo and Jackson had furnished to Young in 1832.

Three auctions generated enough money to settle the estate plus some left over with no apparent heir. The temptation to use those funds fell heaviest on the sanctimonious mission party, which wanted to build a jail. Over the protests of thirty-eight right-minded citizens, proponents constructed the building at Oregon City and soon watched it burn down, torched by an anonymous libertarian.[457]

Waldo, who was determined to collect the money for the old Jackson, Waldo & Young partnership, gathered supporting statements from old mountaineers, including Joseph Gale, Stephen Meek, and Doc Newell. He presented these along with a petition to recover the funds to the provisional government on 11 December 1845. Facing the prospect of paying out money it had already spent, the confounded body referred the matter to a committee of three, two of whom were probably already acquainted with the circumstances from St. Louis or the Oregon Trail. They held that a qualified petition must identify Young, prove the partnership, and show the extent of Young's liability. They declared the supporting depositions inadmissible because they were taken without the state's presence to cross-examine.

Waldo returned to the Clackamas County Court in August 1846, and to the provisional government the following year, with his case in proper order. But an impoverished lawyer, whose incompetence was rewarded by making him a justice of the supreme court, discovered a loophole. J. Quinn Thornton found that the Jackson & Waldo claim failed to properly apply the rules and before an action could be brought, correct names must be used. Faced with beginning the suit "de novo," Daniel finally understood that the government of Oregon was not going to yield money it did not have.[458]

By January 1855 the gold rush had pumped so much cash into the Oregon economy that the territory was feeling flush. When a young Mexican boy presented a baptismal certificate dated 12 April 1833, the government accepted him as the son of Ewing Young by a Taos mother. Sixteen-year-old Joaquin Young left Taos in 1849 with his uncle Juan Cristoval Tafaya and Thomas Boggs. They went to Sonoma, California, where a community of former trappers, many from Oregon, knew about the Young estate.

On 27 June 1852 Charles Beaubien, Christopher Carson, and Manuel Lefebre swore in Taos that Joaquin Young was the issue of Maria Josepha Tafaya and Ewing Young, but they were unable to state specifically when Young had left her. About the same time a baptismal entry was inserted, out of chronological order, into the parish records. Back at San Jose on 1 March 1854 Joseph Gale wrote a supporting document, which Joaquin presented along with his petition to the legislative assembly of Oregon on 1 January 1855. The supreme court awarded him $4,994.64.

It appears that the presentations were fraudulent because Ewing Young was not in New Mexico nine months before the boy's birth. The skin games persisted to the very last.

Notes

Chapter One: "If ever he had a chosen people"

1. Dorothy Davis, *John George Jackson* (Parsons, WV: McClain Publishing Company, 1976), 1, 6, 342 n.1, 2. Hereafter cited as Davis, *JGJ*.

2. Morgan M. Brooks, "Pioneer Settlers of the Buckhannon Valley" (M.A. thesis, West Virginia Wesleyan College, 1934), 120. The descriptions of pioneer life and activities are from Henry Haymond, *History of Harrison County, West Virginia* (Morgantown, WV: Acme Publishing Company, 1910; Parsons, WV: McClain Printing Company, 1973); Roy Bird Cook, *The Family and Early Life of Stonewall Jackson* (Richmond: Old Dominion Press, 1924; Charleston, WV: Education Foundation Inc., 1967). Additional genealogical information came from the Carl D. W. Hays Collection of Jackson Family Papers in the possession of the author; hereafter cited as Hays Collection.

3. Brooks, "Pioneer Settlers," 124-27; Otis K. Rice, *The Allegheny Frontier: West Virginia Beginnings, 1730-1830* (Lexington: The University Press of Kentucky, 1970).

4. Elmer T. Clark, J. Manning Potts, and Jacob S. Payton, eds., *The Journal and Letters of Francis Asbury*, vol. 1 (Nashville: Abingdon Press, 1958), 577.

5. David Lavender, *The American Heritage History of The Great West*, ed. Alvin M. Josephy (New York: American Heritage Publishing Co., 1965), 60-61, 168; David Lavender, *Westward Vision: The Story of the Oregon Trail* (New York: McGraw-Hill Book Company, 1971), 661-64.

6. The tone of this is expressed in Alexander Scott Withers, *Chronicles of Border Warfare*, (1831; new edition ed. Reuben Gold Thwaites, Cincinnati: Stewart & Kidd Company, 1895).

7. At the age of ninety-one Elizabeth dictated her memoir to John George Jackson, which she qualified with the statement, "I will tell it as punctually as I can recollect it but I do not know that I am willing to swear to it." In Davis, *JGJ*, 6.

8. This speculative reconstruction is based on descriptions of life in Haymond, *Harrison County*, 265.

9. Davis, *JGJ*, 23-36.

10. The Indian captives are a fascinating part of the frontier experience. The tribes took them over for adoption to replace lost warriors. Many captives became convinced of the superiority of Indian life and, to the embarrassment of the white community, chose to remain with their adopted brethren. See James Axtell, "The White Captives," Chap. 13 in *The Invasion Within: The Contest of Cultures in Colonial North America* (New York: Oxford University Press, 1985).

11. The children of Edward and Mary Haddon Jackson were George E. Jackson, b. 23 December 1786, d. 26 March 1831; David E. Jackson, b. 30 October 1788, d. 24 December 1837; Jonathan Jackson, b. 25 September 1790, d. 25 March 1826; Rachael Jackson, b. 8 July 1792, d. ?; Mary (Polly) Jackson, b. 19 February 1794, d. 30 August 1840; and Rebecca Jackson, b. 15 September 1795, d. 18 July 1889. After Mary Haddon Jackson's death, Edward married Elizabeth Brake on 13 October 1799 and their children were Katharine Jackson, b. 25 July 1800, d. 3 December 1876; Cummins E. Jackson, b. 25 July 1802, d. 4 December 1849; James Madison Jackson, b. 3 April 1805, d. 27 October 1872; Elizabeth Jackson, b. April 1807, d. 22 February 1849; John E. Jackson, b. 22 January 1810, d. 18 July 1875; Margaret Jackson, b. 2 February 1812, d. ?; Return Meigs Jackson, b. 15 March 1814, d. 6 July 1835; Edward J. Jackson, b. 29 October 1817, d. 21 October 1848; and Andrew Jackson, b. 16 March 1821, d. 31 October 1867. Hays Collection.

12. Davis, *JGJ*, 33; Haymond, *Harrison County*, 260.

13. Edward Conrad Smith, *A History of Lewis County, West Virginia* (Weston: Self-published, 1920), 146-47.

14. Smith, *Lewis County*, 144. Richard Norris settled on the south side of Freeman's Creek and John Norris on Millstone Run. Other immigrants from Farquier and Culpepper counties included the Newton, Minter, and Bailey families.

15. Noble E. Cunningham, Jr., ed., *Circular Letters of Congressmen to Their Constituents, 1789-1829* (Chapel Hill: University of North Carolina Press, 1978), 309-13.

16. Davis, *JGJ*, 110. The connection between Burr and Jackson was Jonathan Dayton, former Speaker of the House, notorious land speculator, and supporter of the former vice-president.

17. J. G. Jackson to C. A. Rodney, 19 April 1807, Ohio Historical Society Library MSS; J. G. Jackson to George Jackson, 18 April 1807, quoted in Davis, *JGJ*, 124-28. *Reports of the Trials of Aaron Burr in the Circuit Court of the United States, Summer Term 1807,* (2 vols.), (Reprint, New York: DeCapo Press, 1969).

Chapter Two: "How my business stands"

18. William J. Petersen, *Steamboating on the Upper Mississippi* (Iowa City: The State Historical Society of Iowa, 1968), 68; Davis, *JGJ*, 150, 232-33. Venture commerce on the Ohio River was nothing new; British traders floated down soon after the conquest of New France in 1760. The prominent Pittsburgh trading firm of Bayton, Wharton, and Morgan even entertained the idea of establishing a separate western province. Ironically, one of those disappointed opportunists, George Morgan, blew the whistle on Burr's scheme.

19. Smith, *Lewis County*, 146, 147; Cook, *Stonewall*, 36.

20. Earle H. Morris, ed., *Marriage Records of Harrison County, Virginia [West Virginia] 1784-1850* (Fort Wayne Public Library, 1966), 65, 73. A conflicting record that David Jackson and Juliet Norris were married by Joseph Cheuvront on 3 November 1811 is not supported by other family evidence, and Juliet refuted it in a pension application that she filed many years later.

21. Haymond, *Harrison County*, 178; Hays Collection. The embarrassing stockings were preserved, but shrinkage spoiled any notion that they might provide a clue to Jackson's actual size.

22. David Sleeth vs. Edward Jackson Heirs, Bill of Particulars, 1828, Hays Collection.

23. Quoted in Barbara W. Tuchman, *The March of Folly* (New York: Alfred A. Knopf, 1984), 132.

24. Jackson vs. Gamble, June 1813, Ste. Genevieve County Court Records; National Archives Record Group 75, Fort Madison folder, drawer 43; also quoted in Donald Jackson, *Thomas Jefferson & the Stony Mountains: Exploring the West from Monticello* (Urbana: University of Illinois Press, 1981), 219; Reuben Gold Thwaites, *How George Rogers Clark Won the Northwest* (Chicago: A. C. McClung & Company, 1903), 323; *The History of Jo Davis County, Illinois* (Chicago: H. F. Kett & Company, 1878), 227.

25. Harrison County Court Minute Book 1811-1812, (15 June 1812), 388; also quoted in Haymond, *Harrison County*, 225.

26. J. G. Jackson to James Madison, 31 August 1812, in Davis, *JGJ*, 203, 375 n.62.

27. Davis, *JGJ*, 204-7. The congressman also offered to pay them from his own funds.

28. Haymond, *Harrison County*, 306-11; the volunteers returned by way of Zanesville, Ohio, where the congressmen told Jonathan Jackson on 22 November to return to Clarksburg while he remained in Ohio.

29. National Archives Record Group 94, microcopy M233, roll 7; Francis B. Heitman, *Historical Register and Dictionary of the United States Army*, vol. 2 (Washington, D.C.: 1903), 567; DEJ to Juliet Jackson, 7 August 1813; this and the letters to Juliet that follow are part of the Hays Collection.

30. Jackson family memento. My particular appreciation to Comdr. Elmer M. Jackson, Jr., who located and furnished a color copy.

31. National Archives Record Group 94, no. 5900, filed with 331904, A. G. O; Veteran's widow pension application of Juliet Jackson, 14 November 1853, Lewis County Court Records.

32. Davis, *JGJ*, 212, 228, 257-58. Jonathan married Julia Beckwith Neale of Parkersburg on 28 September 1817 and fathered the mighty "Stonewall" of Civil War fame.

33. Smith, *Lewis County*, 147, 162-69, 177.

34. George E. Jackson Estate Papers, Hays Collection.

35. The maiden name of George's wife, Helen, was McClanihan. The name of their daughter, Helen McGreggor Jackson, also identified a famous riverboat of the era.

36. Clarence E. Carter, ed., *The Territory of Illinois, 1814-1818*, vol. 17 in *The Territorial Papers of the United States* (Washington, D.C.: Government Printing Office, 1969), 371-72.

Chapter Three: "Mr. Henery leaves here by land"

37. Two excellent studies are Gregory M. Franzwa, *The Story of Ste. Genevieve* (St. Louis: Patrice Press Inc., 1967), and Lucille Basler, *The District of Ste. Genevieve, 1725-1980* (Ste. Genevieve: Self-published, 1980).

38. Malcomb J. Rohrbough, *The Land Office Business* (New York: Oxford University Press, 1968), 102-8.

39. Potosi took its name from a fabulous Peruvian (now Bolivian) gold mine. Within a radius of thirty miles were forty lead mines, most just shallow open pits worked by independent operators who sold their ore to Moses Austin. Henry R. Schoolcraft, *A View of the Lead Mines of Missouri* (New York: Charles Wiley & Co., 1819; Arno Press, 1972), 48-49.

40. The Chouteau family of St. Louis developed a debt interest in Julien Dubuque's Spanish mining grant and after his death sold it to a combination of St. Louis opportunists including John Smith T., who organized a strong-arm mining expedition in the spring of 1811. Thomas M. Marshall, *Life and Letters of Frederick Bates*, vol. 2 (St. Louis: Historical Documents Society, 1926), 90.

41. Mike Fink and John Smith, the stuff of Missouri folklore, came into western mythology on the coattails of Davy Crockett. See Daniel J. Boorstin, "Heroes and Clowns: Supermen from a Sub-literature," in *The Americans: The National Experience* (New York: Vintage Books, 1965); Henry Nash Smith, *Virgin Land: The American West as Symbol and Myth* (Cambridge: Harvard University Press, 1950).

42. What follows is a reconstruction based on documented information in Richard Oglesby, *Manuel Lisa and the Opening of the Missouri Fur Trade* (Norman: University of Oklahoma Press, 1963); and the same author, "Pierre Menard, Reluctant Mountain Man," *The Bulletin of the Missouri Historical Society* 24 (October 1967): 13-19. Confirming evidence also comes from the British traders on the North Saskatchewan River. See Elliott Coues, *The Manuscript Journals of Alexander Henry and David Thompson, 1799-1814* (Minneapolis: Ross & Haines, 1897; Ross & Haines, 1965), 720, 733-36.

43. The family of George and Elizabeth Henry came to the western marches of Penn's colony from northern Ireland and lived at York Furnace during the French and Indian Wars. Near the end of the Indian Rebellion of 1763, their son George married Margaret Young and the couple had six children; Andrew was born on 15 August 1775. York County, Pennsylvania Historical Society, Henry Family File, Marther (Steward) Fulcher, "George and Elizabeth Henry at Chanceford," 1 July 1975. At age eighteen Andrew Henry fell in love with a girl who his parents found unacceptable; he left home when they forbade the match. Henry was established at Ste. Genevieve by February 1803. Two years later he approached Louis Dufreuil Villars, a former officer of the Louisiana Regiment, for the hand of his daughter, Marie. Her mother was of the highly respected Valle family of Ste. Genevieve, an excellent social connection. The couple married on 16 December 1805. The marriage was a romantic disaster and the couple had separated by the following January; their divorce became final on 15 October 1807. Missouri Historical Society Alphabetical Files, Henry Family, statements of Mrs. George Henry, George Brackenridge pocket notebook.

44. Oglesby, *Manuel Lisa*, 69-70.

45. Oglesby, "Pierre Menard," 13-19.

46. The symbiosis is explained in Arthur J. Ray, *Indians in the Fur Trade: Their Role as Trappers, Hunters and Middlemen in the Lands Southwest of Hudson Bay, 1660-1870* (Toronto: University of Toronto Press, 1974). In early 1802 the Gros Ventre emphatically demonstrated their rejection of intrusion into tribal hunting reserves. See Alice M. Johnson, ed., *Saskatchewan Journals and Correspondence: Edmonton House 1795-1800, Chesterfield House 1800-1802* (London: The Hudson's Bay Record Society, 1967), 311 n.4, 321 n.5, 313-16, 317 n.1.

47. Thomas James, *Three Years Among the Indians and Mexicans* (Waterloo, IL: 1846; New York: Lippincott, 1962).

48. Reuben Lewis to Meriwether Lewis, Three Forks, 10 April 1810, Missouri Historical Society, Meriwether Lewis Papers in Dale L. Morgan, ed., *The West of William H. Ashley* (Denver: The Old West Publishing Company, 1964), xxxiii n.16. Many of the citations in my notes refer to this annotated collection of documents—hereafter cited as Morgan, *The West of Ashley*—from the archives of the Missouri Historical Society. Trusting the scholarship of Mr. Morgan, my references are to the documents as published.

49. A hill in the Hoback River exit from Jackson's Hole bears his name.

50. *St. Louis [Louisiana] Gazette*, 26 October 1811.

51. Henry told Brackenridge that the route selected by Lewis and Clark was perhaps "the very worst." Henry Marie Brackenridge, *Views of Louisiana* (Pittsburgh: 1814; Chicago: Quadrangle Books, Inc., 1962).

> "Mr. Henry, a member of the Missouri company and his hunters, have discovered several passes, not only very practicable, but even in their present state, less difficult than those of the Allegheny Mountains. These are considerably south of the source of the Jefferson River. It is the opinion of the gentleman last mentioned, that loaded horses and even wagons, might in its present state, go in the course of six or eight days, from a navigable point on the Columbia, to one on the waters of the Missouri—thus rendering an intercourse between settlements which may be formed on the Columbia, more easy than between those on the heads of the Ohio and the Atlantic states. Mr. Henry wintered in a delightful country, on a beautiful, navigable stream."

52. Thomas Biddle to Col. Henry Atkinson, 29 October 1819, in Morgan, *The West of Ashley*, 64, xlix-li.

53. Dorothy B. Dorsey, "The Panic of 1818 in Missouri," *Missouri Historical Review* 29, 2 (January 1935): 79.

54. Eugene C. Baker, ed., "The Austin Papers, Part I," *The American Historical Association Annual Report* 2 (1917); Thomas James, *Three Years Among the Indians*; Jackson Family Papers, Hays Collection. (Waterloo, IL: 1846; New York: Lippincott, 1962).

55. Ste. Genevieve County Archives, University of Missouri, Columbia, Microfilm F712, F713. The original documents are retained in the Ste. Genevieve County courthouse.

Chapter Four: "All the high points of the mountains were in view"

56. John E. Sunder, *Joshua Pilcher: Fur Trader and Indian Agent* (Norman: University of Oklahoma Press, 1968), 32-36.

57. Richard M. Clokey, *William H. Ashley: Enterprise and Politics in the Trans-Mississippi West* (Norman: University of Oklahoma Press, 1980), 45-46, 52, 62-64.

58. Richard Oglesby, "The Fur Trade as Business," *The Frontier Re-examined*, ed. John Francis McDermott (Urbana: University of Illinois Press, 1967), 117.

59. Atkinson to John C. Calhoun, Secretary of War, 25 January 1822 in Morgan, *The West of Ashley*, 1. *See also*, Roger L. Nicols, *General Henry Atkinson: A Western Military Career* (Norman: University of Oklahoma Press, 1965), 82.

60. W. Edwin Hemphill, ed., *The Papers of John C. Calhoun*, 17 vols. (Columbia: University of South Carolina Press, 1972), 6:633.

61. Ibid., 7:2. A notation on Ashley's license indicates that a similar document was also issued to Henry.

62. John Hendrick Weber, born at Altoona near Hamburg when it was still part of the Kingdom of Denmark, commanded a sailing vessel on the Baltic Sea before the Napoleonic wars. He lived in Ste. Genevieve by 1805, when he was a witness at Henry's wedding. During the War of 1812 he served in Captain McNair's company, which guarded the northern approaches to St. Louis. He killed an Indian in hand-to-hand combat. "Three Generations in the Span of a Continent: The Zumwalt Family," *Missouri Historical Review* (April 1954): 260-61.

63. Accounts, Petitions, etc., 1821-23 Court Records, Washington County, Missouri; Washington County Deeds, B52. Henry and Weber sold land on 1 March 1822 for $1,650, but Henry left his wife with just $200, which suggests that the rest of the money went into the Ashley-Henry business.

64. Probate Court, Ste. Genevieve, Missouri, George E. Jackson Estate Papers, show David protected his brother's property from attachment by some clever rental transactions.

65. Basler, *The District of Ste. Genevieve*, 105; 1822 Tax Book, Ste. Genevieve County, Missouri.

66. George also executed a note attesting receipt of the slaves: "Received of David E. Jackson two Negroes slaves the Property of Edward Jackson to wit Jack & Aleck which I am to Pay at the Rate of sixty Dollars per year Pay tax Cloathing and Risk of sickness But should either Die or Run away then my hire ceases to be Paid on the one so Dieing or absconding to wit thirty Dollars I am to Keep said Negroes until said D E Jacksons Return unless Called on by Edward Jackson for said Negrois Provid nevertheless Im Not to Pay Hire to None else than to David unless By his order. April the 1st 1822, [signed] George E. Jackson." Hays Collection.

67. Hempstead to Pilcher, 3 April 1822, in Morgan, *The West of Ashley*, 3. Daniel Potts put the number of men leaving St. Louis at one hundred. See Potts to Brother, 16 July 1826 in Donald McKay Frost, *Notes on General Ashley, the Overland Trail, and South Pass* (Worcester, MA: The American Antiquarian Society, 1945), 59.

68. O'Fallon to Secretary of War, St. Louis, 9 April 1822, in Morgan, *The West of Ashley*, 6.

69. Later references to a black companion support the speculation about Jim. Taking personal slaves up the Missouri was not unusual, as evidenced by Lewis and Clark's man, York. Freehearty, killed at Three Forks in 1810, was apparently accompanied by a slave. In 1829-30 Jedediah Smith had a slave with him.

70. *St. Louis Enquirer*, 13 April 1822, in Frost, *Notes on Ashley*, 68. *Franklin Intelligencer*, 30 April 1822. Williams previously trapped for the Missouri Fur Company south of the Big Horn post and may have even penetrated into the Green River valley.

71. Alberta Wilson Constant, *Paintbox on the Frontier: The Life and Times of George Caleb Bingham* (New York: Thomas J. Crowell Company, 1974), 25-32.

72. Potts to Cochlen, 7 July 1824. The five letters of Daniel Potts appear to be the only first-hand account of field operations between 1822 and 1828. Frost published those recovered from the *Philadelphia Gazette and Daily Advertiser* issues of 14 November 1826, 27 September 1827, and 19 October 1827. The September-October 1947 issue of *Yellowstone Nature Notes* 21 published two more that had survived in family hands. The letters are: Potts to Thomas Cochlen, Rocky Mountains, 7 July 1824; Potts to Robert Potts, Rocky Mountains, 16 July 1826; Potts to Robert Potts, Sweet Lake, 8 July 1827; Potts to Dr. Lukens, Sweet Lake, 8 July 1827; Potts to Robert Potts, St. Louis, 13 October 1828.

73. A. Bulgar, Governor of the District of Assiniboia, Notice of 10 June 1823, *Public Archives of Canada Publication* 9 (Ottawa, 1914), which called for the arrest of Kenneth McKenzie, Wm. Laidlaw, and James Murdock [Kipp?], former HBC employees who had absconded.

74. The early history of Mandan visitations is traced in W. Raymond Wood and Thomas D. Thiessen, eds., *Early Fur Trade on the Northern Plains: Canadian Traders Among the Mandan and Hidatsa Indians, 1738-1818* (Norman: University of Oklahoma Press, 1985).

75. See "Account of Ashley & Henry for Property Lost to the Indians, 1822-1823," and "Deposition of Joshua Griffith, St. Louis, January 12, 1824," in Morgan, *The West of Ashley*, 70-72. Two individual hunters also lost animals, which suggests some degree of self-financing among the hunters.

76. Russell Reid and C. G. Gannon, eds., "Journal of the Atkinson-O'Fallon Expedition," *North Dakota Historical Quarterly* 4 (October 1929): 41.

77. In his 1830s recollection of the Ashley-Henry effort, Jedediah Smith left many details to be filled in by Ashley, who failed to add them. See Maurice S. Sullivan, *The Travels of Jedediah Smith: A Documentary Outline including the Journal of the Great American Pathfinder* (Santa Ana, CA: The Fine Arts Press, 1934), 1, 8, 160 n.5.

78. Clokey, *William H. Ashley*, 70-73, states that forty-six more men were recruited in St. Louis. Some of Ashley's two crews may have turned back, but deserters from Henry's party, like Potts, were picked up en route.

79. O'Fallon to Ramsay Crooks, Fort Atkinson, 10 July 1822, in Morgan, *The West of Ashley*, 17-18.

80. "Genl Wm. H. Ashley and Major Henry have now ninety-seven men at or near the mouth of the Yellowstone and intend to take on from one to two hundred more next spring." (Duff Green to Calhoun, Chariton, Missouri, 3 January 1823, in Hemphill, *Papers of John C. Calhoun*, 6:403.)

81. Sullivan, *Travels of Jedediah Smith*, 8; Morgan, *The West of Ashley*, 237 n.115, 283 n.181.

82. Potts to Cochlen, 7 July 1824, *Yellowstone Nature Notes*; Sullivan, *Travels of Jedediah Smith*, 9.

83. This speculation is based on actions of the Smith-Fitzpatrick party when it entered this same area the following year.

Chapter Five: "This territory being trapped by both parties"

84. Donald McKenzie, "Journal of Occurrences, Bow River Expedition," Hudson's Bay Company Archives (hereafter cited as HBCA) B34/a/4, fols. 13-13d, Provincial Archives of Manitoba, Winnipeg.

85. McKenzie to Hunt, Fort Nez Perces, 20 April 1821; McKenzie to Hunt, Hudson's Bay, 30 July 1822, MS 246, Oregon Historical Society, Portland; Milo Milton Quaife, ed., *Adventures of the First Settlers on the Oregon or Columbia River* (New York: Citadel Press, Inc., 1969); Kenneth A. Spaulding, ed., *Alexander Ross: The Fur Hunters of the Far West* (Norman: University of Oklahoma Press, 1956). Ross, *First Settlers*; Ross, *Fur Hunters*, 186-86.

86. Weapons trade did not receive the kind of attention given the liquor business, but Thomas Hempstead let slip a clue in his 5 May 1823 letter to Pilcher. Ashley had been allowed to buy guns that his supplier, Bostwick, brought over the Allegheny Mountains for the Missouri Fur Company. The great demand resulted in even used and repaired weapons sold to the Indians. See Hempstead to Pilcher, St. Louis, 5 May 1823, in Morgan, *The West of Ashley*, 8-9.

87. McKenzie, "Chesterfield House Journal," HBCA B34/a/4, fols. 13-13d. On 25 November 1822 Sarsi Indians reported that the Piegans were trading with the Americans "and the Americans gave them to understand that they intended to Establish a Post at the

Bears [Marias] River above the Belly where they intended to trade largely and supply the natives at a lower rate than the European traders." Edmonton House Journal, HBCA B60/a/21, fol. 7.

88. McKenzie, B34/a/4, fol. 31d.

89. McKenzie, B34/a/4, fol. 21; John Edward Harriot, "Memoirs of Life and Adventures in Hudson's Bay Territories, 1819-1825," Coe Collection of Western American History, Yale University Library, New Haven, CT.

90. Ray, *Indians in the Fur Trade*, 195-216.

91. Edmonton House Journal, 25 March 1823, HBCA B60/a/22, 26; Governor Simpson's Dispatch, 10 August 1832, HBCA A12/1, 460.

92. Spokane House Journal 1822-23, HBCA B208/a/1, fols. 12, 13.

93. "Deposition of Hugh Johnson, January 13, 1824," in Morgan, *The West of Ashley*, 72. The Indians could have been the River Crows, who had a nearby winter camp, or the Blackfoot and Gros Ventre scouts who were watching it.

94. This promising opportunity for some field archaeology brings up the unresolved question of how many men Henry took up the river. Dale L. Morgan, *Jedediah Smith and the Opening of the West* (New York: Bobbs-Merrill Company, 1953), 63, says eleven, but that must have been just the boat party because each hunter would not have had fifteen traps. Henry must have taken at least a third of the ninety-seven men available to him. The fourth of May was late in the trapping season, and his hunters may have been scattered.

95. *St. Louis Enquirer*, 13 April 1822, and Potts to Cochlen, 7 July 1824, in Morgan, *The West of Ashley*, 6-7.

96. This conclusion is based on sources placing both Smith and Jackson downriver later at the Arikara fight. See note 102 below, which begins, "Jackson's participation . . . "

97. *Missouri Republican*, 15 January 1823, in Morgan, *The West of Ashley*, 19; Clokey, *William H. Ashley*, 85-89.

98. Charles L. Camp, ed., *James Clyman, Frontiersman: The Adventures of a Trapper and Covered-Wagon Emigrant as told in his Own Reminiscences and Diaries* (Portland: Champoeg Press, 1960), 5-6. Clyman wrote this memoir at Napa, California, in spring 1871. These documentary sources are not as immediate as they seem. They often reflect the imperfect memories of men well after the events they recall.

99. John E. Sunder, *Bill Sublette, Mountain Man* (Norman: University of Oklahoma Press, 1959).

100. LeRoy R. Hafen, *Broken Hand: The Life of Thomas Fitzpatrick, Mountain Man, Guide and Indian Agent* (Denver: The Old West Publishing Company, 1973); St. Francois County folder, Tax Lists, Missouri Historical Society, St. Louis. A Thomas Fitzpatrick was on the tax roll of 1822 but not the following year.

101. Frank Triplett, *Conquering the Wilderness: or New Pictorial History of the Life and Times of the Pioneer Heros and Heroines of America, &c, &c* (Minneapolis: L. M. Ayer Publishing Co, 1889). Guaranteed to outrage modern sensibilities, this book accurately represents attitudes of its time. Triplett interviewed the eighty-four-year-old Eddie in 1883, three years after the Missouri Historical Society published Waldo's recollections.

102. Jackson's participation in the battle derives from William Waldo's recollections. Waldo was intimately familiar with Jackson as a neighbor in western Virginia, from his brother David Waldo's association with him, and from personal acquaintance. See Stella

Drumm, ed., "Recollections of a Septuagenarian by William Waldo of Texas," *Missouri Historical Society Glimpses of the Past* 5 (April-June 1938): 38. Smith is portrayed kneeling over the fallen Gibson while angels hover around in an unintentionally hilarious painting that hangs in the South Dakota State Capitol. It is reproduced in Sullivan, *Travels of Jedediah Smith*, f. 10. Camp, *James Clyman*, 8-12, gives a vivid remembrance of the battle. See also William H. Ashley's letters to the *Missouri Republican*, 4 June 1823; to Major Benjamin O'Fallon, 4 June 1823; and to a gentleman in Franklin, Missouri, 7 June 1823, all in Morgan, *The West of Ashley*, 25-31.

103. "Account of Ashley & Henry for Property Lost to the Indians, 1822-1823," in Morgan, *The West of Ashley*, 70.

104. The color portrait of Iron Shirt painted in 1833 by artist Karl Bodmer speaks for itself. It is reproduced as the frontispiece in Morgan, *The West of Ashley*; see also, Davis Thomas and Karin Ronnefeldt, *People of the First Man* (New York: E. P. Dutton, 1976), 134; and David Hunt, et al., eds., *Karl Bodmer's America* (Lincoln: University of Nebraska Press, 1984), 246.

105. Edmonton House Journal, 28 November 1823 and 16 March 1824, HBCA B60/a/22, 26d-28, and 48d.

106. Pilcher to O'Fallon, Fort Recovery, 23 July 1823, which forwards Gordon to Pilcher, Fort Vanderburgh (Mandan villages), 15 June 1823, in Morgan, *The West of Ashley*, 48-50. About a thousand pelts believed taken from Americans were later traded at Edmonton House by individual Indians who brought them in small lots.

107. A. P. Nasatir, "The International Significance of the Jones and Immell Massacre and of the Aricara Outbreak of 1823," *Pacific Northwest Quarterly* 30 (January 1939): 80-107.

108. "Ashley & Henry's Second License to Trade with the Indians, March 12, 1823," and Ashley to Col. John O'Fallon, Fort Brassaux, 19 July 1823, in Morgan, *The West of Ashley*, 47-48.

109. Col. Henry Leavenworth to O'Fallon, 21 July 1831; Ashley to O'Fallon, 4 June 1823; and Ashley to a gentleman in Franklin, Missouri, 7 June 1823, all in Morgan, *The West of Ashley*, 52, 27-31. Morgan incorrectly identified this George Jackson as a Booneslick settler (see p. 294 n.235), but according to the *Missouri Intelligencer*, 8 July 1823, that man had been appointed as administrator of an estate.

110. For evidence supporting Jackson's loan to Wheeler, see DEJ to his son, Edward J. Jackson, 12 December 1837, Hays Collection.

111. Spokane House Journal 1822-23, HBCA B208/a/1, fols. 12, 13; "Spokane Report 1822-23," HBCA B208/e/1, fol. 4. The fourteen were J. Gardipee, Francois Wm. Hodgens, Pierre Cassawasa, Francois Method, J. McLeod, Thos. Nakarsheta, Patrick O'Conner, Jos. St. Armand, Ignace Sokhonie, his stepson, Louis St. Michael, Franc H [X] Frenestoresue, Lazard Teycaleyecourigi, and Ignace Tahekeurate. Gardipee and St. Michael had been robbed by the Crows in 1813.

112. O'Fallon to Pilcher, Fort Atkinson, 1 August 1823, in Morgan, *The West of Ashley*, 51.

113. "Spokane Report 1822-23," HBCA B208/e/1, fol. 3d. states: "The custom of giving debts has not yet been introduced in this district. furs are paid for as presented. we are in the habit of advancing large supplies to freemen who are old Canadian and Iroquois—many of them having large families, wander about like Indians and adopt their manner of life. these people generally summer in the Snake country well stocked in some parts with beaver and near the buffalo."

114. J. Cecil Alter, *James Bridger: Trapper, Frontiersman, Scout and Guide* (Columbus, Ohio: Long's College Book Company, 1951), 25-36.

115. The Mike Fink legend began after his death as a by-product of a book inflating Davy Crockett. See Daniel J. Boorstin, *The Americans: The National Experience* (New York: Vintage Press, 1965), 327.

116. "Names of Persons Killed belonging to the parties of Wm. H. Ashley and Smith, Jackson & Sublette, &c, &c." Morgan, *Jedediah Smith*, 344. It is possible that they were stragglers from the Missouri Fur Company's Musselshell group.

117. "Spokane Report 1822-23," HBCA B208/e/1, fol. 4; Servant's Accounts, Canadians, 1821-39, HBCA B239/x/2, fol. 53; McDonald to John George McTavish, Spokane House, 5 April 1824, HBCA B239/c/a, fols. 140-140d. McDonald referred to the American trappers who came upriver after Lewis and Clark. He was with David Thompson when the property of the slain Charles Courtin was distributed.

118. Ashley to *St. Louis Enquirer*, 17 November 1823, in Morgan, *The West of Ashley*, 63-64.

Chapter Six: "They have traversed every part of the country"

119. J. N. B. Hewitt, ed., *Journal of Rudolph Friederich Kurz* (Lincoln: University of Nebraska Press, 1970), plates 1, 6, 11.

120. Leavenworth to Maj. Gen. Alexander Macomb, Fort Atkinson, 20 December 1823, in Morgan, *The West of Ashley*, 68. This cites the report of Henry's activities brought in by Fitzgerald and the two Harrises who left the major on the Big Horn.

121. I have no direct proof of Jackson's role and base this on the reasoning that he had prior preparation for his later superintendence and a good background in pioneer business. Near the end of his life Jackson was still concerned about his field account books.

122. Leavenworth to Macomb, 20 December 1823, in Morgan, *The West of Ashley*, 68, repeating the news from Henry's messengers sent back from the mouth of the Powder.

123. DEJ to Edward J. Jackson, 12 December 1837, in the Hays Collection. See also "Memorandum by General Clark" in Morgan, *Jedediah Smith*, 342.

124. Potts to Cochlen, 7 July 1824, *Yellowstone Nature Notes*.

125. Black's identity is puzzling. He was still traveling with Smith in 1829 (when Joe Meek told about stealing a porcupine from "a negro boy, belonging to Jedediah Smith") but was with Jackson in spring 1830. Black's Fork of the Green River is named for him.

126. Morgan, *Jedediah Smith*, 78-86; Camp, *James Clyman*, 15-20.

127. The allure of Indian values and lifestyle often burdened whites on the frontier, and they occasionally lost children to that other world. Stories from David's Uncle Brake, who had been a former captive, may have preconditioned David's attitudes toward Indians.

128. Morgan, *The West of Ashley*, 245 n.169, speculates that Eddie, Branch, and Stone were not with Smith from the beginning.

129. See Frederick Merk, *Fur Trade and Empire: George Simpson's Journal . . . 1824-1825* (Cambridge: Harvard University Press, 1931), 191, 193-94, 195.

130. *St. Louis Enquirer*, 7 June 1824, in Morgan, *The West of Ashley*, 76, 77-78; Morgan, *Jedediah Smith*, 106-9.

131. O'Fallon to Superintendent of Indians William Clark, Council Bluffs, 9 July 1824, in Morgan, *The West of Ashley*, 82-83.

132. Baker, "The Austin Papers," citing John Hawkins to Col. Stephen F. Austin, Prearie Spring, County of Washington, 21 September 1824. This valuable document rehabilitates Henry's maligned reputation as a founder of the trade. See also, J. B. Meetch to John Davis, Perry Township, St. Francois County, Missouri, 4 October 1824, Yale University Library, Coe Collection MSS; and *Arkansas Gazette*, 16 November 1824, both in Morgan, *The West of Ashley*, 255, 97.

133. Hawkins to Austin, 21 September 1824.

134. The circumstances of the documents' creation may explain the contesting versions. "Solitaire" (John S. Robb) contributed his edification of Fitzpatrick to the *St. Louis Weekly Reveille* of 1 March 1847, when the admirers of the deceased Ashley were appropriating discovery for their hero. Robb had access to his editor, Keemle, or other unnamed witnesses, possibly Eddie or Caleb Greenwood, who had returned from California in summer 1846 accompanied by James Clyman. After visiting friends and family in Wisconsin, Clyman returned early in 1848 through St. Louis, where he must have seen the Solitaire article. When Clyman dictated his remembrances at Napa in 1871 he may have been trying to refute those previous opinions. See Hafen, *Broken Hand*, 338-42, for the complete Solitaire statement and Camp, *James Clyman*, 7-29, for Clyman's narrative.

135. Virginia Cole Trenholm and Maurine Carley, *The Shoshonis: Sentinels of the Rockies* (Norman: University of Oklahoma Press, 1964), 22-40; Brigham D. Madsen, *The Northern Shoshoni* (Caldwell, ID: The Caxton Printers Ltd., 1980); Ake Hultkrantz, "The Shoshones in the Rocky Mountain Area," in *Shoshone Indians* (New York: Garland Publishing Company, 1974). According to information shared by Merle Wells, Shoshoni is a French and English designation of Indians that the Spanish, using a Ute derivation, knew as Comanche. After they obtained horses, the bands that expanded into Texas became known as Comanche while those who expanded into Dakota, Montana, Saskatchewan, and Alberta were identified as Shoshoni but usually called Snakes.

136. Camp, *James Clyman*, 25-26.

137. One informant, favoring Fitzpatrick, stated that Smith did not even make the trip up the Wind River valley, staying instead in the winter camp to tend the worn-out horses and mules. Solitaire, "Major Fitzpatrick: The Discoverer of South Pass," *St. Louis Weekly Reveille*, 1 March 1847, in Hafen, *Broken Hand*, 339-40.

138. Camp, *James Clyman*, 20-25. Note that Clyman does not name Smith in the party that attempted Union Pass.

139. Rollins, Philip Ashton, ed., *The Discovery of the Oregon Trail: Robert Stuart's Narrative* (New York: Charles Scribners Sons, 1935), 154, identifies a place fifteen miles up Hoback River that the returning Astorians saw in 1812 as "Henery's Hill."

140. Potts to Cochlen, 7 July 1824, *Yellowstone Nature Notes*.

141. Clokey, *William H. Ashley*, 120, 132.

142. Ibid., 122-33. It is possible that Ashley-Henry agreed not to bring out an outfit in summer 1824 and hoped to squeak by with the supplies on hand. But that does not answer how they expected to bring out the returns, or why Henry sent two expensive letters to his partner.

143. O'Fallon to Clark, Council Bluffs, 9 July 1824; O'Fallon to Atkinson, Fort Atkinson, 15 July 1824; Graham to Clark, St. Louis, 28 July 1824; *St. Louis Enquirer*, 14 June 1824, 19 July 1824, all in Morgan, *The West of Ashley*, 81-87.

144. Hawkins to Austin, 21 September 1824; Potts to Cochlen, 7 July 1824; *Yellowstone Nature Notes*; Potts to Brother, Rocky Mountains, 16 July 1826; Frost, *Notes on Ashley*, 56-59. Henry provided a contingency plan for the hunters if he was unable to supply them, but Potts, buoyed by his success at trapping, was prepared to stay for two years and expected to earn $1,200.

145. About sixteen men may have stayed on the Yellowstone. Some were probably free hunters formerly associated with the Missouri Fur Company.

146. Hafen, *Broken Hand*, 39-41, 340. Solitaire placed Tom's cache in the canyon between the Sweetwater and Goat Island. Lucien Fontenelle's pack string took forty-five days to complete the 1,400-mile round trip, which showed that Ashley could have gotten a supply column up the Platte in time for the rendezvous.

147. Frost, *Notes on Ashley*, 134, cites the 21 September 1824 *Arkansas Gazette*, which was picked up by the *National Intelligencer*, 25 September 1824. The *St. Louis Enquirer* article of 16 November 1824 was picked up by *Nile's Weekly Register*, 4 December 1824. Morgan, *The West of Ashley*, 257 n.22, made a convoluted argument that appears to be an attempt to discredit Andrew Henry's perception of the overland route.

148. Returning from the upper Snake River in 1811, Henry told Henry Marie Brackenridge that the upper Missouri-Snake portage hoped for by President Jefferson was possible, but optimism about Snake River navigation turned to pessimism after the overland Astorians reported their experience. Henry's statement shows he was interested in a transcontinental connection.

149. William Carr Lane to Wife, 31 August 1824, in Morgan, *The West of Ashley*, 87; J. E. B. Austin to Austin, Hazel Run, 6 September 1824; John Hawkins to Austin, 21 September 1824, in Baker, "Austin Papers." The scene in the warehouse is from Clokey, *William H. Ashley*, 133.

150. Brackenridge's Interview with Mrs. George Henry, Missouri Historical Society, Henry Family File.

151. Clokey, *William H. Ashley*, 136 n.43.

152. Three children were born to Andrew and Mary Henry: Patrick in 1826, Mary in 1830, and George, born eight months after the death of his father on 10 June 1832. Before his death Henry selected a burial site for himself in a corner of his property. After his estate was settled, only $150 remained for the widow, who had to face the consequence of marriage to a man of integrity. Perhaps that was a reason that the grave site was soon forgotten.

153. Historians who find problems with the integrity of Andrew Henry have attempted to diminish his character. The 18 June 1833 obituary that appeared in the *Missouri Republican* described Henry as "a man much respected for his honesty, intelligence and enterprise," which was the view that the fur trade historian Chittenden adopted in his 1902 publication. Louis Houck, *A History of Missouri* vol. 3, (Chicago, 1908), 95-97, began restating the facts concerning Henry. When Walter B. Douglas edited Thomas James's *Three Years Among the Indians and Mexicans* (St. Louis, Missouri Historical Society) in 1916, he could not resist adding, "the tradition still lingers that he was his own worst enemy."

Chapter Seven: "The grand rendezvous of the persons engaged in that business"

154. Ashley to Gen. Henry Atkinson, St. Louis, 1 December 1825, in Harrison Clifford Dale, ed., *The Ashley-Smith Explorations and the Discovery of a Central Route to the Pacific 1822-1829* (Glendale: The Arthur H. Clark Company, 1941), 153.

155. Potts to Brother, Rocky Mountains, 16 July 1826, in Frost, *Notes on Ashley*, 59.

156. Charles L. Camp, ed., *George C. Yount and his Chronicles of the West* (Denver: The Old West Publishing Company, 1966), 76-77.

157. Howard R. Lamar, *The Trader on the American Frontier: Myth's Victim* (College Station: Texas A & M University Press, 1977), 17, 21, 25, notices the ancient plains patterns. W. Raymond Wood, "Plains Trade in Prehistoric and Protohistoric Intertribal Relations," in *Anthropology in the Great Plains* (Lincoln: University of Nebraska Press, 1980), 99, 102-3, and map, shows patterns of intertribal trade that came from the Dalles of the Columbia River fisheries through this intermountain Shoshoni exchange point. Other trade fairs were held near the Walla Walla River, in the Grand Ronde Valley, on the Boise River, and near the mouth of the Portneuf.

158. William H. Goetzman, "The Mountain Man as Jacksonian Man," *American Quarterly* 15 (Fall 1963): 404-5.

159. HBCA B202/a/1, published as T. C. Elliott, "Journal of Alexander Ross—Snake Country Expedition," *Oregon Historical Quarterly* 14 (December 1913): 383-85.

160. Finan McDonald, "Spokane District Journal," HBCA B208/a/1 and HBCA B202/a/1; Simpson to Ross, 29 October 1824, 11 January 1825, D4/5; Alexander Kennedy to Simpson, Spokane, 12 April 1823, cited as HBC Journal no. 606 in Merk, *Fur Trade and Empire*, 193-94.

161. Elliott, "Journal of Alexander Ross"; Morgan, *Jedediah Smith*, 127-29, 398 n.30.

162. Elliott, "Journal of Alexander Ross"; HBCA B202/a/1, 55d in Morgan, *Jedediah Smith*, 128-30.

163. Potts to Brother, 16 July 1826, in Frost, *Notes on Ashley*, 56-59.

164. E. E. Rich, ed., *Peter Skene Ogden's Snake Country Journals: 1824-25 and 1825-26* (London: The Hudson's Bay Record Society, 1950), 43.

165. When Col. Edward Jackson learned that his son was going into the mountains he deeded property directly to his grandchildren as a form of life insurance for David. Hays Collection.

166. Rich, *Peter Skene Ogden*, 43-46.

167. Elliott, "Journal of Alexander Ross," states in HBCA B202/a/1: "It is evident part of [our deserters of 1822] have reached the American posts on the Yellowstone and Big Horn with much fur. I suspect these Americans have been on the lookout to decoy more."

168. That unavoidable courtesy was not the reason Governor Simpson replaced Ross with Ogden, since he made that decision before the two rival parties even met. It had to do with Ross's regrettable habit of sending suggestions up the chain of command.

169. "Made Beaver" was an accounting term based on the value of a prime beaver pelt but applicable to many other furs.

170. Elliott, "Journal of Alexander Ross," HBCA B202a/1.

171. Ogden's most recent biographer is Gloria Griffin Cline, *Peter Skene Ogden and the Hudson's Bay Company* (Norman: University of Oklahoma Press, 1974).

172. See Merk, *Fur Trade and Empire*, which was published when the conservative HBC still kept most of its records close to the vest.

173. Elliott, "Journal of Alexander Ross," HBCA B202/a/1; Flathead Post Journal, B69/a/ 1; Merk, *Fur Trade and Empire*, 263.

174. The HBCA documentation of the Snake Brigade is in Ogden's 1824-25 Snake Country journal, B202/a/2, and "Journal of William Kittson," B202/a/3. Both of these are published in Rich, *Peter Skene Ogden*; excerpts have also appeared in David E. Miller, ed., "Peter Skene Ogden's Journal of his Expedition to Utah in 1825," *Utah Historical Quarterly* 20, 2 (April 1952), which clarifies the geography. See also, David E. Miller and David H. Miller, "Appendix A, Some Revisions to Ogden's 1824-25 Route," in Glyndwr Williams, ed., *Peter Skene Ogden's Snake Country Journals, 1827-28 and 1828-29* (London: Hudson's Bay Record Society, 1971), 169-72.

175. David J. Weber, *The Taos Trappers: The Fur Trade in the Far Southwest, 1540-1846* (Norman: University of Oklahoma Press, 1968), 74-76; William S. Wallace, "Antoine Robidoux," in LeRoy R. Hafen, ed., *The Mountain Men and the Fur Trade of the Far West* vol. 4, (Glendale: The Arthur H. Clark Company, 1965-72), 261-62.

176. Ogden to Governor, Chief Factors, and Chief Traders, East Fork of the Missouri, 10 July 1825, HBCA D4/119, fols. 10d-11, 12. This was published in Frederick Merk, "The Snake Country Expedition Correspondence, 1824-5," *Mississippi Valley Historical Review* 21 (June 1934): 86-93; and also in Frederick Merk, *The Oregon Question: Essays in Anglo-American Diplomacy and Politics* (Cambridge: The Belknap Press of Harvard University Press, 1946), 86-92.

177. Rich, *Peter Skene Ogden*, 46.

178. It would be convenient to associate John S. and Johnson Gardner with the dedicated frontiersman Benjamin Gardner, who came to Spanish Louisiana with the Bryan family in 1800 and located at Femme Osage near Daniel Boone. Benjamin Gardner often went on hunting expeditions that lasted four or six months. He died in 1805. In March 1811 his Spanish land grant of 750 arpents of land (about 640 acres) was confirmed to him "or his legal heirs." Ten years later the St. Charles post office held a letter for and tried to locate Russell Gardner, and in April 1824 the St. Louis post office published a similar advertisement for Johnson Gardner. Nancy Gardner was appointed executrix of the deceased Mary Gardner on 14 May 1823 and immediately sold a slave to help meet expenses. John S. Gardner was also mentioned in those public notices, which were published in the *Missouri Republican*.

179. Rush Welter, *The Mind of America, 1820-1860* (New York: Columbia University Press, 1975), 73.

180. See Davis, *JGJ*, for the best survey of Jackson family political understanding.

181. Weber had twenty-nine men after losing one, and Smith brought in seven. The camp guard was approximately eleven, of which three or four were leaders and minor investors.

182. Rich, *Peter Skene Ogden*, 233-34.

183. John C. Jackson, "Charles McKay," in Hafen, *The Mountain Men and the Fur Trade* vol. 9, 256.

184. Ogden's letter of 10 July 1825, Merk, *Oregon Question*, 86-92. There is a charming, though apparently false, story that contends Ogden's country wife, Julia Rivet, risked the American guns to recover an HBC horse that held her baby in an attached cradle board.

185. Rich, *Peter Skene Ogden*, 53-54.

186. Provost must have told Gardner about the Atkinson-O'Fallon expedition of 1825, which planned to go to the mouth of the Yellowstone and conclude treaties of amity with most of the river tribes.

187. Merk, *Oregon Question*, 86.

Chapter Eight: "All the men . . . with whom I had concern in the country"

188. The Snake Brigade started with fifty-eight hunters. Following the confrontation with the Americans, Kittson listed twenty-two freemen, eleven engaged men, and six boys, for a total of thirty-nine. After Godin, Gervais, and Sasanare left, the brigade had thirty-six, which raised the number of deserters to twenty-two. Rich, *Peter Skene Ogden*, 235.

189. Morgan, *Jedediah Smith*, 143, 400.

190. Hawkins to Austin, Prearie Spring County of Washington, Missouri, 21 September 1824, in Baker, "Austin Papers."

191. General Ashley recorded his activities in a memo book and also sent a long narrative to General Atkinson in December 1825. The narrative was first published in Dale, *The Ashley-Smith Explorations*, and the diary, after the true author was identified, was published in Morgan, *The West of Ashley*. The manuscript diary is now in the Missouri Historical Society in St. Louis.

192. Morgan, *The West of Ashley*, 118.

193. Camp, *James Clyman*, 38; T. D. Bonner, *The Life and Adventures of James P. Beckwourth* (New York: Harper, 1856; New York: Alfred Knopf, 1931), 41-44.

194. Indians reported "five tents containing 30 to 40 men" to the retreating Ogden. Rich, *Peter Skene Ogden*, 66 n.2; Merk, "Snake Country Correspondence," 91. The actual number of hunters is deducted from the rendezvous accounts.

195. Morgan, *The West of Ashley*, 117, 288 n.205; Fred R. Gowans, *Rocky Mountain Rendezvous: A History of the Fur Trade Rendezvous 1825-1840* (Provo: Brigham Young University Press, 1976), 5-16.

196. Morgan, *The West of Ashley*, 99, 106, 107, 112.

197. Ibid., 97. A clue to the relationship of the former partners, or to the general's public ambitions, lies in Ashley's avoidance of using his former partner's name for this historic stream.

198. Morgan, *The West of Ashley*, 118. The total number of Columbia freemen had increased from twenty-two to twenty-nine, which suggests that the Americans who hunted up the Yellowstone from the Big Horn may have picked up some stray HBC hunters.

199. Quite probably there was another, now missing, account book from the Weber brigade, in Jackson's handwriting, which accounted for the transactions with men who do not appear in Ashley's memo book.

200. Morgan calculated that an average beaver skin weighed 1.66 pounds while a Southwest skin only weighed 1.47. Weight was the determining factor because the furs were used for raw fiber material in the felting process.

201. "Flathead Report 1824-25," HBCA B69/e/1. The company also accepted muskrat, fox, fisher, dressed elk skins, dressed or parchment deerskins, and meat.

214

202. Morgan, *The West of Ashley*, 118-29.

203. Ibid., 122, 124. Ironically, Montour's father retired from the North West Company in 1793 as one of the richest men in Lower Canada.

204. Morgan, *The West of Ashley*, 126, 294 n.235. The original document clearly shows the letter "G." Morgan wrote a lengthy footnote suggesting that Jackson first came to the mountains this year with Ashley, which is odd because Carl Hays confirmed that Morgan had seen the St. Genevieve documents that proved that David went upriver in 1822. See Chapter 4, note 66 above.

205. It appears that Ashley-Henry borrowed around $60,000 for its first two years of operation, which had been reduced by $25,000 in returns when Ashley took over. The furs still cached on the Popo Agie were attributable to outfit 1823-24. The following updates Morgan's annotations (in *The West of Ashley*, 126) on Ashley's weight totals from the rendezvous trading:

> 1567 [skins traded from freemen last fall and others today]
>
> 1800 [45 packs cached on the Popo Agie last year, rounded off]
>
> 120 [Ashley's catch]
>
> 140 [Fitzpatrick's catch]
>
> 3100 [Weber's catch]
>
> 461 [Ham's catch]
>
> 166 [Clyman's catch makes 887 pounds taken by Ashley's men]
>
> 668 [Smith's fall and spring catch]
>
> 675 [the 16 Yellowstone men who still had their fall hunt in cache]
>
> <u>132</u> [Provost's four men, should be 236]
>
> 8829 Ashley's total of his trade.

206. Sunder, *Bill Sublette*, 28-30, 60-61.

207. This description of Ashley's thoughts is based on the following year's developments and the belief that the parties could not have come to a spontaneous transfer of the business in the summer of 1826 without prior consideration.

208. Ashley had left Fort Atkinson on 23 November 1824 with twenty-five hired hands and fifty horses. After the winterkill (of the original stock) he purchased twenty-three more Indian horses and also brought out enough replacements to have twenty-six hired men available to split off into three trapping parties. He contracted with those men to help him return the caravan. There must have been exchanges between those who wanted to remain in the mountains as hunters and some of the returning Ashley-Henry trappers.

209. Sunder, *Bill Sublette*, 28-30, 60-61; Morgan, *The West of Ashley*, 129, 295 n.243. Ogden met some Piegans on Deer Lodge Pass who bragged that a party had recently arrived in their camp with "53 Horses Stolen from the Americans on Bears River." Rich, *Peter Skene Ogden*, 77.

210. Robert Campbell, "A Narrative of Çol. Robert Campbell's Experiences in the Rocky Mountains Fur Trade From 1825 to 1835," St. Louis, Missouri Historical Society MSS, 32; Morgan, *Jedediah Smith*, 407 n.27, 408 n.29. Ashley expected to meet the American Atkinson-O'Fallon expedition that was concluding peace treaties with the Missouri tribes and, in an impressive demonstration of timing, got to the mouth of the Yellowstone just two

days after the arrival of the Army, which gave him and his returns a convoy and transportation on government vessels. See the Dairy of Stephen Watts Kearney, 4 August 1825, Missouri Historical Society MSS.

211. Charles Kelly and Dale Morgan, *Old Greenwood, The Story of Caleb Greenwood: Trapper, Pathfinder and Early Pioneer* (rev. ed., Georgetown, CA: The Talisman Press, 1965), 80-82.

212. The first written record was by Warren Angus Ferris, "Life in the Rocky Mountains," *Western Literary Messenger* (Buffalo, NY: 29 July 1843). "On the 4th [July 1832] we crossed the mountain and descended into a large prairie valley, called Jackson's Big Hole. It lies due east of the Trois Tetons, and is watered by Lewis River. . . . The Hole is surrounded by lofty mountains, and received its name from one of the firm Smith, Sublett and Jackson." David's descendent, Carl D. W. Hays, was quite proud of this, but, being more concerned with the central problem, never got around to visiting that beautiful place.

213. See T. C. Elliott, "Journal of John Work, June 21-Sept 6," *The Washington Historical Quarterly* 5, 2 (April 1914): 333-34, for the record of three of these men who reached the Flathead Post on 5 September 1825.

214. Simpson's fur barrier was designed to protect the fur reserves of New Caledonia, and the intentions of the company in the Snake country were mainly exploitive.

215. Morgan, *The West of Ashley*, 129-30, 295 n.243, misidentified these animals as Ashley's, but the Indians told Ogden that they were taken from the Americans on Bear River.

216. Bonner, *James P. Beckwourth*, 60-61.

217. John S. Galbraith states in the prologue to *The Hudson's Bay Company as an Imperial Factor, 1821-1869* (Berkeley: University of California Press, 1957), "The expansion of the British Empire has been largely motivated by the energies of the mercantile class. Far more important to the shaping of British Imperial policy than the secretaries and undersecretaries of state often credited with its formation were the hundreds of men in the commercial community, most of them unknown to history, who created the conditions upon which that policy was based."

Chapter Nine: "The business of taking furs in the Rocky Mountains"

218. Simpson traveled to London ahead of the fall express from the Columbia District and was unaware of the Ogden incident. [HBC] Governor J. H. Pelly to Hon. George Canning, London, 9 December 1825 in Merk, *Fur Trade and Empire*, 257.

219. Merk, *The Oregon Question*.

220. Bonner, *James P. Beckwourth*, 61.

221. Morgan, *The West of Ashley*, 147-48. James Clyman and Henry G. Fraeb claimed participation in the adventure, but it is unlikely that Black Moses Harris or Luis Vasquez could have taken part since they were with the supply caravan.

222. Rich, *Peter Skene Ogden*, 146.

223. Ibid., 170-71; Merk, *Fur Trade and Empire*, 275. Ogden believed that Jackson and Sublette left the Salt Lake in May with the intention of exploring the Clamimit (Klamath) country, but starvation forced them to abandon the effort.

224. Dale L. Morgan and Carl I. Wheat, *Jedediah Smith and His Maps of the American West* (San Francisco: California Historical Society, 1954), 41.

225. This guess is based on the fact that former Bay men were with the American party, and Jackson and Sublette would have taken a reliable guide on their western tour.

226. Elliott, "Journal of Alexander Ross," 384; Ross, *Fur Hunters*, 266-67; Williams, *Ogden's Snake Country Journals*, 13-14. The exploration of the Boise and Payette rivers is not shown by the tracings on the Gibbs-Frémont map, which shows Ogden's travels. Morgan guessed the route in *Jedediah Smith*, 186-87.

227. Rich, *Peter Skene Ogden*, 149-50.

228. Ashley had been waiting about a month, but not as long as the fifty days that Morgan guessed in *The West of Ashley*, 145.

229. Smith started with fifty men riding, each leading two packhorses. The ten additional animals were used by clerks, hunters, and others, including Robert Campbell, Hiram Scott, Bill Fallon, and A. G. Boone, the grandson of the legend. Ashley joined the party at Grand Island on 1 April 1826.

230. "Narrative of Campbell's Experiences," 11, 14.

231. Potts to Brother, 16 July 1826, Frost, *Notes on Ashley*, 56-59. The general indulged in oratory as Beckwourth remembered his elaborate, probably fictitious, farewell address to the mountaineers, two weeks before the actual agreement was signed. Bonner, *Beckwourth*, 73-74.

232. Morgan, *The West of Ashley*, 153, 305 n.323; Don Berry, *A Majority of Scoundrels: An Informal History of the Rocky Mountain Fur Company* (New York: Harper & Brothers, 1961), 125. There is a discrepancy between the 126 packs estimated by the Missouri newspapers and 123 packs reported by O. N. Bostwick of the American Fur Company on 21 September 1826. Probably the packs weighed fifty pounds each, and a mule could carry three of those, so 123 packs required forty-one animals, plus twenty more for riders.

233. Ashley spent approximately $14,000 to buy 4,667 pounds of beaver and picked up an additional 1,483 pounds from the hired men obliged to turn over half of their catch. The total American hunt of fall 1825 and spring 1826 was about 3,727 beaver.

234. This agreement has not survived, but a parallel contract concerning the resupply arrangements called "Articles of Agreement, 18 July 1826" is in the Missouri Historical Society, Sublette Collection, and has been published in Morgan, *The West of Ashley*, 150-52.

235. "Narrative of Campbell's Experiences," 11.

236. "Articles of Agreement," in Morgan, *The West of Ashley*, 150-52.

237. Ashley to B. Pratte, 14 October 1826, Missouri Historical Society, Ashley Collection, in Morgan, *The West of Ashley*, 158-59, 199.

238. Both men apparently withdrew from the mountains and returned home with Ashley.

239. Rich, *Peter Skene Ogden*, 126-34.

240. Edmonton House Journal, HBCA B60/a/24, 17. Montour's figures suggest that he was counting heavily on his fall and spring hunts. The letter passed through HBC channels creating some interesting reactions to competitive espionage.

241. Rich, *Peter Skene Ogden*, 154-58.

242. Merk, *Fur Trade and Empire*, 277.

243. Smith's memoir of 1830 in George R. Brooks, ed., *The Southwest Expedition of Jedediah Smith* (Glendale: The Arthur H. Clark Company, 1977), 35-36. This is also paralleled in Smith to Gen. William Clark, Little Lake of Bear River, 12 July 1827 in Dale, *The Ashley-Smith Explorations*, 182-90.

244. Brooks, *Southwest Expedition*, 205-13.

245. Potts to Robert Potts, Sweet Lake, 8 July 1827, Frost, *Notes on Ashley*. 60-62.

246. Bonner, *James P. Beckwourth*, 75. Beckwourth was a prodigious liar, recalling incredible details twenty-eight years after the fact, but the evidence from HBC sources supports his statements. The emphasis is mine.

247. Edmonton House Journal, 7 September 1826, HBCA B60/a/24, 2.

248. It was not until 1831 that a significant increase in the mountain arms race resulted from the American Fur Company's establishment at the mouth of the Marias River.

249. As late as 1839 Yellowstone Lake was still called Sublette's Lake. See Carl D. W. Hays, "David E. Jackson," in Hafen, *The Mountain Men and the Fur Trade* vol. 9, reprinted in LeRoy Hafen, ed., *Trappers of the Far West* (Lincoln: University of Nebraska Press, 1983), 84-85.

250. This is taken from the original letter, Potts to Respectid Brother, Sweet Lake, 8 July 1827, now in possession of the Yellowstone Library and Museum Association, as published in *Yellowstone Nature Notes* 21, 5 (September-October 1947): 52-53.

251. "Narrative of Campbell's Experiences," 13-14, 17.

252. Edmonton House Journal, HBCA B60/a/24, 18.

253. "Narrative of Campbell's Experiences," 17-18.

254. Bonner, *James P. Beckwourth*, 75-79.

255. Edmonton House Journal, 17 November 1826, HBCA B60/a/24, 19d.

256. Simpson to HBC, York Factory, 20 August 1826 in E. E. Rich, ed., *Part of Dispatch From George Simpson, Esqr., Governor of Rupert's Land to the Governor and Committee of the Hudson's Bay Company, London* (London: The Hudson's Bay Record Society, 1947), 152-53.

257. T. C. Elliott, "The Journal of John Work, July 5-September 15, 1826," *Washington State Historical Quarterly* 6, 1 (January 1915): 38-41, 43-44.

258. John Grey used Ashley's name as the chief of the American party and forwarded his invitation to come and visit him. Grey's previous connection, Johnson Gardner, had returned to Missouri with Ashley.

259. John Dease to HBC, Athabaska Portage, 15 October 1826, John McLeod Collection, British Columbia Provincial Archives MSS.

260. Kittson to McLeod, Kootenay House, 8 March 1827, McLeod Collection.

261. Dease to McLeod, Fort Colvile, 14 April 1827, McLeod Collection; Colvile District Report, 1827, HBCA B45/e/1.

262. Merk, *Fur Trade and Empire*, 283-84, 287-92.

263. "Narrative of Campbell's Experiences," 15-17.

264. Sublette's narrative of his overland trip of 1827, Missouri Historical Society MSS, in Sunder, *Bill Sublette*, 71-72.

265. Morgan, *Jedediah Smith*, 218-20; Morgan, *The West of Ashley*, 158-59; Berry, *Majority of Scoundrels*, 136-38.

266. "Narrative of Campbell's Experiences," 17-18.

267. Potts to Respectid Brother, Sweet Lake, 8 July 1827. The Blackfeet were ambivalent when they related this experience to the Edmonton trader on 15 January 1828. John Rowand wrote, "a small party of Piegans accompanied by a Blackfoot chief visited a place built by the Americans near a large lake for the purpose of equipping their trappers, and it is there where they saw the grand Camp of Snake Indians encamped *about the house* and Rum like so much water about them." (Emphasis added.) Simpson's Correspondence, HBCA D4/121, 46d.

Chapter Ten: "The Americans have almost resided on these rivers"

268. Sullivan, *The Travels of Jedediah Smith*, 26.

269. Brooks, *Southwest Expedition*, 54-55 n.48. Robeseau returned to the Bear Lake rendezvous and joined Smith's second expedition.

270. The value of the virgin region Smith had left untrapped later proved fruitful by the success of the Snake Brigade trapping in that area.

271. Morgan, *Jedediah Smith*, 230-32; Berry, *Majority of Scoundrels*, 158-59.

272. Sublette Papers, Smith Jackson & Sublette Account with W. H. Ashley, Missouri Historical Society MSS. Also published in Morgan, *The West of Ashley*, 196-97; Morgan, *Jedediah Smith*, 320-22, 421 n.32; and Clokey, *William H. Ashley*, 180 n.80.

273. Brooks, *Southwest Expedition*, 215 and elsewhere; Morgan, *Jedediah Smith*, 236.

274. Ashley Papers, Missouri Historical Society, in Morgan, *The West of Ashley*, 171.

275. Sublette Papers, Missouri Historical Society. Don Berry's discovery of this document caused him to look critically at Ashley's operations in *Majority of Scoundrels*, 159.

276. David Lavender, chapter 23 in *The Fist in the Wilderness* (1964; Albuquerque: University of New Mexico Press, 1979).

277. "Secretary of State, 1827," vol. 6 in *The Papers of Henry Clay*, ed. James F. Hopkins and Mary W. Hargreaves (Lexington: The University Press of Kentucky, 1981), 854-55, 859, 867, 878-79, 907-8; Merk, *The Oregon Question*, 176-78.

278. Edmonton House Journal, HBCA B60/a/24, 19d: D4/121, 46d; U.S. Congress, *House Executive Document 351*, 25th Cong., 2d sess., 228-30, in Morgan, *The West of Ashley*, 168-69.

279. Williams, *Ogden's Snake Country Journals*, 81.

280. Simpson's Correspondence, HBCA D4/121, 14.

281. Williams, *Ogden's Snake Country Journals*, 40 n.1.

282. Ibid., 10-14.

283. Simpson's Correspondence, HBCA D4/121, 45d-46d; Edmonton House Journal, B60/a/25, 34d, 50d.

284. Edmonton House Journal, HBCA B60/a/25, 18d, 34d.

285. Glyndwr Williams, ed., *Hudson's Bay Miscellany 1670-1870*, (Winnipeg: The Hudson's Bay Record Society, 1975), 208.

286. "Narrative of Campbell's Experiences," 21-22.

287. Simpson to HBC, 18 July 1828, HBCA D4/92, 30d-32d.

288. "Narrative of Campbell's Experiences," 16.

289. Ibid., 22-24.

290. Ibid., 24-25.

291. Williams, *Ogden's Snake Country Journals*, 45.

292. Williams, *Ogden's Snake Country Journals*, 46; Simpson to Dease, 17 February 1829, HBCA D4/9, 22.

293. Williams, *Ogden's Snake Country Journals*, 49, 60, 72, for this and the previous paragraph.

294. Ashley to Benton, St. Louis, 20 January 1829, in Morgan, *The West of Ashley*, 187. P. Sublette, P. Ragotte (F. Rashotte), and J. Jondron (J. B. Joundreau) were the men killed in 1828.

295. Williams, *Ogden's Snake Country Journals*, 71, 74, 75, 81-82.

296. "Narrative of Campbell's Experiences," 29-30. Beckwourth also reported a fully inflated version of this.

297. U.S. Senate, *Senate Document 39*, 21st Cong., 2d sess., 7-8, in Morgan, *The West of Ashley*, 175; Sunder, *Joshua Pilcher*, 68.

298. Simpson's Correspondence, HBCA D4/121, 47; Ashley to Gen. Alexander Macomb, Washington, March 1829, in Morgan, *The West of Ashley*, 191.

299. Sunder, *Sublette*, 76.

300. "Narrative of Campbell's Experiences," 30-31.

Chapter Eleven: "For a cause in which they are not concerned"

301. Dease to HBC, Flathead Post, 7 December 1828, HBCA D4/122, 11-12.

302. Ibid.

303. Work to HBC, Fort Colvile, 21 October 1828, HBCA D4/122, 5. Dease to HBC, Flathead Post, 7 December 1828, HBCA D4/122, 11-12; Simpson to Work, Fort Vancouver, 17 November 1828, HBCA D4/16, 9.

304. Dease to HBC, 7 December 1828, HBCA D4/122, 11-12.

305. Smith reached Fort Vancouver on 8 August, which allowed more than enough time for the news to travel upriver to Fort Colvile by the first of November. A Saulteaux Indian trapper named Parsin, who was Jaco Finlay's brother-in-law, went from the west side of the mountains to Edmonton House by 8 October with the news of Finlay's death and a report "that eighteen Americans have been killed," HBCA B60/a/26, 14.

306. McLoughlin to Simpson, Fort Vancouver, 20 March 1827; Dease to HBC, Fort Colvile, 16 April 1827; and McLoughlin to Simpson, Fort Colvile, 17 April 1827, all in HBCA D4/120, 52, 63, 63d.

307. McLoughlin to Simpson, Fort Vancouver, 20 March 1828, HBCA D4/121, 35d.

308. McLoughlin to Simpson, Fort Vancouver, 20 March 1827, HBCA D4/120, 15.

309. Simpson to McLoughlin, York Factory, 10 July 1826, HBCA D4/6, 10; Simpson to Grant, York Factory, 15 July 1826, HBCA D4/6, 26d-27.

310. HBCA B223/b/4, fols. 18d-19, in Williams, *Ogden's Snake Country Journals*, 122 n.3.

311. HBCA D4/92, 40, in Williams, *Ogden's Snake Country Journals*, 122 n.3.

312. Simpson to [Dease] John Work, Fort Vancouver, 17 November 1828, HBCA D4/16, 9-9d.

313. HBCA D4/122, 11d; Fort Colvile Journal 1830-31, B45/a/1, 3d, 15d, 20d; McLoughlin to Heron, 14 October 1830, B223/b/6, 19d.

314. Dease to HBC, Flathead Post, 17 January 1829, HBCA D4/122, 21d; Sunder, *Joshua Pilcher*, 70-72. Pilcher's letter was dated Flathead Post 30 December, but Simpson sent his February response to Flathead Lake.

315. HBCA D4/122, 121d; Sunder, *Joshua Pilcher*, 70-72; Merk, *Fur Trade and Empire*, 307-8.

316. Dease noted that the Flatheads left for the Horse Plains on 20 December and did not plan to return until 25 March. For the logical location of the American camp, I am indebted to Mr. Thane White of Dayton, Montana.

317. Information about the St. Regis Grey family was gathered by James Anderson, who studied the métis that settled at the mouth of the Kaw River in present Kansas. Two imperfect biographies of John Grey are in Dale Morgan and Eleanor Towles Harris, *The Rocky Mountain Journal of William Marshall Anderson: The West in 1834* (San Marino, CA: The Huntington Library, 1967), and Merle Wells, "Ignace Hatcheoraughnasha (John Grey)," in Hafen, *The Mountain Men and the Fur Trade* vol. 7, 161-75.

318. Paul C. Phillips, ed., *Life in the Rocky Mountains by W. A. Ferris* (Denver: The Old West Publishing Company, 1940), 318; Francis Fuller Victor, *The River of the West: Life and Adventures [of Joe Meek]* . . . *A Mountain-man and Pioneer* (Hartford: 1870; Columbus, OH: Long's College Book Company, 1950), 104.

319. Sublette Papers, Jackson & Sublette Accounts, Missouri Historical Society MSS. The boy apparently boarded with Sublette's brother-in-law, Grove Cook.

320. Malcomb McLeod, *Peace River: A Canoe Voyage from Hudson's Bay to the Pacific . . . in 1828* (Rutland, VT: Charles Tuttle Company, 1971).

321. Pombert was in California in 1827 and may have preceded Smith, since the accounts of the 1826 party do not list him. See Morgan, *Jedediah Smith*, 419.

322. The most recent and complete study of Smith's retreat is Bob Zybach, "A. Black, Jedediah Smith, and the Location of the Hudson's Bay Company Pack Trails in Northwest Oregon in 1828," unpublished MS, copy in author's possession.

323. Records of McLeod's expeditions, which represent a good part of the few surviving from Fort Vancouver, are in HBCA B223/a/2 (1826), B223/a/4 (1826-27), and B223/a/5 (1828). The journal of the recovery is published in Sullivan, *The Travels of Jedediah Smith*, 112-35, as is Smith's journal up to 3 July.

324. Simpson to Smith, Fort Vancouver, 26 December 1828 and 29 December 1828, HBCA D4/9, 13-17d. Also in Merk, *Fur Trade and Empire*, 302-07.

325. Williams, *Ogden's Snake Country Journals*, 123.

326. Simpson's Correspondence, HBCA D4/122, 24, 24d, 34d, 42.

327. At least 589 large and small beaver were recovered, as well as a few otter skins and 38 horses valued at $8 each. That amounted to £541.0.6 (£486.18.5 Halifax or Canadian currency) or $2,369.60. Two hundred dollars may have paid for recovered gear.

328. Volume of letters, 12 August 1828 to 20 March 1829, forwarded to London by Governor Simpson 1829, HBCA D4/16, 20d-22. Emphasis added.

329. Simpson's Correspondence, HBCA D4/16, 20. Also in Sunder, *Pilcher*, 70.

330. E. E. Rich, *The History of the Hudson's Bay Company* vol. 2 (London: The Hudson's Bay Record Society, 1928-29); John S. Galbraith, *The Little Emperor: Governor Simpson of the Hudson's Bay Company* (Toronto: Macmillan of Canada, 1976).

331. Dease to HBC, 17 January 1829, HBCA D4/122, 21d; Pilcher to Secretary of War, 1830, U.S. Senate, *Senate Document 39*, 21st Cong., 2d sess., 7-8.

332. The site has been identified by U.S. Forest Service archaeologist Mark J. White.

333. Sunder, *Pilcher*, 72.

334. Gloria Ricci Lothrop, ed., *Recollections of the Flathead Mission by Fr. Gregory Mengarini, S. J.* (Glendale: The Arthur H. Clark Company, 1977), 171-72.

335. Burt Brown Barker, *Letters of Dr. John McLoughlin Written at Fort Vancouver 1829-1832* (Portland: Oregon Historical Society, 1948), 1-5.

336. Some information relative to Colvile District by John Work, April 1830, HBCA, B45/e/3:

Spokane [Colvile] District returns for 1823-1829

	1823	1824	1825	1826	1827	1828	1829
Colvile	1609	1442	886	1100	1143	1034	849
Flatheads	1472	2009	1468	960	1400	928	1621
Kootenay	1139	*	950	1028	1198	836	827
MB Totals	4220	3451	3304	3088	3741	2798	3297

* in 1824 the Kutenais traded at Flathead Post and no separate MB amounts were kept. My emphasis is to suggest that the Americans were making inroads with Indians who usually traded with the HBC.

337. Dease to McLoughlin, Fort Colvile, 15 August 1829, HBCA D4/123, 22d; Colvile District Report by John Work, April 1830, B45/3/3, 12d; Work to Rowand, Fort Colvile, 19 September 1829, D4/122, 74.

338. Rich, *Part of Dispatch From George Simpson*, 55, 57, 63.

339. Simpson to McLoughlin, Fort Vancouver, 15 March 1829, in Merk, *Fur Trade and Empire*, 308-9.

340. Fort Vancouver Correspondence 1829-30, HBCA B223/b/5, 20.

341. McLoughlin to McLeod, Fort Vancouver, 1 February 1830, McLeod Collection.

Chapter Twelve: "An acceptable service to the administration"

342. Joe Meek reported the meeting on the east side of the Tetons in Victor, *River of the West*, 58; Dorothy O. Johansen, ed., *Robert Newell's Memoranda: Travles in the Territory of Missourie; ect...* (Portland: The Champoeg Press, 1959). George W. Ebberts, "A Trapper's Life in the Rocky Mountains from 1829 to 1839," Bancroft Library MSS.

343. "Narrative of Campbell's Experiences," 31-33, for this and the following paragraph.

344. Ibid., 31-34

345. Johansen, *Newell's Memoranda*, 31; Ashley to Thomas H. Benton, St. Louis, 20 January 1829, in Morgan, *The West of Ashley*, 186; SJ&S to Gen. William Clark, 24 December 1829, "A brief sketch of accidents, misfortunes, and depredations committed by Indians, &c. on the firm of Smith, Jackson & Sublette, Indian traders on the East & west side of the Rocky Mountains, since July 1826 to the present," in Morgan, *Jedediah Smith*, 337-43.

346. Victor, *River of the West*, 59; Johansen, *Newell's Memoranda*, 31.

347. Ebberts, "Trapper's Life"; Victor, *River of the West*, 82.

348. Edward Jackson Estate Papers, Probate Court, Lewis County, Virginia.

349. SJ&S to Gen. William Clark, 24 December 1829, in Morgan, *Jedediah Smith*, 337-42.

350. Morgan, *Jedediah Smith*, 342; Sunder, *Bill Sublette*, 83; Berry, *Majority of Scoundrels*, 234-35, 240-41.

351. The resulting misadventures of the Rocky Mountain Fur Company were graphically chronicled in Bernard DeVoto, *Across the Wide Missouri* (New York: Houghton Mifflin Company, 1947), and Berry, *Majority of Scoundrels*.

352. SJ&S to Clark and Smith to Clark, Smith to his parents, Smith to Ralph Smith, East side of Rocky Mountains, 24 December 1829, in Morgan, *Jedediah Smith*, 337-42, 349-54.

353. London Correspondence Inward 1823-1843, HBCA A12/1, 330. Emphasis added.

354. Morgan, *Jedediah Smith*, 309, 350-54.

355. Victor, *River of the West*, 82-85; Johansen, *Newell's Memoranda*, 31.

356. U.S. Congress, "Licenses to Trade with the Indians," *House Document 41*, 21st Cong., 2d sess., in Morgan, *Jedediah Smith*, 315.

357. Morgan, *The West of Ashley*, 199; Richard E. Ahlborn, ed., *Man Made Mobile: Early Saddles of Western North America* (Washington: Smithsonian Institution Press, 1980), 41-44; personal discussion with Bill McGaw of El Paso, a man who knows just about everything about horses.

358. Victor, *River of the West*, 85.

359. Lavender, *Fist in the Wilderness*, 392.

360. Yount also named Smith, but Morgan says he was in the Yellowstone country. Morgan, *Smith*, 313-15.

361. Camp, *George C. Yount*, 67-76, 79, 81. Camp has reservations about the veracity of Yount, who dictated his recollections to a friend in 1855.

362. Black, the only survivor of the Umpqua massacre to return to the mountains, apparently described the livestock potential that Smith twice attempted but never realized.

363. Kittson to Rowand, Kootenais, 12 August 1830, HBCA B76/a/1, 15d; Simpson's Correspondence, D4/a25, 59; D4/97, 12-12d. Some of the Iroquois hunters returned to Bear River from the Wind River rendezvous of 1830. Phillips, *Life in the Rocky Mountains*, 59, 67-68.

364. Snake Brigade Journal Reports, HBCA B208/e/1, 4d; B202/a/2; B223/d/19, 7d-8; B223/d/19; Francis D. Haines, ed., *The Snake Country Expedition of 1830-1831: John Work's Field Journal* (Norman: University of Oklahoma Press, 1971).

365. Morgan, *Jedediah Smith*, 322.

366. *Missouri Intelligencer*, 9 October 1830.

367. Frost, *Notes on Ashley*, 142-44.

368. Morgan, *Jedediah Smith*, 322.

369. U.S. Senate, *Senate Document 39*, 22d Cong., 2d sess., in Morgan, *Jedediah Smith*, 343-48. Ashley was the obvious pipeline to the administration, but Jackson enjoyed several connections: Albert Gallatin, a former associate of his uncle George Jackson; his cousin John George Jackson, then a federal judge; and John Scott, the senator from Ste. Genevieve, Missouri.

370. Morgan and Wheat, *Smith and His Maps*, 32-33.

371. "Captain Jedediah Strong Smith, A Eulogy," *Illinois Magazine* (June 1832).

372. Morgan and Wheat, *Smith and His Maps*, 59, and the "Frémont-Gibbs-Smith Map" in the book's pocket.

373. See discussions in Smith, *Virgin Land*, and Boorstin, *The Americans*.

374. Morgan, *Jedediah Smith*, 433 n.37.

Chapter Thirteen: "The earnest pursuit of wealth"

375. Morgan, *Jedediah Smith*, 359; Sunder, *Bill Sublette*, 94.

376. U.S. Land Patent 2340, vol. 5, p. 333, 11 February 1832, signed 1 May 1833.

377. Sunder, *Bill Sublette*, 93 n.8; Governor John Miller to the governors of Santa Fe, Chihuahua, Sonora, and others of the Mexican Republic, Sublette Missouri Historical Society.

378. George Jackson Estate Papers, Ste. Genevieve Archives.

379. Hays, "David Jackson," 227; George Jackson Estate Papers. Minter appears to have been from western Virginia.

380. Reminiscences of J. J. Warner, E 65 n.29, Bancroft Library MSS.

381. L. P. Marshall to Gamble, 26 March 1833, Hamilton Gamble Papers, Missouri Historical Society.

382. Instruction of Fitzpatrick to Sublette, Santa Fe, 28 August 1831, Sublette Papers; Missouri Historical Society. Hafen, *Broken Hand*, 93 n.11, indicates that Fitzpatrick arrived in Lexington a few days before 11 May.

383. St. Francois County Tax Lists, Missouri Historical Society. John Minter was a non-resident in 1827 who owned lands worth $210. The following year his holding increased, but he was skipped for assessment in 1830. In 1831 Delilah Minter was listed as the owner of the property.

384. John O'Fallon to Robert Campbell, St. Louis, 30 June, 1831, Campbell Collection, Missouri Historical Society.

385. Milton Milo Quaife, ed., *The Commerce of the Prairies*, by Josiah Gregg (1926; University of Nebraska Press, 1967), 61, makes the shortcut fifty miles. Two and a half weeks later, when a second caravan passed, so much rain had fallen that a wagon was upset and its cargo got soaked.

386. These were the Gros Ventre of the South Saskatchewan River who were noticed departing in January 1830 and did not return until January 1834. Simpson's Correspondence, HBCA D5/2, 43d; D4/126, 63.

387. Mexican Archives of New Mexico (hereafter cited as MANM) roll 14, nos. 314-17; David J. Weber, *The Taos Trappers: The Fur Trade of the Far Southwest* (Norman: University of Oklahoma Press, 1971), 144.

388. Quaife, *Commerce of the Prairies*, 78.

389. Total duties in 1830-31 were $10,581 (or $31,882) and in 1831-32 were $31,314. By 1832 Mexican officers who previously complained of being overworked servicing *estrangeros* were willing to admit that the customs were profitable.

390. David Lavender, *Bent's Fort* (1954; Lincoln: University of Nebraska Press, 1972), 134, 412 n.6.

391. Quaife, *Commerce of the Prairies*, 100.

392. Camp, *George C. Yount*, 81; Weber, *Taos Trappers*, 144.

393. Hafen, *Broken Hand*, 98 n.17, 99 n.21; Sublette Papers, Missouri Historical Society.

394. Account with the RMFCo., 15 July 1832, Sublette Papers, Missouri Historical Society.

395. Bancroft Library, Vallejo Documents, tomo, 30, 1830-32, 135, 241; Harlan Hague, *The Road to California: The Search for a Southwest Overland Route, 1540-1848* (Glendale: The Arthur H. Clark Company, 1978), 181. Young's biographers are Kenneth L. Holmes, *Ewing Young: Master Trapper* (Portland: Binford & Mort, 1967); Harvey L. Carter, "Ewing Young" in Hafen, *The Mountain Men and the Fur Trade*, reprinted Hafen, *Trappers of the Far West*.

396. James W. Goodrich, "In Earnest Pursuit of Wealth: David Waldo in Missouri and the Southwest, 1820-1878," *Missouri Historical Review* 66 (January 1972): 61 n.15; and Goodrich's unpublished dissertation, University of Missouri, 1967.

397. Floyd F. Ewing, Jr., "The Mule as a Factor in the Development of the Southwest," *Arizona and the West* 5 (Winter 1963): 318; LeRoy R. Hafen and Ann W. Hafen, *Old Spanish Trail, Santa Fe to Los Angeles* (Glendale: The Arthur H. Clark Company, 1954), 171; Eleanor Lawrence, "Mexican Trade Between Santa Fe and Los Angeles, 1830-1848," *California Historical Society Quarterly* 10 (March 1931): 28.

398. Sublette Papers, Missouri Historical Society.

399. Hays, "David E. Jackson," 35.

400. Robidoux and Campbell to Governor, Santa Fe, 18 September 1830, MANM; Request of David Waldo, Santa Fe, 17 September 1831, and response of Governor Chavez, 19 September 1831, in Weber, *Taos Trappers*, 184.

Chapter Fourteen: "The facility of crossing the continent"

401. H. H. Bancroft, *History of California* vol. 2 (San Francisco: The History Company, 1886), 147; Bancroft Library, Vallejo Documents, tomo 30, 1830-32; Sublette Collection.

402. Arizona Pioneers' Historical Society (Tucson), Holliday Collection MSS; "Reminiscences of Jonathan Trumbull Warner," Bancroft Library MSS; "Reminiscences of Early California from 1831 to 1846," *Annual Publications of the Historical Society of Southern California, 1907-1908* (Los Angeles, 1909), 176-93.

403. L. L. Waldo to David Waldo, Chihuahua, 14 January 1832, Jackson County Historical Society, Waldo Letters.

404. William Cochrane McGaw, *Savage Scene: The Life and Times of James Kirker, Frontier King* (New York: Hastings House, 1972), 72, 78, 87-96.

405. Archivo Historico de Estado, Hermosilla, Sonora, Asuntos Indigenas, through the courtesy of Fr. Kieran McCarty, O.F.M., The University of Arizona, Tucson; C. L. Sonnichsen, *Tucson: The Life and Times of an American City* (Norman: University of Oklahoma Press, 1982).

406. Fr. J. M. Carillo, F.S.C.J., *San Antonio de Pala* (Newport Beach: Paisano Press, 1959), 9.

407. Bancroft, *History of California* vol. 3, 181-221.

408. Bancroft Library, Vallejo Documents, tomo 25, 1830-32, 280.

409. Jackson to Cooper, Mission San Gabriel, 24 December 1831, Hays Collection. This is the first document in ten years that confirms Jackson's business activities in his own hand.

410. Bancroft, *History of California* vol. 2, 729, and vol. 3, 755.

411. Bancroft, *History of California* vol. 3, 406 n.46; Morgan, *Jedediah Smith,* 413 n.5.

412. Morgan, *Jedediah Smith,* 206, 416 n.27. Sublette finally received the bill, which he divided into three precisely equal amounts of $33.33.

413. Bancroft, *History of California* vol. 3, 726; Bancroft Library, Nasario Galindo MSS.

414. Bancroft Library, Nasario Galindo MSS.

415. Jackson to Cooper, San Miguel, 22 February 1832, Vallejo Documents, tomo 31, 1833-35; Miscellaneous Register of Brands & Marks, 1828-34, Provincial State Papers, Benica, I, Bancroft Library.

416. Bancroft, *History of California* vol. 2, 683-84, 690, and vol. 3, 724, 726. In that year mission herds declined by 1,073.

417. Jackson to Cooper, San Miguel, 22 February 1832. Captain Cooper continued to be interested in horses and in October 1833 hired Job F. Dye to drive 217 brood mares to his "El Sur" ranch where he conducted a general stock business. See Job F. Dye, *Recollections of a Pioneer* (Los Angeles: Glen Dawson, 1951), 30.

418. Hays, "David E. Jackson," 237.

419. Weber, *Taos Trappers,* 148, identifies twenty-nine of the thirty-six men, including Moses Carson, Job F. Dye, Joseph Gale, Pauline Weaver, and Young's apparent brother-in-law, José Teforia.

420. Hays, "David E. Jackson," 237-38.

421. Guesswork using Weber, *Taos Trappers,* 148, and supported in part by D. E. Jackson to E. J. Jackson, 12 December 1837, Hays Collection.

422. Ralph P. Biedler, ed., "Cooke's Journal of the March of the Mormon Battalion, 1846-1847," in *Exploring Southwest Trails, 1846-1854* (Glendale, 1938), 166.

423. John Walton Caughey, *History of the Pacific Coast* (Los Angeles: 1933). Carl Hays requested documentation from Caughey in 1964 but did not receive an answer.

424. Historical notes at Casa Grande National Monument. See Hays, "David E. Jackson," in Hafen, *Trappers of the Far West,* 94 n. 24.

425. Asuntos Indigenas, MANM.

426. Proceedings against Ewing Young, Santa Fe, regarding contraband goods confiscated, 12 July-25 July 1832, MANM, microfilm 15, frames 162-69; Weber, *Taos Trappers*, 149-51.

427. William K. Rule to David Waldo, St. Louis, 17 April 1832, Waldo Papers, Missouri Historical Society.

428. L. L. Waldo to David Waldo, Chihuahua, 14 January 1832, Jackson County Historical Society, Waldo Letters; Stella D. Hare, "Jedediah Smith's Younger Brother, Ira," *The Pacific Historian* II (Summer 1967): 44.

429. Weber, *Taos Trappers*, 152.

430. Quaife, *Commerce of the Prairies*, 214; "Alphonso Wetmore's Diary, Wetmore to Secretary of War Lewis Cass, Franklin, Missouri, 11 October 1831" in Archibald Butler Hubert, ed., *Southwest on the Turquois Trail* (Denver Public Library: 1933); U. S. Bureau of Indian Affairs, *Osage Agency 1842-46*, National Archives, microfilm M234, roll 632.

431. Edgely W. Todd, ed., *The Adventures of Captain Bonneville, U. S. A.: In the Rocky Mountains and Far West*, by Washington Irving (Norman: Univ. of Oklahoma Press, 1961).

432. Waldo W. Rosebush, *Frontier Steel: The Men and Their Weapons* (Spokane: Eastern Washington Historical Society, 1958); D. E. Jackson to E. J. Jackson, 12 December 1837, Hays Collection.

433. John Francis McDermott, ed., *The Western Journals of Washington Irving* (Norman: University of Oklahoma Press, 1944), and *A Tour on the Prairies*, by Washington Irving (Norman: University of Oklahoma Press, 1956); George F. Spaulding, *On the Western Tour with Washington Irving: The Journal and Letter of Count de Pourtales* (Norman: University of Oklahoma Press, 1968); Stanley T. Williams and Barbara D. Simpson, *Washington Irving on the Prairie, Or a Narrative of a Tour of the Southwest in the Year 1832* (New York: American Book Company, 1937).

434. "Recollections of a Septuagenarian by William Waldo," *Missouri Historical Society Glimpses of the Past*, 60.

435. *St. Louis Times*, 2 March 1833; *Columbus (Ohio) Monitor*, 3 April 1833. Both references through the courtesy of Fred A. Rosenstock.

Chapter Fifteen: "Should my case be favored by feelings"

436. D. E. Jackson Estate Papers, Ste. Genevieve Archives.

437. The Missouri Census suggests that William Pitt Jackson may have traveled west as early as 1830.

438. U.S. Land Patent 2346.

439. Sunder, *Bill Sublette*, 116-22.

440. Morgan, *Jedediah Smith*, 323, 433 n.32, put Jedediah's share of the partnership at $17,604.33 and one-third of the RMFCo. debt, which increased by interest to a total to $23,148.46.

441. W. P. Jackson to Capt. John Norris, Paris, Tennessee, 1 January 1834, Hays Collection.

442. Ibid. Ray, apparently a member of Congress during the 1814 session, had lived in the same boardinghouse with J. G. Jackson.

443. Sunder, *Bill Sublette*, 134; Simpson's Correspondence, HBCA D4/126, 61.

444. See DeVoto, *Across the Wide Missouri*, or various other books, for the story of the declining fur trade.

445. W. P. Jackson to Mary J. Hays and Nancy N. Jackson, Valle Mines, St. Francois, Missouri, 1 February 1835, Hays Collection.

446. W. P. Jackson to E. J. Jackson, Pototoc, 15 November 1835, Hays Collection.

447. Soap and a little wine are also included in the Boggs & Lecompte Store accounts, 26 September-7 November 1835, Hays Collection.

448. D. E. Jackson Estate Papers, Ste. Genevieve Archives; D. E. Jackson to E. J. Jackson, 12 December 1837, Hays Collection. Chapman owed land near the St. Francois property but was forced to sell part of it in 1833 and live on the rest until his death in 1843.

449. D. E. Jackson Estate Papers, Ste. Genevieve Archives, for this and the subsequent paragraph on collecting debts.

450. *Ladies Indispensible Assistant—And Complete System of Home Medicine—and one of the best systems of cookery ever produced* (New York: E. Hutchinson, 1852), 16-18, for this and the following quote.

451. Joseph G. Baldwin, *The Flush Times of Alabama and Mississippi: A Series of Sketches* (New York: Hill & Wang, 1957), 64-65.

452. Victor, *River of the West*, 72.

453. Original and photocopy in Hays Collection.

Epilogue

454. Comdr. Elmer Martin Jackson, Jr., *Keeping the Lamp of Remembrance Lighted* (Hagerstown, MD: Hagerstown Bookbinding and Printing Co. Inc., 1985), 44, 55.

455. D. E. Jackson Estate Papers, Ste. Genevieve Archives; Circuit Court Records, St. Francois County, Ste. Genevieve Archives; copies in Hays Collection.

456. Ste. Genevieve Deed Book D, 19-20.

457. *The Oregon Archives including the Journals, Governor's Messages and Public Papers of Oregon* (Salem: Asahel Bush, 1853), 110.

458. *Oregon Spectator*, 24 June 1847; "Waldo vs Estate of Ewing Young in Clackamus County Court," *Records of the Oregon Supreme Court* (Portland: Stevens Ness, 1938); Unidentified news clipping pertaining to J. Quinn Thornton, Oregon Historical Society Scrapbook 116.

Bibliography

Manuscript Sources

Archives of California Collection. Bancroft Library, Berkley, California.

Ashley Papers, Campbell Collection, Chouteau Collection, Fur Trade Collection, Sublette Papers, Waldo Papers. Missouri Historical Society, St. Louis.

Barker Collection. University of Oregon, Eugene.

Biedler, Ralph P., ed. "Cooke's Journal of the March of the Morman Battalion, 1846-1847." *Exploring Southwest Trails, 1846-1854*. Glendale, 1939.

British Columbia Archives. Victoria, British Columbia.

California Mission Archives. Santa Barbara, California.

Coe Collection of Western American History. Yale University, New Haven.

Public Archives of Manitoba, Hudson's Bay Company Archives. Winnipeg, Manitoba.

Ritch Papers. Huntington Library, Los Angeles.

Missouri State Historical Society. Columbia, Missouri.

Stearns Collection. Jackson County (Missouri) Historical Society.

New Mexico State Archives. Santa Fe.

Oregon Historical Society. Portland.

Public Records

St. Francois County, Missouri.

Ste. Genevieve County, Missouri.

Washington County, Missouri.

Newspapers

Arkansas Gazette.

Columbus (Ohio) Monitor.

Franklin (Missouri) Intelligencer.

Missouri Republican.

National Intelligencer.

Nile's Weekly Register.

Philadelphia Gazette and Daily Advertiser.

St. Louis Enquirer.

St. Louis (Louisiana) Gazette.

St. Louis Times.

St. Louis Weekly Reveille.

Periodicals

Brooks, Morgan M. "Pioneer Settlers of the Buckhannon Valley." M.A. thesis. West Virginia Wesleyan College, 1934.

Carter, Harvey L. "A Reply" [to Goetzman's "A Note on 'Stereotypes of the Mountain Man'"]. *Western Historical Quarterly* 6 (July 1975).

———, and Marcia C. Spencer. "Stereotypes of the Mountain Man." *Western Historical Quarterly* 6 (January 1975).

Dorsey, Dorothy B. "The Panic of 1818 in Missouri." *Missouri Historical Review* 29 (January 1935).

Drumm, Stella, ed. "Recollections of a Septuagenarian by William Waldo of Texas." *Missouri Historical Society Glimpses of the Past* 5 (April-June 1938).

Elliott, T. C. "Journal of Alexander Ross—Snake Country Expedition." *Oregon Historical Quarterly* 14 (December 1913).

———. "The Journal of John Work, July 5-September 15, 1826." *Washington State Historical Quarterly* 6 (January 1915).

Ewing, Floyd F., Jr. "The Mule as a Factor in the Development of the Southwest." *Arizona and the West* 5 (Winter 1963).

Goetzman, William H. "A Note on 'Stereotypes of the Mountain Man.'" *Western Historical Quarterly* 6 (July 1975).

———. "The Mountain Man as Jacksonian Man." *American Quarterly* 14 (Fall 1963).

Goodrich, James W. "In Earnest Pursuit of Wealth: David Waldo in Missouri and the Southwest, 1820-1878." *Missouri Historical Review* 66 (January 1972).

Hare, Stella D. "Jedediah Smith's Younger Brother, Ira." *The Pacific Historian* 11 (Summer 1967).

Jackson, John C. "Brandon House and the Mandan Connection." *North Dakota History* 49 (Winter 1982).

Lawrence, Eleanor. "Mexican Trade Between Santa Fe and Los Angeles, 1830-1848." *California Historical Society Quarterly* 10 (March 1931).

Merk, Frederick. "The Snake Country Expedition Correspondence, 1824-25." *Mississippi Valley Historical Review* 21 (June 1934).

Miller, David E, ed. "Peter Skene Ogden's Journal of his Expedition to Utah in 1825." *Utah Historical Quarterly* 20 (April 1952).

Nasatir, A. P. "The International Significance of the Jones and Immell Massacre and of the Aricara Outbreak of 1823." *Pacific Northwest Quarterly* 30 (January 1939).

Oglesby, Richard. "Pierre Menard, Reluctant Mountain Man." *The Bulletin of the Missouri Historical Society* 24 (October 1967).

Reid, Russel, and C. G. Gannon, eds. "Journal of the Atkinson-O'Fallon Expedition." *North Dakota Historical Quarterly* 4 (October 1929).

Yellowstone Nature Notes 21 (September-October 1947).

Books

Ahlborn, Richard E., ed. *Man Made Mobile: Early Saddles of Western North America.* Washington: Smithsonian Institution Press, 1980.

Alter, J. Cecil. *James Bridger: Trapper, Frontiersman, Scout and Guide.* Columbus, OH: Long's College Book Company, 1951.

Baker, Eugene C., ed. "The Austin Papers, Part I, 1789-1824." In *American Historical Association Annual Report.* Vol. 2. Washington, D.C., 1917.

Bancroft, H. H. *History of California.* 2 vols. San Francisco: The History Company, 1886.

Basler, Lucille. *The District of Ste. Genevieve, 1725-1980.* Ste. Genevieve: self-published, 1980.

Berry, Don. *A Majority of Scoundrels: An Informal History of the Rocky Mountain Fur Company.* New York: Harper & Brothers, 1961.

Biedler, Ralph P., ed. "Cooke's Journal of the March of the Mormon Battalion, 1846-1847." *Exploring Southwest Trails, 1846-1854.* Glendale, 1939.

Bonner, T. D. *The Life and Adventures of James P. Beckwourth.* 1856. Reprint. New York: Alfred Knopf, 1931.

Brackenridge, Henry Marie. *Views of Louisiana.* 1814. Reprint. Chicago: Quadrangle Books, 1962.

Brooks, George E., ed. *The Southwest Expedition of Jedediah Smith.* Glendale: Arthur H. Clark Company, 1977.

Camp, Charles. "The DTP Letters." In *Essays for Henry R. Wagner.* San Francisco: N. p. 1947.

————, ed. *James Clyman, Frontiersman.* Portland: Champoeg Press, 1960.

————, ed. *George C. Yount and His Chronicles of the West.* Denver: Old West Publishing Company, 1966.

Carillo, J. M. *San Antonio de Pala.* Newport Beach: Paisano Press, 1959.

231

Clark, Elmer T., J. Manning Potts, and Jacob S. Payton, eds. *The Journal and Letters of Francis Asbury.* Vol. 1. Nashville: Abingdon Press, 1958.

Cline, Gloria Griffin. *Peter Skene Ogden and the Hudson's Bay Company.* Norman: University of Oklahoma Press, 1974.

Clokey, Richard M. *William H. Ashley: Enterprise and Politics in the Trans-Mississippi West.* Norman: University of Oklahoma Press, 1980.

Constant, Alberta Wilson. *Paintbox on the Frontier: The Life and Times of George Caleb Bingham.* New York: Thomas J. Crowell Company, 1974.

Cook, Roy Bird. *The Family and Early Life of Stonewall Jackson.* 1924. Reprint. Charleston, WV: Education Foundation, 1967.

Coues, Elliott. *The Manuscript Journals of Alexander Henry and David Thompson, 1799-1814.* 1897. Reprint. Minneapolis: Ross & Haines, 1965.

Cunningham, Nobel E., Jr., ed. *Circular Letters of Congressmen to their Constituents, 1789-1829.* Chapel Hill: University of North Carolina Press, 1978.

Dale, Harrison Clifford, ed. *The Ashley-Smith Explorations and the Discovery of a Central Route to the Pacific 1822-1829.* Glendale: Arthur H. Clark Company, 1941.

Davis, Dorothy. *John George Jackson.* Parsons, WV: McClain Publishing, 1976.

DeVoto, Bernard. *Across the Wide Missouri.* New York: Houghton Mifflin Company, 1947.

Dye, Job F. *Recollections of a Pioneer.* Los Angeles: Glen Dawson, 1951.

Ekberg, Carl J. *Colonial Ste. Genevieve: An Adventure on the Mississippi Frontier.* Gerald, MO: The Patrice Press, 1985.

Frost, Donald McKay. *Notes on General Ashley, the Overland Trail and South Pass.* Worcester, MA: The American Antiquarian Society, 1945.

Galbraith, John S. *The Little Emperor: Governor Simpson of the Hudson's Bay Company.* Toronto: Macmillan of Canada, 1976.

Gowans, Fred R. *Rocky Mountain Rendezvous: A History of the Fur Trade Rendezvous 1825-1840.* Provo: Brigham Young University Press, 1976.

Gregory, Jack, and Dennard Strickland. *Sam Houston with the Cherokees, 1829-1832.* Austin: University of Texas Press, 1967.

Hafen, LeRoy R., ed. *The Mountain Men and the Fur Trade of the Far West.* 10 vols. Glendale: Arthur H. Clark Company, 1965-72.

———. *Broken Hand: The Life of Thomas Fitzpatrick, Mountain Man, Guide and Indian Agent.* Denver: Old West Publishing Company, 1973.

———, and Ann W. Hafen. *Old Spanish Trail, Santa Fe to Los Angeles.* Glendale: Arthur H. Clark Company, 1954.

Hague, Harlan. *The Road to California: The Search for a Southwest Overland Route, 1540-1848.* Glendale: Arthur H. Clark Company, 1978.

Haines, Francis D., ed. *The Snake Country Expediton of 1830-1831: John Work's Field Journal*. Norman: University of Oklahoma Press, 1971.

Hargraves, Mary W. M., and James F. Hopkins, eds. *The Papers of Henry Clay*. Vol. 6. Lexington: University Press of Kentucky, 1987.

Haymond, Henry. *History of Harrison County, West Virginia*. 1910. Reprint. Parsons, WV: McClain Printing Company, 1973.

Heitman, Francis B. *Historical Register and Dictionary of the United States Army*. Vol. 2. Washington, D.C., 1903.

Hemphill, W. Edwin, ed. *The Papers of John C. Calhoun*. Vol. 6. Columbia: University of South Carolina Press, 1972.

Hewitt, J. N. B., ed. *Journal of Rudolph Friederich Kurz*. Lincoln: University of Nebraska Press, 1970.

The History of Jo Davis County, Illinois. Chicago: H. F. Kett & Company, 1878.

Holmes, Kenneth L. *Ewing Young: Master Trapper*. Portland: Binford & Mort, 1967.

Houck, Louis. *A History of Missouri*. Vol. 3. Chicago: 1908.

Hubert, Archibald Butler, ed. *Southwest on the Turquois Trail*. Denver: Denver Public Library,1933.

Hultkrantz, Ake. "The Shoshones in the Rocky Mountain Area." In *Shoshone Indians*. New York: Garland Publishing Company, 1974.

Jackson, Donald. *Thomas Jefferson & the Stony Mountains: Exploring the West from Monticello*. Urbana: University of Illinois Press, 1981.

Jackson, Elmer Martin, Jr. *Keeping the Lamp of Rememberance Lighted*. Hagerstown, MD: Hagerstown Bookbinding and Printing Company, 1985.

James, Thomas. *Three Years Among the Indians and Mexicans*. 1846. Reprint. New York: Lippincott, 1962.

Johansen, Dorothy O., ed. *Robert Newell's Memoranda: Travles in the Territory of Missourie; ect. . .* Portland: The Champoeg Press, 1959.

Josephy, Alvin M., Jr. *The Nez Perce Indians and the Opening of the Northwest*. New Haven: Yale University Press, 1965.

Joslyn Museum. *Karl Bodmer's America*. Lincoln: University of Nebraska Press, 1984.

Kelly, Charles, and Dale Morgan. *Old Greenwood, The Story of Caleb Greenwood: Trapper, Pathfinder and Early Pioneer*. Revised edition. Georgetown, CA: The Talisman Press, 1965.

Kreidborg, Marvin A., and Merton G. Henry. *History of Military Mobilization of the United States Army, 1775-1945*. Washington, D.C.: Department of the Army Pamphlet 20-212, June 1955.

Ladies Indispensible Assistant—And Complete System of Home Medicine—and one of the best systems of cookery ever produced. New York: E. Hutchinson, 1852.

Lavender, David. *Bent's Fort*. 1954. Reprint. Lincoln: University of Nebraska Press, 1972.

———. *The American Heritage History of The Great West*. New York: American Heritage Publishing Company, 1965.

———. *Westward Vision: The Story of the Oregon Trail*. New York: McGraw-Hill Book Company, 1971.

Madsen, Brigham D. *The Northern Shoshoni*. Caldwell, ID: Caxton Printers, 1980.

Marshall, Thomas M. *Life and Letters of Frederick Bates*. Vol. 2. St. Louis, 1926.

McDermott, John Francis, ed. *A Tour on the Prairies*, by Washington Irving. Norman: University of Oklahoma Press, 1956.

———, ed. *The Western Journals of Washington Irving*. Norman: University of Oklahoma Press, 1944.

McDonald, Lois Halliday. *Fur Trade Letters of Francis Ermatinger*. Glendale: Arthur H. Clark Company, 1980.

McGaw, William Cochrane. *Savage Scene: The Life and Times of James Kirker, Frontier King*. New York: Hastings House, 1972.

McLeod, Malcomb. *Peace River: A Canoe Voyage from Hudson's Bay to the Pacific . . . in 1828*. Rutland, VT: Charles Tuttle Company, 1971.

Merk, Frederick. *Fur Trade and Empire: George Simpson's Journal . . . 1824-1825*. Cambridge: Harvard University Press, 1931.

———. *The Oregon Question: Essays in Anglo-American Diplomacy and Politics*. Cambridge: The Belknap Press of Harvard University Press, 1946.

Morgan, Dale L. *Jedediah Smith and the Opening of the West*. 1953. Reprint. Lincoln: University of Nebraska Press, 1969.

———, ed. *The West of William Ashley*. Denver: Old West Publishing Company, 1964.

———, and Carl I. Wheat. *Jedediah Smith and His Maps of the American West*. San Francisco: California Historical Society, 1954.

———, and Eleanor Towles Harris. *The Rocky Mountain Journal of William Marshall Anderson: The West in 1834*. San Marino: The Huntington Library, 1967.

Morris, Earle H., ed. *Marriage Records of Harrison County, Virginia [West Virginia], 1784-1850*. Fort Wayne: Fort Wayne Public Library, 1966.

Nicols, Roger L. *General Henry Atkinson: A Western Military Career*. Norman: University of Oklahoma Press, 1965.

Oglesby, Richard. "The Fur Trade as Business." In *The Frontier Re-examined*. Urbana: University of Illinois Press, 1967.

———. *Manuel Lisa and the Opening of the Missouri Fur Trade*. Norman: University of Oklahoma Press, 1963.

The Oregon Archives including the Journals, Governor's Messages and Public Papers of Oregon. Salem: Asahel Bush, 1853.

Petersen, William J. *Steamboating on the Upper Mississippi*. Iowa City: The State Historical Society of Iowa, 1968.

Phillips, Paul C., ed. *Life in the Rocky Mountains by W. A. Ferris*. Denver: Old West Publishing Company, 1940.

Quaife, Milo Milton, ed. *Adventures of the First Settlers on the Oregon or Columbia River*. Reprint. New York: Citadel Press, 1969.

————, ed. *The Commerce of the Prairies*, by Josiah Gregg. 1926. Reprint. Lincoln: University of Nebraska Press, 1967.

Ray, Arthur J. *Indians in the Fur Trade: Their Role as Trappers, Hunters and Middlemen in the Lands Southwest of Hudson Bay, 1660-1870*. Toronto: University of Toronto Press, 1974.

Records of the Oregon Supreme Court. Portland: Stevens Ness, 1938.

Reports of the Trials of Aaron Burr in the Circuit Court of the United States, Summer Term 1807. 2 vols. Reprint. New York: DeCapo Press, 1969.

Rice, Otis K. *The Allegheny Frontier: West Virginia Beginnings, 1730-1830*. Lexington: University Press of Kentucky, 1970.

Rich, E. E. *The History of the Hudson's Bay Company*. London: The Hudson's Bay Record Society, 1928-29.

————, ed. *Part of Dispatch From George Simpson, Esqr., Governor of Rupert's Land to the Governor and Committee of the Hudson's Bay Company, London*. London: The Hudson's Bay Record Society, 1947.

————, ed. *Peter Skene Ogden's Snake Country Journals: 1824-25 and 1825-26*. London: The Hudson's Bay Record Society, 1950.

Rohrbogh, Malcomb J. *The Land Office Business*. New York: Oxford University Press, 1968.

————. *The Trans-Appalachian Frontier: Peoples, Societies, and Institutions, 1775-1850*. New York: Oxford University Press, 1978.

Rollins, Philip Ashton, ed. *The Discovery of the Oregon Trail: Robert Stuart's Narratives*. New York: Charles Scribner's Sons, 1935.

Rosebush, Waldo W. *Frontier Steel: The Men and Their Weapons*. Spokane: Eastern Washington Historical Society, 1958.

Schoolcraft, Henry R. *A View of the Lead Mines of Missouri*. 1819. Reprint. Arno Press, 1972.

Smith, Edward Conrad. *A History of Lewis County, West Virginia*. Weston: Self-published, 1920.

Sonnichsen, C. L. *Tucson: The Life and Times of an American City*. Norman: University of Oklahoma Press, 1982.

Spaulding, George F. *On the Western Tour with Washington Irving: The Journal and Letter of Count de Pourtales*. Norman: University of Oklahoma Press, 1968.

Sullivan, Maurice S. *The Travels of Jedediah Smith: A Documentary Outline including the Journal of the Great American Pathfinder*. Santa Ana, CA: The Fine Arts Press, 1934.

Sunder, John. *Joshua Pilcher: Fur Trader and Indian Agent*. Norman: University of Oklahoma Press, 1968.

———. *Bill Sublette, Mountain Man*. Norman: University of Oklahoma Press, 1959.

Thomas, Davis, and Karin Ronnefeldt. *People of the First Man*. New York: E. P. Dutton, 1976.

Thwaites, Reuben Gold. *How George Rogers Clark Won the Northwest*. Chicago: A. C. McClung & Company, 1903.

———, ed. *Maximillian's Travels in the Interior of North America*. Vols. 22-24. Cleveland: Arthur H. Clark Company, 1909.

Todd, Edgely W., ed. *The Adventures of Captain Bonneville, U. S. A.: In the Rocky Mountains and Far West*, by Washington Irving. Norman: University of Oklahoma Press, 1961.

Trenholm, Virginia Cole, and Maurine Carley. *The Shoshonis: Sentinels of the Rockies*. Norman: University of Oklahoma Press, 1964.

Triplett, Frank. *Conquering the Wilderness: or New Pictorial History of the Life and Times of the Pioneer Heros and Heroines of America, &c, &c*. Minneapolis: L. M. Ayer Publishing Company, 1889.

United States Congress. *Abridgement of the Debates in Congress from 1789 to 1856*. Vol. 7. New York: D. Appleton & Company, 1860.

Victor, Francis Fuller, *The River of the West*, 1870. Reprint. Long's College Book Company, 1950.

Weber, David J. *The Taos Trappers: The Fur Trade in the Far Southwest, 1540-1846*. Norman: University of Oklahoma Press, 1968.

Williams, Glyndwr, ed. *Hudson's Bay Miscellany, 1670-1870*. Winnipeg: The Hudson's Bay Record Society, 1975.

———, ed. *Peter Skene Ogden's Snake Country Journals, 1827-28 and 1828-29*. London: The Hudson's Bay Record Society, 1971.

Williams, Stanley T., and Barbara D. Simpson. *Washington Irving on the Prairie, Or a Narrative of a Tour of the Southwest in the Year 1832*. New York: American Book Company, 1937.

Withers, Alexander Scott. *Chronicles of Border Warfare*. Edited by Reuben Gold Thwaites. Cincinnati: Stewart & Kidd Company, 1895.

Wood, W. Raymond. "Plains Trade in Prehistoric and Protohistoric Intertribal Relations." In *Anthropology in the Great Plains*. Lincoln: University of Nebraska Press, 1980.

———, and Thomas D. Thiessen, eds. *Early Fur Trade on the Northern Plains: Canadian Traders Among the Mandan and Hidatsa Indians, 1738-1818*. Norman: University of Oklahoma Press, 1985.

Index

Shoshone (Snake), 52-53, 73, 82, 96, 105-6, 133, 139
Shreve, Henry M., 18
Simpson, George (HBC), 54, 84, 104, 116, 125, 129, 140, 143, 146, 150, 157
Sioux, 43, 46, 61
Slaves, 27, 43, 75, 168, 176, 190, 196
Smith, Austin, 170, 172-73
Smith, Ira, 165, 183
Smith, Jedediah Strong, 47, 55, 58, 61, 70-72, 80, 82, 96-97, 112, 122, 139, 144, 145, 158-59, 168
Smith, Peter, 170, 172, 183
Smith, Jackson & Sublette, 98, 107, 118, 122, 124, 132, 156, 187
Smith's River, 54
Snake. See Shoshone
Snake country, 105-7
Snake Hunting Brigade (HBC), 85, 100, 111, 112, 126, 127, 145
Snake Hunting Brigade (NWCo.), 52
Snake River, 34, 52, 72, 93, 105, 155
Soledad Mission, 180
South Pass, 80, 162
Spokane House (HBC), 54, 64, 84
Stephens, Aaron, 57
Sublette, Milton Green, 56, 143, 155, 157, 160
Sublette, Pinckney W., 119, 126, 134
Sublette, William Lewis, 56, 61, 70, 97, 118, 158, 168, 193
Sublette & Campbell, 187-88
Sweetwater River, 73, 74

Taforia, José, 181
Talbot, Levi, 48, 60
Taos, New Mexico, 171
Teton Mountains, 34, 140
Tevanitagon, Old Pierre, 81, 92, 95, 111, 130
Teycateycowige, Lazard, 85, 86, 88

Three Forks of Missouri River, 33, 34, 55, 60, 100, 114-16
Tildon, William P., 45, 75
Togwotee Pass, 4, 98, 161
Tracy & Wahrendorff, 76
Tullock, Samuel, 119, 124, 126, 127, 133, 154, 159

Umpqua River massacre, 139, 141, 144

Vanderberg, William Henry, 133, 160
Virgin, Thomas, 68

Wagons (first time in Rocky Mountains), 159, 161-62
Waldo, Daniel, 172, 182, 193, 198
Waldo, David, 172, 182, 193
Waldo, William, 57, 173, 183-84, 188, 192
Waldo family, 12, 172
Warner, Jonathan Trumbull, 169, 177, 178, 181
Weaver, Pauline, 181-82
Weber, John H., 42, 47-48, 54, 68, 74, 76, 80, 83, 92, 96-97, 101, 105, 118
Weber Canyon, 87, 128
Weber River, 83, 87
Wheeler, Oliver, 62, 68-69, 193
Williams, Ezekiel, 45
Willow Valley. See Cache Valley
Wind River, 49, 54, 69, 71-72, 73, 154
Wolfskill, William, 171-72
Work, John (HBC), 116, 118, 139, 146, 150
Wyeth, Nathaniel, 188

Yellowstone country, 40, 114
Yellowstone (Sublette) Lake, 99, 114
Yellowstone River, 34, 46-47, 55, 154
Young, Ewing, 172, 174, 180-82, 193, 198, 199
Yount, George C., 80, 160, 172-73

241